Getting Started

Online
Personal
Finance

The Getting Started In Series

Getting Started in
Online
Personal
Finance

Brad Hill

John Wiley & Sons, Inc.

New York • Chichester • Weinheim • Brisbane • Singapore • Toronto

Published by John Wiley & Sons, Inc.
Published simultaneously in Canada.

Library of Congress Cataloging-in-Publication Data:
Hill, Brad, 1953–
    Getting started in online personal finance / Brad Hill.
      p. cm.
    Includes index.
    ISBN 0-471-38809-2 (pbk. : alk. paper)
    1. Finance, Personal—Computer network resources. 2. Investments—Computer network resources. I. Title.
    HG179 .H468 2001
    025.06'6332024—dc21   00-042292

Printed in the United States of America
10 9 8 7 6 5 4 3 2 1

Acknowledgments

M any thanks to my agent, Nicholas Smith of Altair Literary Agency.

Thanks also for the saintly patience of Debra Englander at John Wiley & Sons.

Contents

Introduction

Since 1995, tectonic shifts have rocked the financial services industries. Institutions have not always enjoyed the changes wrought by technology. But individuals, increasingly empowered by personal computers and the Internet, are on firmer ground than ever before.

The revolution started with basic family accounting. Home computers raised balancing the checkbook to new heights and simplified everything from budgeting to preparing taxes.

Investing, the most complex and tradition-bound area of personal finance, was next. Some cracks had appeared in the institutional wall when online services attained some popularity in the early 1990s. The World Wide Web broke the field wide open to new realities and started a profound rewiring of Wall Street that is still a story being told.

Other financial realms, particularly banking, felt pressure to lumber onto the information highway, as virtual banks started attracting attention and customers. Virtual insurance brokers and lending companies popped up.

Today there is almost no aspect of daily financial life that cannot be enhanced or completely given over to specialized online services. The number of useful sites is growing so fast that you need a book to guide you through the thicket.

Now, there's an idea! This book is your companion to understanding a few basic and crucial points:

✔ How you can move your money management online.

✔ Why you might want to.

✔ Where the good services are.

WHAT YOU NEED TO KNOW

Happily, you barely need to know anything to get started with online personal finance. You certainly do not need much money.

This book does not teach basic Internet navigation skills. So if you are a newcomer to the online scene and do not yet know a Back button from a hyperlink, you may have to get a little help moving around the sites recommended in these pages. Alternatively, you can read these chapters without going online at all and acquire a sense of what online finance has to offer, and whether it is up your alley. For people with pretty normal finances and average Internet experience, everything between these covers is a piece of cake. The glossary explains any terms that might be unfamiliar—and readers are hereby permitted to skip to the end whenever needed.

What do you need to benefit from personal finance on the Internet?

✔ A desire to simplify your life.

✔ A willingness to try new ways of managing your money.

✔ An interest in growing money faster.

If you meet those considerations, you're in for a an enlightening read—possibly a life-changing one.

HOW THIS BOOK IS ORGANIZED

This book covers seven tracts in the landscape of online finances. These territorial zones overlap each other in various ways but are distinguished by specific services and dedicated online niches:

1. Banking

2. Bill management

3. Insurance

4. Loans

5. Mortgages

6. Credit

7. Investing

It is not necessary to read the book in sequence. However, it may prove useful to keep in mind these chapter groupings:

✔ Chapter 1 covers some general principles of getting started and describes general finance resources on the Web.

✔ Chapters 2, 3, and 4 deal with the related fields of online banking and bill management. Many virtual banks help their customers pay bills. Chapter 2 explains how it all works; Chapter 3 concentrates on dedicated bill-paying services; and Chapter 4 helps you choose a good online bank.

✔ Chapters 5 and 6 pair up to cover online insurance.

✔ Chapters 7 and 8 are likewise a team, the first describing online lending in general and the second covering the growing field of online mortgages.

✔ Chapter 9 deals with online credit cards.

✔ Chapters 10 and 11 work in tandem to point out investing resources and help you shop for an online broker.

A REVOLUTION IN THE WORKS

It is almost embarrassingly facile to say the Internet has wrought a revolution. I say it anyway because the transformation of personal finance is too deep for moderate description.

This revolution is all about individuals, and that is what makes it so much fun to participate in. If the Internet has proven to be good at anything, it is bringing individuals more directly in touch with the services they need. Shorten the distance between consumer and service, and that service inevitably becomes cheaper. That's one big advantage to online finances—the services cost less, from bank fees, to stock commissions, to mortgage rates.

Even if price were not affected, this revolution would be worth it strictly on the basis of choice. Never have individuals had greater selection. The Internet has made services cheaper and removed geographical restrictions. A person's bank need not be located down the street anymore.

And let us not forget convenience. Online services, when chosen and managed properly, can save people time and hassle.

Today is a good day to join this peaceful and productive revolution. It is happening right through the personal computer.

Chapter

Moving Your Money Online: An Overview

Between the dawn of personal computing, when early adopters proudly brought home clunky machines to help balance the checkbook, and the early 21st century, a lot has happened to personal finance. The Internet has happened, for one thing. (Actually, the Internet has been happening for decades, but until the *World Wide Web* was invented few people knew about it or used it.) Internet-enhanced personal finance has brought an astounding range of alternatives and opportunities into the hands of average people.

World Wide Web the hyperlinked portion of the Internet. Other distinct portions of the Internet include e-mail and Usenet newsgroups. The Web is distinguished by its navigation system, which is based on clickable links (hyperlinks), each of which displays a new screen, or destination.

Following is a short list of basic money-management services you can find online, each of which is used by thousands or millions of people:

✔ *Investing.* Online investing is the most mature of the many Internet financial services, having been started by a couple of pioneering companies in pre-Web cyberspace. Currently there exist over 150 *online brokers* and an astounding number of free information and research sources. Online brokers are financial institutions whose customers buy and sell securities using personal computers. Most, but not all, online brokers use the Web browser as an interface. These institutions differ from traditional brokers by charging lower fees and offering less personalized service. More than any other single factor, online brokers have revolutionized the investment industry. In addition to investment brokers, online insurance brokers and online loan brokers assist in other areas of personal finance.

online broker broker that provides on-screen interfaces for buying and selling stocks, mutual funds, and other securities. Low fees, account convenience, and more direct access to the securities markets give online brokers (or brokerages) an advantage over their brick-and-mortar cousins.

✔ *Banking.* Online banking got a late start compared to investing, but it is coming on strong in terms of availability, convenience, popularity, and innovation. Now it is getting easier to link banking and investing accounts for seamless transfers.

online banking involves access to checking and savings accounts through a personal computer. Typically, online banking services include access to account statements, money transfer functions, and online check writing. Traditional banks often provide customers with online account access; virtual banks exist online only, without walk-in branch offices.

✔ *Bill paying.* Related to online banking, and usually incorporated into virtual bank accounts, Internet bill payments can be accomplished by companies dedicated to this service, or by bank.

✔ *Insurance.* Shopping for life and property insurance through a computer is now feasible. The same Internet advantages of selection and price leveraging that benefit online bookstores apply to online insurance brokers.

✔ *Borrowing.* All kinds of lenders are putting up virtual storefronts. The most sophisticated and rewarding type of online borrowing for most people involves real estate mortgages. Financing a home can be accomplished from query to closing through Internet sources.

✔ *Credit cards.* It is no surprise that credit card companies have established *online application* procedures—it is just a matter of making the forms available in browser format. The advantages? *Instant approval* notification in many cases, plus on-screen statements.

online application   Internet forms submitted to virtual banks, insurance brokers, and other financial institutions. These forms require pretty much the same information as paper applications. Online applications result in the initiation of an online account, a price quote, or the preapproval of a loan.

instant approval   instant acceptance of new accounts available through some online application procedures, especially credit card applications. The approval may be displayed on the screen in which you completed the application or sent by e-mail.

All these opportunities add up to a revolution. You may subscribe to the French expression, "The more things change, the more they remain the same." And it is true—the underpinnings of banking, investing, and lending remain the same as ever. But thanks to the Internet, these basic financial services cater more to individual choice and personal access than ever before.

With so many services proliferating on the Net, questions abound. How do you choose among competing companies? What are the advantages of opening online accounts or applying to online lenders? Are there dangers to all this? And above all, how on earth does a person get started?

SAFETY AND SECURITY

Ever since the World Wide Web made the online realm a commercial one, a certain equation has held true for many people: Money + Internet = Fear. Occasional media stories about computer *hackers* do not ease anybody's nerves, and the grass-roots nature of the Web's historical develop-

hackers   individuals who interrupt, steal, or alter the flow of information in a network. Most hacking is illegal and involves remotely breaking into other people's computers. In theory, hackers can pirate financial information, but actual losses due to hacking are extremely rare.

ment is enough to give any thinking person pause. Are online accounts safe depositories for people's money? Are online interfaces to those accounts secure and private?

One important fact holds true for online bank and *brokerage* accounts: They are no different from the accounts opened in physical offices. Money is essentially data, and has been so for many years.

brokerage   a company that serves as an intermediary between a consumer and a financial service. A brokerage can help consumers purchase and sell stocks, options, insurance, real estate, and loans.

When you open an account at a physical bank branch, your *assets* become bookkeeping notations in that bank's computers. An account opened in an Internet bank or brokerage is no more exposed to network piracy than an account that "resides" down the street at a local branch office. It is accessing accounts through the Internet that exposes them to small windows of opportunity for pirates.

assets   property, investments, and cash that have worth. An asset can be anything, from a certificate of deposit to a family heirloom. For most people, assets are measured by totaling personal property, investments, and deposits, then subtracting debts.

Institutions that provide online interfaces to your money deal with safety issues in two basic ways:

1. *Insurance.* Online brokers typically provide transparent, free, automatic insurance protection to their accounts from the *SIPC* (Securities Investor Protection Corporation) and, in some cases, other sources, as well. (Unfortunately, SIPC does not cover losses from betting on that Lithuanian semiconductor stock.) Online banks use the *FDIC* (Federal Deposit Insurance Corporation) in the same way.

SIPC Securities Investor Protection Corporation. The SIPC insures brokerage accounts—not against bad investing but against brokerage failure.

FDIC Federal Deposit Insurance Corporation. The FDIC insures deposit accounts (checking and savings) against bank failure.

2. *Technology.* All Internet finance institutions guard against the violability of your on-screen transactions by putting interface screens in an *encrypted* environment. This means that when a person types a password, or views account balances, or enters transfer amounts and account numbers, the information is scrambled to a degree almost impossible for a third party to decipher. Encryption technology is a big gun aimed at a tiny threat—the truth is, the chance of a network pirate snooping on a person's account is minuscule.

Encryption with Muscle

Modern Web browsers have encryption built in. If person uses version 4.x, 5.x, or later of Netscape Navigator or Microsoft Internet Explorer (the two most popular browsers), some encryption is available without doing anything. The strongest encryption level is 128-bit. To see if your browser has 128-bit security, pull down the Help menu and search under "encryption." The resulting screen tells how to upgrade to 128-bit (it is easy and free) if necessary.

encryption scrambling of data for security. Encryption does not protect information from being intercepted on a network, but it can stop that information from being read or used. Encryption exists for all kinds of online content, including e-mail. Web sites and browsers use encryption to protect all kinds of personal information that people type when applying for and using online finance accounts.

Perhaps the best argument for the safety of online finance lies in numbers. In the online investing realm, several million people keep some or all of their assets in Internet accounts, and all industry studies predict the number of people and assets will grow like gangbusters during the first half of this decade. I have never heard of a network attack on personal assets. Safety is not a concern that should stop anyone from opening an account.

ADVANTAGES OF ONLINE ACCOUNTS

What is so great about conducting personal finance online anyway? The traditional methods work pretty well for a lot of people, after all.

Fortunately, taking your money online is not an all-or-nothing proposition. Some aspects of the experience may delight and relieve you, while others just prove annoying or unnecessary. Certain benefits seem worth a learning curve, and others do not.

Presumably readers of this book have some interest in online finances. The following six basic advantages are what people can expect from transferring some or all of their finances online. Later chapters delve into more detailed pros and cons of individual services.

1. *Access convenience.* Home access to account balances, banking statements, investment activity, loan application status, and other bookkeeping details of personal finance is probably the biggest attraction and the main reason so many people are moving their money online.

2. *Integration convenience.* People who use stand-alone *financial software* for balancing the checkbook, tracking deductible expenses, and

financial software   financial software, or accounting software, is a program that resides on a person's computer and helps manage his or her accounts. When using this book it is important to understand the difference between stand-alone programs that are bought and installed in a computer and Internet programs that people use interactively when online. Web sites and their features are also software, but people do not own them or house them in their computers.

completing tax returns enjoy the convenience of (in some cases) being able to transmit online account information directly into their software.

3. Price. This is another big item on many priority lists. *Online accounts* tend to charge lower service fees, since the overhead of running an online operation is less costly than for a *brick-and-mortar* shop. Discounted brokerage commissions are the most dramatic and publicized cost savings in the virtual finance realm, but banks, credit cards, and lenders offer good online rates, too.

online accounts   refers to online access to accounts. Financial accounts always exist in the computers of real institutions. Online accounts are those accessed through an online interface, and offline accounts are accessed through branch offices, ATM machines, and other offline means. Many modern financial accounts can be accessed by both online and offline methods.

brick-and-mortar   a slightly derogatory term that refers to physical institutions such as banks. Brick-and-mortar companies have not extended their services to the online realm. Those that have are known as click-and-mortar businesses, offering both online and offline access to accounts.

4. *Selection.* We are entering a new world that can be visualized as a global supermarket of financial products. Never in history have regular folks had access to so many ways of storing, investing, leveraging, and otherwise manipulating money. From stocks, to bonds, to options, to funds, to currencies, to commodities, to banks, to Realtors, to lenders, to credit cards, to insurance *brokers*—the variety is dizzying. And while not everyone is online yet, almost every financial institution not yet there has plans to get there soon.

> **broker** a intermediary between a consumer and a financial service. Stock brokers (human or virtual) connect investors to the stock market; insurance brokers match consumers to insurance providers; loan brokers create relationships between borrowers and lenders. Although the Internet is famous for removing intermediaries, many types of online brokerages are thriving.

5. *Control.* Along with vast selection, online institutions offer unprecedented control for the individual financier. There is an account type for every person, except perhaps those who prefer keeping cash under a mattress. As usual, the investment field is the most mature when it comes to account control, but banks, credit cards, and lenders are now rolling out specialized account types representing various financial goals and lifestyles.

6. *Innovative features.* Online brokers and banks position themselves on technology's cutting edge when it comes to financial services. Online brokers provide unprecedented information streams and access to securities markets; online banks are developing new ways to enhance online shopping, bill paying, and mobile money management. For anyone exploring the wired lifestyle, online finance is both a convenience and a lot of fun.

GETTING STARTED

Enough background. Enough theory. Let us get down to practical matters. How does a person get started in the convenient, cost-effective, varied world of online personal finance? What is the best area to wade in to first? How can people best match their experience with computers and the Internet (if any) to the many choices in online personal finance? This section contains general suggestions and presents broad alternatives; later chapters offer specific solutions, institutions, and Web sites.

In the past, the barrier to entering a brave new world of online personal finance was higher than it is today. Opening an online account used to require a greater familiarity with Internet navigation than it does now. While today people can wade slowly into these new waters, back then it was more like a dive into the deep end.

Part of the reason for today's user-friendliness lies in the fact that more familiar account types (credit cards, checking accounts, mortgages) are available online. Another reason going online is easier than it used to be: Familiar institutions are creating online interfaces to accounts people may already have, enabling them to glide smoothly into the virtual environment.

The first factor in choosing an on-ramp to online finance should be your degree of computer and Internet experience.

STARTING WITH LITTLE OR NO INTERNET EXPERIENCE

If you have just bought your first computer, or recently established your first Internet access, it is probably best not to start virtual money management by opening a sophisticated online brokerage account or by shopping for a mortgage through the Web. High-tech investing and navigating through on-screen lending forms do not provide novices with peaceful, happy experiences.

The easiest way to get a computer and the Internet involved with your finances is to access accounts you already have electronically. Whether you can do this right now or not depends on the banking, brokerage, or credit card institution. (Even phone and utility companies are putting account statements online and inviting online payments.) Increasingly, physical institutions are creating online interfaces for their customers, and in some cases even providing custom-made software. These *click-and-mortar* institutions, especially banks, make it relatively easy to get started with online statements and bill paying.

click-and-mortar   traditional financial institutions that have extended their products and services to the virtual space. Such institutions have not abandoned their physical presence (the mortar) but have added online interfaces (the clicks). Institutions that have not (yet?) ventured online are called *brick-and-mortar* companies, and the term is not entirely complimentary.

The best way to know whether your accounts have as-yet hidden on-line access is to ask your bank, brokerage, or credit card company. You also may have received notices about online services offered by your bank or credit card company, or even a software disk. Brick-and-mortar institutions offer online services to their customers in two basic ways:

1. *On the Web.* The more common of the two ways involves setting up an Internet site on the Web and letting customers create their own access path to their accounts. Customers do this by making up a *user name* and *password*, the two private keys to online money accounts. The beauty of using the Web as an account environment is that no additional software is required—you do not need to install a disk and learn a new program. The downside is that Internet access is not completely reliable, nor is Web-site stability, so occasionally there may be brief times when your on-screen account information is not available for some reason. But for most institutions, most of the time, reliability is not an issue.

user name   part of a two-step security process for accessing online accounts. Most online banks and brokerages protect the privacy of your account with a user name and password. In most cases, both can be of your choosing, although some brokerages assign user names and passwords at first, then let customers change them.

password   used to access online accounts. Passwords and user names form a two-step key that opens the door to an online account. Passwords never appear on-screen; when you type your password a series of asterisks appears instead, shielding your private password from curious eyes.

2. *With special software.* The alternative to Web-based account access is a stand-alone program, installed on your computer, that connects directly with the institution's computer. For some time, this solution seemed preferable from the institution's viewpoint, because it could avoid copying all its account information into Web format. (Also, customers who do not like the Internet might feel more comfortable outside of the Web browser.) But in the last two years there has been a trend away from stand-alone access programs in online banking. As the Internet has become more ubiquitous, customers want to be able to see their accounts from any computer (while traveling, for example) without depending on a particular software program. Some new online brokerages use stand-alone programs.

At the most basic level of financial online service, you get access to account information—basically, viewing your up-to-date statement on the screen. That service alone is worth a lot. For many people, gone are the days of driving to a bank branch or ATM machine and ordering a printout of that day's account statement to see if a check has cleared. With the right setup, you can accomplish that chore by logging on to the Internet and clicking a few on-screen *links*.

links (more formally: hyperlinks)   on-screen navigation items that take you to new destinations on the Web. Links can be words or images and are distinguished by the changing shape of the mouse cursor on most computers. Text links are often (but by no means always) underlined.

PC Banking and Internet Banking

These two online banking terms are easy to confuse. PC banking refers to stand-alone programs that are installed in a PC and connect directly to the bank—bypassing the Internet. They use a different log-on phone number, provided by the bank. Accordingly, you must log off the Internet to do your banking. Internet banking, which has become much more prevalent, uses the Web as the primary interface, so you can accomplish your banking chores while logged on to the Internet in the normal fashion. Both types of interactive banking are considered part of online banking, which is a generic term that refers to accessing your account through a home computer.

If your bank lacks online services, either through special software or the Internet, you cannot view your accounts through a computer. To get online access, either you can wait until industry consolidation and modernization strikes your neck of the woods, or you can open an account elsewhere—which, admittedly, may not be worth the trouble for a variety of reasons. (Chapter 2 discusses the pros, cons, and choices of online banking.) The same holds true for credit card accounts.

If it is investing activity that you want to move online, and your broker has not yet joined the information age, other ways of tracking your investments are available. Numerous Web-based, free portfolio services allow you to replicate the data of your brokerage account—including holdings, transaction dates, transaction prices, commission rates, and all kinds of *real-time* performance information. The missing link in this scenario is the ability to buy and sell securities through the computer. To actually get your hands on your money through the computer, you need a brokerage that offers some kind of online service. (Chapter 10 discusses the ins and outs of moving investments online.)

real time   refers to financial information that is absolutely current. In the world of online finances, often price, portfolio, and account information is delayed for one reason or another. Obviously delayed information is inferior to real-time information, but the distinction matters more in some situations than in others. Delayed quotes are a nuisance for online traders, for example, whereas mutual fund prices delayed until the end of the day generally do not cause any grief. Real-time information is sometimes available as a subscription product, but in many areas of online finance is becoming cheap or free.

The upshot of all this for the Internet newcomer is that if your current financial institutions offer any kind of online service, using those services is probably the easiest way to get started—easier than signing on with a new institution. You have enough to learn without closing accounts and opening new ones. As time goes on, and you get a grip on the depth of the World Wide Web, you may develop good reasons for opening new accounts. Then many of the chapters in this book will point you in the right direction.

Filling Out Forms

Forms collect information and submit it for review. (See Figure 1.1.) Online forms work pretty much like the familiar paper ones, in terms of what content they request. The main difference lies in how you fill them out—typing instead of writing and moving the mouse cursor from one form field (the space in which you answer each question) to another. (Hint: If you do not like using the mouse constantly, the Tab key moves the cursor from one form field to the next.)

Online forms are ubiquitous, especially in financial sites. You fill them out when applying for anything, even free, everyone-accepted services. Small forms request your user name and password when looking at your accounts. Getting instant insurance quotes online is convenient, but you pay for that convenience by filling out lengthy forms—sometimes stretching over several Web pages.

Another hint: Internet Explorer version 5 keeps track of form entries for you, if you give it permission in the Internet Options panel. Activating this feature makes quicker work of forms. Explorer does not fill them in for you, but it does supply a list of previously entered responses to whatever field you are on. So, for example, when entering your user name for any account, just press the Arrow Down key to see your list of user names stored by Explorer, and select the correct one for that account. Once you get the hang of this feature, it's a time-saver. And rest easy: Explorer does not store passwords, so no one can break into your accounts on your computer.

STARTING WITH ONLINE EXPERIENCE

If you have used a computer for a while and are pretty familiar with Internet navigation, the starting points in online personal finance are more varied. Like an experienced rock climber, you may not care to hike up gradual slopes to get to the good stuff—the vertical walls are where the action is. The Web is not hard. Most online financial services are easily navigated by anyone with the following two basic skills:

1. *Exploring the Web.* This experience includes basic daily surfing, clicking links, opening new browser windows, and keeping track of multiple passwords.

2. *Completing online forms.* Expect to see lots of online *forms* when you get involved with virtual banks, brokerages, and lenders. They are just like physical forms except you do not use a pen, and the mouse cursor must be in the right place. If you have ever registered for any free site on the Web, you know about online forms.

If you can work the Web, the idea of setting up a dedicated virtual account does not seem so daunting, and you may be aware of the advantages of such an account.

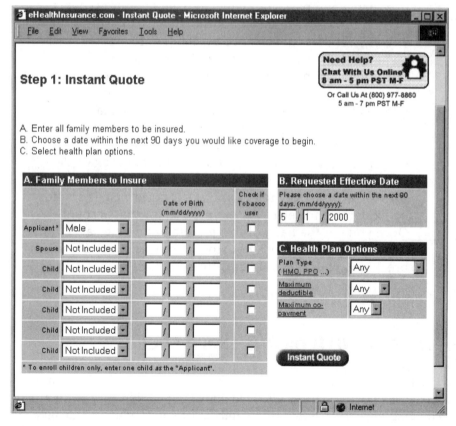

FIGURE 1.1 On-screen forms collect information for financial accounts and applications, in this case a request for a health insurance quote.

(Reprinted with permission of eHealthInsurance.com.)

forms   documents that collect and submit information. Financial institutions use online forms to gather information about you and submit that information as part of the application process. Short forms are used for all sorts of tasks, including entering your user name and password when logging on to an account. Long forms are used to apply for credit cards, online banking accounts, and instant insurance quotes.

STARTING POINTS FOR ONLINE FINANCE

Many of the personal finance sites covered in this book are particular to one type of service, such as investing, mortgage lending, or insurance. This section details a few more general destinations that deal broadly with financial issues.

OnMoney (www.onmoney.com)

OnMoney is, at the time of this book's publication, one of the great personalization *portals* on the Web. (See Figure 1.2.) What does that mean? That you can turn OnMoney into an information site that is uniquely yours, tracking and organizing many aspects of your online life. Obviously, given its name, OnMoney is mostly concerned with organizing the financial aspects of online life. But the service is growing quickly to include more personal facets of the wired lifestyle.

OnMoney took a great idea and charged onto the Internet with it before anyone else could catch up. The site aims to allow members to track

portal   home-base Internet destinations that link to all kinds of information, both within the site and elsewhere on the Web. The big generic portals, such as Yahoo! and Excite, provide many types of information on almost every subject imaginable. Smaller portals also exist, focusing on specific topics and industries. This book refers to financial service portals in the fields of online banking, investing, insurance, and loans.

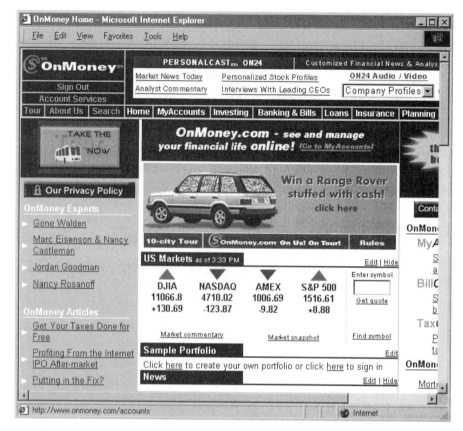

FIGURE 1.2 OnMoney.com is a jam-packed finance portal that consolidates all your online account statements.

(Reprinted with permission of OnMoney.com.)

all their online financial accounts in a single location. If you are just getting started in online banking, investing, bill paying, and insurance, you may not realize what this concept implies. Daily tracking of multiple accounts, each with its own special user name and password, is an arduous chore. OnMoney consolidates everything to a single personalized page.

If the idea still does not seem revolutionary to you, remember that many enthusiasts of online finance have multiple bank accounts, multiple investment accounts, and multiple credit cards. There are good reasons not to consolidate the accounts themselves and great need for a way to consolidate access to the accounts. OnMoney provides that organizational force.

Account consolidation is a feature that may make you want to use OnMoney often as you wade deeper into online finance. In the meantime, there are plenty of good reasons to use the site as a general financial information portal. Each section of the OnMoney landscape—Saving, Credit, Loans, Mortgages, Online Banking, and others—spins off a distinct universe of information, interactive tools, and links to other sites.

Yodlee (www.yodlee.com)

Yodlee provides a similar service as OnMoney and seeks to help you consolidate your financial account summaries onto a single secure page. Yodlee's charter is broader than OnMoney's, and the site invites you to register many types of online accounts. In addition to financial accounts, you can add Web-based e-mail and message boards, online calendars, news sources, shopping services (i.e., a personal account page at Amazon.com), and travel pages (i.e., an itinerary page at Expedia.com).

Adding accounts is faster and easier than at OnMoney, but at this writing there is not as great a selection of institutions. In comparative testing of the two sites, Yodlee won gigantic favor by automatically listing

How Secure Are OnMoney and Yodlee?

OnMoney and Yodlee, and services like them that doubtless will emerge, raise the question of network security starkly. You cannot help but wonder if your personal information is safe as you enter your account numbers and passwords into the OnMoney pages to set up your account consolidation.

Technology solutions to questions of security do exist. Any reputable account consolidator implements such solutions. OnMoney, for example, uses VerticalOne, a prominent online security provider. All your account screens that appear through the OnMoney site are pulled from the VerticalOne security fortress. The pages that accept your account password data are secured, and the information is strongly encrypted. OnMoney publishes privacy and security verification statements on the site.

If you get jittery, remember that entering account information at OnMoney is not essentially different from entering it at the account's institution. In other words, there is no difference, from a technology and security viewpoint, to accessing your account on the secure pages of an online bank and accessing it on the secure pages of OnMoney.

multiple accounts at single institutions without the need to enter individual account numbers—only the user name and password for access to the institution site was required.

Account displays at Yodlee are reasonably clear and load quickly. When you want to see transaction data from any account, it pops up in a separate window.

All in all, Yodlee provides excellent consolidation of personal online accounts, with an imaginative (if not yet comprehensive) array of account types.

Gomez.com (www.gomez.com)

Gomez is the leading decision center for several kinds of online financial services as well as other types of consumer services, including shopping and travel agents. The company develops and employs special methodologies for researching and ranking financial services. Gomez reviews and rates the following types of online service:

- ✔ Banks
- ✔ Investment brokers
- ✔ Insurance providers and brokers
- ✔ Mortgage companies

Within each of the above sections, Gomez determines a ranked list based on several criteria including ease of use, customer confidence, onsite resources, relationship services, and overall cost. Gomez tries out the services and interviews their customers. The reviews are brief (perhaps too brief) and present both pluses and minuses of each reviewed site.

Gomez is considered an indispensable destination for anyone who uses online financial services. The site is an especially important destination for newcomers. Gomez is a respected force in the industry and a consumer's best friend.

TheWhiz.com (www.thewhiz.com)

TheWhiz.com is an interactive digital magazine about money and personal finance. The main sections—Banking, Credit, Insurance, Investing, Real Estate, Spending, and others—open to feature-rich departments with feature articles and various help tools.

Most finance sites have an assortment of *online calculators*, interactive tools that help you budget, see amortization schedules, and make decisions. The calculators at theWhiz.com are many, varied, and sometimes

online calculators interactive tools that help determine one's financial goals and their attainability. Presented within the Web browser, these calculators often are small Java programs that take up to a minute to appear. Popular and useful online calculators help users plan retirement, figure out affordable mortgage scenarios, compare auto loan and leasing possibilities, and calculate the advantages of Roth IRA accounts.

entertaining in the way they present results. Some can be life-changing—look at one called "The True Cost of Paying the Minimum," which invites you to enter the interest rate, balance, and minimum monthly payment of your credit card. Another page then presents a table showing how much you would save in the long run if you paid a little more each month. The results can be staggering.

A free weekly newsletter is delivered via e-mail on demand. Usefully, all previous site articles are archived for reading at any time. If the home page seems overwhelming—it contains almost too many choices—go first to the Site Map page, which presents your choices more plainly.

Bankrate.com (www.bankrate.com)

Much more than just a bank site, as the name implies, Bankrate.com (see Figure 1.3) is one of the best sites around for general information about online personal finance. An impressive range of articles covers auto loans, banking, credit cards, individual retirement accounts (IRAs), money markets, mortgages, online financial services, personal loans, and much more.

When it comes to finding rates for all kinds of financial products, Bankrate's state-by-state approach lets you specify a town; then the site presents an extensive table of possible institutions, their products and interest rates, and links to their sites. This is not an application site but an information portal. To fill out an online application, you must proceed to the institution's site.

The Moving On section is all about relocation and provides one of the best such resources on the Web, including state profiles; school system report cards; regional costs of banking, housing, and moving; and planning guides.

Message boards provide a community feeling to Bankrate.com, and

FIGURE 1.3 Bankrate.com covers lending, insurance, banking, and credit with news and online tools.

(Reprinted with permission of Bankrate.com, a publication of iLife.com, Inc.)

message boards interactive community features that allow users to engage in protracted written discussions. Financial message boards transpire on the Web and in the Usenet portion of the Internet and are especially popular among investors. Community sites allow investors to share research and discuss their stock picks.

unlike many Web-based forums, this community space is really used. The boards are good places to ask questions and pick up on the buzz about various online banks and brokerages.

Financecenter.com (www.financecenter.com)

Financecenter is an information and solutions portal with strong and weak points. As a solutions provider that connects you to online applications to various financial products, the site tends to farm visitors out to affiliated lenders, banks, and brokerages. When it comes to information, however, Financecenter is more original and vital.

The site is divided into broad sections—autos, homes, investing, credit cards, credit lines, insurance, budgeting, savings, and retirement. Within each section are an assortment of drop-down menus of two types: ClickCalcs and ClickDeals. ClickDeals lead to affiliated sites, and Click-Calcs selections display a tremendous assortment of interactive tools and decision assistants.

You could spend hours immersed in this site, emerging with your financial goals sharpened and your knowledge enhanced.

YouDecide (www.youdecide.com)

YouDecide is a decision center and financial service broker that aims to match your needs with the best provider of auto loans, auto insurance, homeowner's insurance, online banking, credit cards, home equity loans, stock brokerage, and health insurance.

YouDecide uses a number of questionnaires and selection forms to determine your needs and goals. The problem with the system, at the time of this writing, is a decided lack of *provider* affiliations, which results in limited choices. But the site may expand its relationships as time goes on.

provider an institution that renders concrete service—such as a bank, a direct lender, and a virtual investment brokerage. Many of the sites described in this book act as intermediaries between you, the visitor/shopper, and providers affiliated with the intermediary site. Other sites profiled are produced by providers themselves to market their services directly to consumers.

There is a distinction to be drawn, in the online universe, between brokers and providers. Providers are the institutions that render concrete service. Many of the sites described in this book act as intermediaries between you and providers affiliated with the intermediary site. Insurance brokers and loan brokers are examples; of course, brokerage is a service as well, but not one that provides the disaster coverage or writes the loan check.

Other sites in this book are produced by the providers themselves to market their services directly to consumers.

The Money Page (www.moneypage.com)

The Money Page, billed as the "Consumer Guide to Investment, Banking and Finance," is basically a link hub to finance destinations on the Web. The site is partitioned into eight sections—Consumer Credit, Electronic Money, Investor's Guide, Real Estate, and others—each of which is further subdivided into categorized links.

A little descriptive content would be welcome and would enliven the unadorned links on this site. For example, under "online trading," a long list of online stock brokers can leave the newcomer as baffled as before. Still, this is a good resource to all kinds of financial information (not service) sites.

CALCULATORS

Online calculators are first-rate Web destinations that are easily lost in the shuffle, buried as they usually are within larger sites. You might want to bookmark one or more calculator pages. These interactive tools not only help you define financial goals and set budget limits but get you thinking about your assets and liabilities more deeply than you might do otherwise.

Forbes Toolbox (www.forbes.com/tool/ html/toolbox.asp?category=calculators)

From this page Forbes links you to 12 calculators. From asset allocation to life insurance, from college savings to tax rates, these tools are not the most complex around, but the short forms are something of a relief. One nice feature in most of the calculators is that the form displays on the results page, so you can tweak your input numbers without backtracking.

Allstate Calculators and Tools (www.allstate.com/tools)

The Allstate Insurance company provides about 20 interactive tools that go beyond insurance calculations. Drop-down menus divide these calculators into three areas: auto planning, home planning, and life and estate planning. Framing the tools as questions ("How much should I put down?" "What will it take to save for a home?") lends a practical quality to these pages.

Each calculator is presented with an input screen, a results screen, and a graph screen. This layout makes it easy to change input values after seeing the results. The graphs display the results visually.

Kiplinger Calculators (www.kiplinger.com/calc/calchome.html)

The Kiplinger calculators are presented in the same user-friendly, ask-a-question manner as the Allstate tools, and in fact the two companies use the same behind-the-scenes technology for their forms and results. The difference is in the calculators themselves—Kiplinger has constructed different ones, and more of them. This page is a terrific resource.

Some of these calculators deal with beguilingly subjective topics such as "Is your broker worth the big bucks?" Kiplinger builds some thoughtful questions into the forms that get you thinking beyond the numbers. The extensive range of tools covers 10 main subject areas, including Investments, Saving and Borrowing, Insurance, and Spending.

USA Today Money Calculators (www.usatoday.com/money/calculat/mcfront.htm)

USA Today is known for it is data-intensive publications, so it is no surprise that the USA Today Web property would offer some calculators. One might wish there were more of them or that they were more sophisticated. Still, the seven tools help you determine monthly loan payments, figure out tuition costs, compare leasing and buying a car, and review retirement investing scenarios. They are a good place to get started.

Chapter
2

Understanding Online Banking

Banking is the most universal of the financial services. For centuries banks have provided an alternative to putting cash under the mattress. Secure storage has always been the main selling point of banks. In recent decades, as competition among banks grew, features such as interest growth of deposits attracted customers. Then cash machines and fancy *savings accounts* gave stored cash new liquidity and growth potential.

savings account   traditionally, an alternative to a checking account, where you can stash money you will not need for a while. Savings accounts generally pay higher interest rates than checking accounts but offer lower yields than CDs and money market accounts. Savings accounts may or may not require a minimum balance.

Now the Internet brings a whole new range of attractions to bear on the banking scene. Safe, secure, inexpensive, convenient, powerful banking options are available to anyone with a computer, online access, and a willingness to try new methods of personal finance.

As discussed in Chapter 1, traditional banks often provide the easiest entree to online banking by providing online services to their preexisting accounts. For newcomers to the Internet (and anyone else), activating online banking services that already exist can be the smoothest way to glide into virtual finance.

This chapter details questions and considerations to keep in mind when shopping for an online banking account. Some of the factors and selling points described in this chapter relate primarily to the pure-Internet *virtual banks*, but you can apply the information even if you are evaluating your present institution and its online services.

virtual banks   some terms do not have industry-wide, exact meanings. For the purposes of this book, a virtual bank is a branchless institution that operates online and only online. Click-and-mortar banks that have branch offices and on-screen services are considered online banks but not virtual banks.

TWO TYPES OF ONLINE BANKS

As with other financial institutions, banks that offer online services come in two basic flavors:

1. *Click-and-mortar banks.* Some traditional banks provide their customers with online access to their account statements, *online transfers* between accounts at that bank, and *online bill-paying* systems. Other features may be available. In addition to these interactive computer services, click-and-mortar banks continue operating their branch offices and *ATM networks*.

online transfer   a method of moving money from one Internet-accessed account to another. Ideally, online transfers are as easy as using a mouse and occur within minutes. When implemented well, online transfers between two accounts at a single institution occur almost instantly.

2. *Virtual banks.* Although they are backed by physical offices and real people, virtual banks have no walk-in facilities and operate their customer services entirely on the Internet. Standard online services are provided, as with the click-and-mortars, plus certain distinguishing features.

online bill paying   one of the most popular and intriguing aspects of Internet banking, online bill-paying services let the bank (or independent company) write and send the check for standard monthly bills. Some bills can be paid electronically, using fast bank transfers. Whichever method is used, the advantage is freedom from manually writing and sending checks. Online bill-paying interfaces are partly automated and easy to use.

ATM networks   automated teller machine systems. Traditional banks either own or are affiliated with networks of ATM machines, offering customers a way to get cash without paying an annoying service charge. Most virtual banks do not enjoy such network ownerships or affiliations; thus they cannot offer their customers no-fee ATM access. Some, however, rebate the cost of using the ATM networks of other banks.

When traditional banks provide online service these days, it usually is delivered on the Internet, but that was not always the case. Until recently, many banks favored giving their customers stand-alone software packages that had to be installed on the computer. These programs, which are still used occasionally, dial a telephone number at the bank to connect

Is Your Bank Wired for Business?

Not every traditional bank has entered the new millennium wired for the future, providing basic online banking services for its customers. How do you know if your bank provides online statements, transfers, and bill paying? If it does, you've probably received numerous invitations to activate your online access. (Banks want their customers to use online services; they are cheaper for the bank than staffing elaborate walk-in offices.) If you are not sure, just call the bank or ask a teller.

users to their accounts—you have to disconnect from the Internet and let the program dial its own number to accomplish your banking.

The Web is a much more convenient medium for delivering banking services, and most click-and-mortar banks have switched over. Virtual banks, of course, exist only on the Internet.

At first glance, there may seem little difference between the online services of a traditional bank and the features of a virtual bank. In fact, virtual banks distinguish themselves in a number of ways, positive and negative. But whether you stay with your current bank or move to a virtual bank, you can expect to find a few basic, nearly universal features relating to statements, transfers between accounts, and bill paying.

✔ *Online statements.* The monthly task of balancing the checkbook by hand is but a dim memory for millions of people. Online statements, by themselves, justify the entire online banking revolution. (See Figure 2.1.) Ideally, online statements are updated immediately following every account event, such as a deposit or ATM withdrawal. At the very least, they are updated daily—still a vast improvement over the old-style monthly paper statement.

✔ *Transfers between accounts.* If you have a checking account plus a savings account of some kind (traditional savings, *money market*, or *CD account*), your bank certainly allows transfers between the accounts, subject to whatever withdrawal restrictions apply to the savings accounts. Online banking makes sweet, short work of such transfers, usually accomplishing them with a couple of mouse clicks. (See Figure 2.2.) If the system is well implemented, the statements of both accounts reflect the transfer immediately. (All of this is true only if the accounts are housed at the same bank. Do not expect to find easy transfers between institutions.)

money market account   deposit account that pays a modest investment return approximating the yield of a Treasury bond. In fact, money market accounts are partly invested in Treasuries and other kinds of conservative debt. People often use these safe accounts as temporary depositories for spare cash, located in both banks and investment brokerages. Some online brokers automatically sweep spare cash into a money market account, where it remains available for investments.

FIGURE 2.1   Online bank statements are often easier to fathom than traditional paper statements.

(Copyright First Internet Bank of Indiana.)

CD account   an account that holds certificates of deposit (CDs), which are low-yield, conservative investments. The certificates give the issuing institution (usually a bank or virtual bank) access to your money for a predetermined period, during which time the bank hopes to create a better return than it is paying you. CD yields are on the low side compared to many other investments, but they are extremely safe and a popular way to park money that is not needed immediately.

FIGURE 2.2 Online cash transfers between two accounts at the same institution are almost effortless and very fast.
(Copyright First Internet Bank of Indiana.)

✔ *Online bill paying.* Like the increasingly arcane drudgery of balancing the checkbook, writing checks is fast becoming a moldering anachronism. Online bill paying allows you to enter all your bill-paying information and let the bank write the checks for you. The service is sometimes free but always cheap. (See Chapter 3 for a more detailed discussion.)

Virtual banks go the extra mile with online services, because they have nothing *but* online services. All virtual banks provide online statements, transfers between accounts, and online bill paying. Additionally, the Internet-only banks distinguish themselves with innovative features, free or very cheap checking, high-yield accounts, and—on the downside—the logistic difficulty of getting money in the account.

Virtual Savings Accounts

Online banks offer the same type of savings accounts as traditional banks, although the *interest rates* may differ. In both online and traditional banks, the three most common savings accounts are:

1. *Traditional savings accounts.* In these accounts, your money is completely liquid and available. There may or may not be a minimum balance requirement to lock in a certain interest rate.

2. *Money market accounts.* These are really a type of investment account, almost like a mutual fund. Deposits are invested in a pool of conservative, ultra-safe securities, including Treasury bonds and commercial debt. Money market accounts have both minimum deposit requirements and duration requirements—you cannot take the money out before the term is up.

3. *Certificate of deposit (CD) accounts.* A CD is a purchased product, with a term and an interest yield, but often the bank holds the CDs themselves and passes the interests to depositors. There may by minimum deposit requirements and early-withdrawal penalties.

These accounts generally operate the same way online as offline. One difference is that online banks tend to offer higher interest yields, but that disparity is more pronounced with checking accounts.

interest rate defined percentage at which money appreciates (grows) over one year. The extra money is called interest, and can accrue (in the case of a savings account, e.g.) or be owed (as in the case of a mortgage). Accordingly, a high interest rate is favorable for savings accounts, and a low interest rate is sought for loans of all kinds.

Virtual Deposits

How do you get money into a virtual bank account? That question vexes not only customers, but the banks themselves. Unless and until some new technology saves the day, most people settle for mailing checks. Some virtual banks can arrange electronic transfers of funds, but that still requires a traditional checking account as resting place for your money. *Direct deposit* is possible at some banks, but the "deposit problem" is the main drawback to a virtual bank compared to a click-and-mortar solution.

direct deposit   paperless method of depositing regular paychecks into a bank account. Direct deposit has been used for years in certain high-volume administrative situations, such as Social Security payments. The method has gained additional popularity with the advent of virtual banking, where direct deposit is sometimes the easiest way to get money into the online account.

GOING LOCAL; GOING VIRTUAL

If virtual banks were identical to click-and-mortar institutions in banking features, there would be no compelling reason for anyone to use an Internet-only bank. Why give up the comforting physicality of a walk-in bank if there is not something to gain?

Virtual banks offer some advantages to physical banks; the question is whether those advantages are significant enough to lure you away from your present bank.

Virtual banks save money by not building and maintaining branch offices. They are primarily Internet companies and secondarily banks. The traditional, brick-and-mortar counterparts are primarily banks and secondarily Internet companies—to whatever extent they offer online services.

Virtual banks pass their savings to you in the form of attractive *deposit yields*, and many people regard this aspect of virtual banking to be its most appealing factor. High checking and savings interest is certainly one

All or Nothing? Not.

When wrestling with the question of whether to take the plunge and open a virtual bank account, remember that it need not be a plunge at all—rather, you can wade in gradually. Most virtual banks have very low minimum initial deposit requirements, if any. Some people open online bank accounts the way they buy new gadgets—if it costs only a hundred dollars to open an account, and you can always get that money back, why not?

Even if you do not become a bank-hopper, it makes sense to audition a virtual bank by opening a small account and trying the online features for a while. Some of those features—in particular, online bill paying—require a bit more commitment. But you can get the feel of the place with any old account.

deposit yield   percentage of gain on deposited money. Deposit yield differs from dividend yield associated with some stocks.

compelling reason to bank virtually. Along the same lines, virtual banks generally do not charge any fees for checking.

Virtual banks play a strong hand when it comes to innovative features that enhance the digital lifestyle. From sophisticated *bill management* to online safe deposit boxes, the Internet-only banks are positioned on the cusp of the future. Being Internet companies, these institutions have an advantage in introducing and distributing new online services.

Local click-and-mortars have their advantages, too. In addition to basic online service, the concept of the branch office is making a comeback in the face of virtual banking. Physical banks provide multiple ways of making a deposit: walk-in, drive-through, ATM. Compared with the difficulty of depositing into an Internet account (discussed later in this chapter), click-and-mortar banking is pretty convenient.

Which style of online banking is better for you? Consider how you currently do business with your bank. If you use direct deposit, it may not

bill management   usually refers to online services that receive, schedule payments for, and send payments to pay a person's monthly and sporadic bills. The most sophisticated online bill-management services take near-total control of recurring bills, storing them and notifying customers when bills have arrived and when payments are due. Such services usually cost less than $10 a month.

matter where your bank is located—even in cyberspace. Likewise, if you enjoy being on the forefront of technology, virtual banking is the way to go.

Table 2.1 outlines the comparative selling points of virtual and click-and-mortar banking.

DECIDING WHAT YOU NEED

The first step in knowing what kind of online banking service is best for you is deciding what is missing from your current banking experience.

Table 2.1 Pros and Cons of Banking Styles		
	Virtual Banks	*Click-and-Mortar Banks*
Advantages	▪ Low or nonexistent fees ▪ High yields, sometimes even on checking accounts ▪ High-tech and innovative services	▪ Get started in online banking without opening a new account ▪ Integration of all existing accounts into one online service ▪ Branch offices, ATM networks, and other physical perks
Disadvantages	▪ Difficult deposits ▪ No bank-owned ATM networks ▪ No branch offices for customer service and other transactions	▪ Relatively high account expenses ▪ Relatively low account yields ▪ Not as high tech, and sluggish compared to Internet speed

Account Access

For many people, the online, up-to-date access to account statements is the deal-closer. That single feature is a blessing to anyone who dreads balancing a checkbook. The always-open nature of online banking is by itself a lifestyle revolution. If examining the statement and making fund transfers at all hours is primarily what you need, your current bank may already be up to speed.

Bill Paying

Perhaps online bill paying attracts your attention. No doubt about it, having your bank write your checks for you is quite appealing. Your current bank may have an online bill-paying system ready for you, but it may not be as slick as virtual bank alternatives. Furthermore, there are the independent online bill management services to contend with. (See Chapter 3.) So if you seriously want to virtualize your bill-paying methods, shop carefully. You have many options.

Investing

How does investing fit into your picture? If you have a *brokerage account* at a nonbanking institution and are happy with the setup, no problem. If you invest through your current bank, you might not want to break up that synergy by shifting your checking to a virtual bank. On the other hand, some virtual banks offer brokerage services, too, just as many online brokers provide basic banking features. The relationship of your banking and investing accounts represents the most complex chemistry in the personal finance universe. At its heart is how you move money between investing accounts and *deposit accounts*—traditionally a sore point.

brokerage account   investment accounts through which securities are bought, held, and sold. They are called brokerage accounts because traditionally such accounts have been administered by trained securities brokers, agents who accessed the trading markets on the behalf of individual investors. Such human agents may or may not intervene in modern online brokerage accounts. Where such assistance exists, it is invisible, and customers use on-screen interfaces to buy and sell securities.

deposit account one of several types of account in which cash is placed with some degree of liquidity (availability). Typical deposit accounts include checking accounts, traditional savings accounts, certificate of deposit (CD) accounts, and money market accounts.

Keeping both types of account in one institution makes life easier, especially if you access the accounts online.

Deposit Question

The deposit question is sometimes the deciding factor in choosing how to bank. As technology stands now, getting money into a virtual banking account is the hardest part of the equation.

If you receive regular paychecks from a single source, you may be able to arrange to have them deposited directly into a virtual account. Talk to both your employer and the bank about this possibility—direct deposit is not usually a problem on the bank's end.

If you receive your income from multiple sources, and if those sources change, you have little choice but to use a walk-in account. You also may use a virtual bank for the convenience of its online features. In that case, you can send checks from your walk-in account to the virtual account, an awkward but workable (and fairly common) double-deposit scenario.

OPENING AN ACCOUNT

Opening an account at an online bank is not much different, or harder, than starting an account at a walk-in bank. It is easier, really, when you consider the time saved by not having to walk in—you can finish the application from your home computer (see Figure 2.3), then mail your initial deposit.

There are three basic methods of initiating online services for your banking activities. You can : (1) stay with your present bank; (2) move to a different local bank; or (3) use a virtual bank.

Staying with Your Present Bank

Staying put is an option if your bank provides online account services. If it does, you have probably been solicited to use them, through brochures

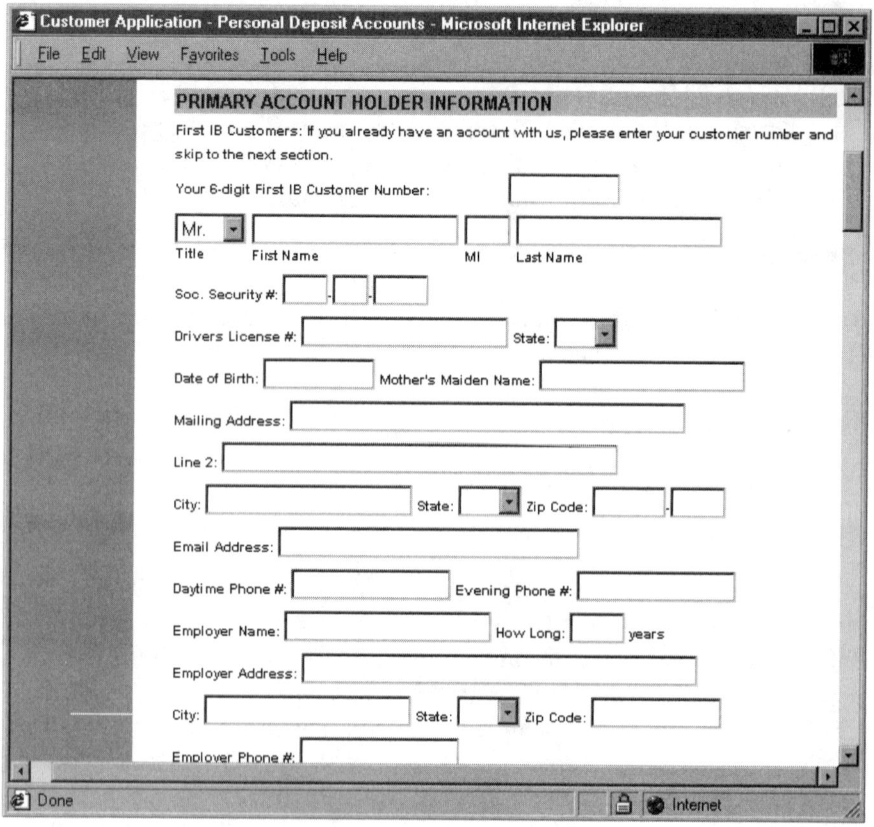

FIGURE 2.3 Opening an online bank account means filling out an on-screen form—and it is much longer than the excerpt shown here.
(Copyright First Internet Bank of Indiana.)

that come with your statement and are posted in the bank's lobby. If you are not sure about the status of online services, just call the bank and ask. If online account access is a reality, chances are you will need to do nothing more than log onto a Web site with a bank-supplied password and begin using it. (The password may be included on your mailed statement, or you may need to get one assigned to you.)

Moving to a Different Local Bank

If your current bank does not offer online services, you may not want to abandon the convenience of walk-in (and drive-through) banking for computer access to your account. An option is to move your account to another local bank that does offer online services. Call around and see what your options are. You may be able to open a new local account on-line, or, of course, you can do it in person.

Using a Virtual Bank

Branchless virtual banks use on-screen application forms. You simply fill them out online and send them in using the on-screen Submit button. (Some banks may allow you to print out the forms and mail them in, but virtual banks do not encourage this and doing so is more difficult for you.) The bank may or may not look at your credit report—it will if you're applying for overdraft protection or a credit card.

It is all too easy to make mistakes when filling out online forms. Some banks use "intelligent" forms that realize when certain information is impossible (like a birth date in the future) and do not let you proceed without fixing it. Just about all banks present your input information for your examination before you submit it.

New accounts at virtual banks are often verified within minutes, using e-mail notification. If your credit situation cannot be approved instantly, the process may take a couple of days, and you are then notified either by e-mail or through a postal communication. Either way, you need to fund the account somehow, either by sending a check or beginning a direct paycheck deposit system.

ONLINE BANKING RESOURCES

The following sites deliver basic news, tutorials, and interactive tools to help you learn about and make the most of online banking.

Electronic Payments: A Consumer's Guide (www.paytips.org/consumer.htm)

This nonprofit site offers information, advice, and consumer rights related to electronic payments and deposits. Interesting statistics (50 percent of the U.S. workforce deposits paychecks electronically—a good system to use for virtual banking) are presented in the spirit of consumer advocacy. Be sure to read the Consumer Tips section, which lists basic user-protection rules for online banking. The site answers several questions you may have about consumer rights in the realm of direct deposits, direct payments, and debit cards. A brief list of consumer-advocacy links rounds out the site.

Online Banking Report (www.onlinebankingreport.com/home)

The Online Banking Report is a trade newsletter designed primarily for professionals in the field. Consumers can use the Find an Online Bank link, which offers a list of 100 top banks and a search engine for prowling through the database of online banking services. Of some interest is the newsletter, which deals with every factor of online banking, from interest rates to electronic cash, and is written understandably. It is not free, though; in fact, it costs $695 a year. So make sure you are *very* interested in the subject before you subscribe.

Yahoo! Banking News (biz.yahoo.com/news/banking.html)

Yahoo!, the master information-gathering portal, continually updates wire service reports throughout the day. Because of Yahoo!'s particular method of sorting its huge volume of news sources, the topicality of this page is not precise. Some of the headlines (see Figure 2.4) relate specifically to online banking or single institutions, while others cover broader economic news that affects the banking industry generally. The lack of precision is rather an advantage when browsing, and the concise display of headlines is efficient.

BankSite (www.banksite.com)

The upshot of this site: bad design, all-purpose content. The site's divisions offer worldwide bank directories, loan qualification calculators, and an interest rate monitor. Most interesting is the discussion forum, in which participants chew over banking issues, complain about individual institutions, and even plead for private loans.

Banking on the WWW (www.wiso.gwdg.de/ifbg/banking.html)

This site is a link directory with no original content. The top directory level divides into categories—Guides and General Information, Banks of the World, Academic Research, Banking and Finance in Electronic Media, and a few less relevant ones. The Miscellaneous section contains what might be the most interesting links, covering such topics as offshore banking, online bankruptcy files, and electronic payments.

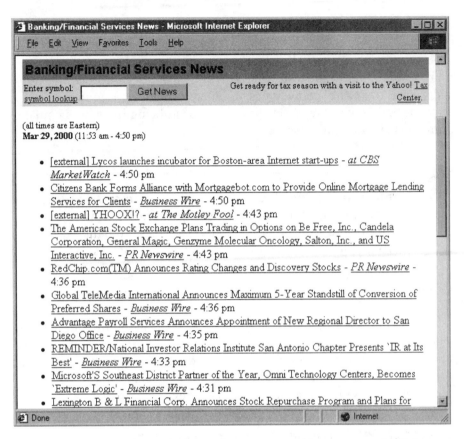

FIGURE 2.4 Yahoo! Banking News features an unglamorous and efficient display of headlines related (sometimes loosely) to online banking.
(Reprinted with permission of Yahoo!)

FDIC (www.fdic.gov/bank/individual/index.html)

The Federal Deposit Insurance Corporation (FDIC) insures the deposit accounts of most banks. The FDIC brand on a bank is a sign of account security and also bank legitimacy. That affirmation might not seem like a problem with walk-in banks, but it is an issue with cyber banks. The FDIC site delivers information about its member banks and lets you search for any individual bank's member status. As you prowl around the database, you get information about the bank's assets, liabilities, number of deposits, branch offices—and all the data are accompanied by links to glossary definitions.

DEPOSIT RATE RESOURCES

The Internet shines at delivering and sorting large amounts of information, and it is put to the test when delivering *bank rate* information. Consider that there are many types of interest-yielding accounts (money market, basic savings, and certificate of deposit being the most popular), hundreds of banks, and constantly shifting rates.

> **bank rates**   interest rates paid by banks on certain types of accounts. Traditionally, banks pay interest on savings accounts and other long-term deposits. Online banking has started a new tradition of paying attractive interest on checking account deposits.

The following sites provide comparative rate-shopping information. The fact that so much rate reporting exists should not necessarily be an encouragement to jerk your money around from one institution to another. But maintaining a basic awareness of the kaleidoscopic range of interest rates helps make the most of your money.

Bank-CD Rate Scanner (www.bankcd.com)

This site generates weekly updates of the CD rates at about 3,000 banks. (All banks on the list are FDIC insured.) For a subscription fee, you can receive e-mail delivery of the weekly list, but that is probably not necessary unless you are an extremely active investor in certificates of deposit. As a no-charge visitor, you can get daily updates of the highest-rate deposit accounts, but you must request to have the list e-mailed. All of this is a bit awkward. While the subscription rate is justified by the comprehensiveness and immediacy of the rate scan, the following sites dish out their information at no charge.

Money-Rates.com (www.money-rates.com)

An attractively designed site and a veritable information portal about bank account yields. Somewhat educational in tone, articles and links describe how yields work and how the annual percentage yield (APY) is derived. Key interest rates as set by the Federal Reserve are listed as well as economic indicators that affect the cost of money generally. The rate tables are extensive, dividing into three categories: money markets, savings accounts, and CD accounts. Institutions are linked from the tables. All of this is free, but the site also offers two subscription e-mail products: Internet Banking Report and CD Rates Weekly.

RateNet (www.rate.net)

Unlike Money-Rates.com, which presents comparative tables of institutions with high rates, RateNet encourages you to select an institution first. Once you do, the site delivers information on the full range of that bank's products—savings accounts, CD accounts, money markets. The site assists in locating banks by providing a geographic directory; you drill through it starting with a clickable map of the United States. For comparative purposes (without which the information would be less useful), data on each bank are ranked within its state and nationally. Mortgage products, auto loans, and credit cards are covered, making RateNet an exceptionally complete resource. Around the edges of this core service, graphs and top-10 lists complete an informative experience.

FISN (www.fisn.com)

The Federally Insured Savings Network (FISN) is a certificate of deposit broker that finds the best rates and markets those products to its customers. This site is not a comparative information resource as Money-Rates.com and RateNet are. But it does present its best findings in various categories, which makes for a useful comparison against whatever rates you are considering or receiving. The company reports on the best fixed term, callable (you can bail out early), and jumbo (high minimum investment) CDs.

Bankrate.com (www.bankrate.com)

Bankrate.com is mentioned in Chapter 1. The site earns its placement here due to its coverage of savings, money markets (deposit accounts and mutual funds), and checking/ATM fees. A drop-down menu on the home page invites you to choose among these and other products. Then more menus let you sort information by geography, bank name, minimum deposit, and APY. The upshot is a dynamic source for comparing bank account features. Tables displaying results (see Figure 2.5) are informative and list the contact phone number of each bank.

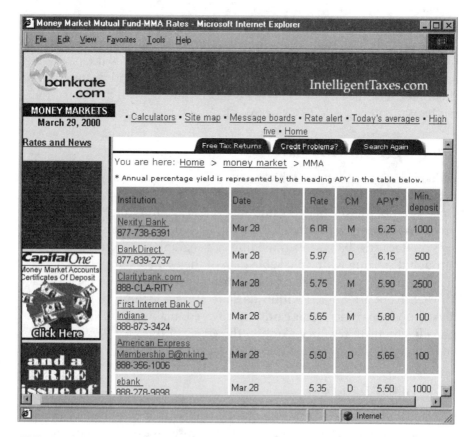

FIGURE 2.5 Among its many services, Bankrate.com displays current money market rates sorted by annual percentage yield (APY).

(Reprinted with permission of Bankrate.com, a publication of iLife.com, Inc.)

BanxQuote (www.banx.com)

BanxQuote is a personal finance information-comparing portal of uneven quality, but it should not be ignored. The banking area, which is low on the home page (scroll down), lets you search for money markets and CDs. The drop-down menus require that you select an amount (to distinguish between jumbo and nonjumbo products), a location (by state), and a term (between one month and five years). The results page lists the bank and the specific time of the rate quote—sometimes mere minutes before your search. Minimum deposit and interest rate are listed, as well. The results page automatically updates every minute, so as not to miss the next big rate quote.

GUIDES FOR BEGINNERS

The sites in this section tutor new and prospective users of online banking services.

InvestorGuide Banking
(www.investorguide.com/banking.htm)

The banking portion of the InvestorGuide site may not be much to look at, but it gives you a lot to explore by means of extensive link lists. Starting things off is a huge list of banks with online services. Such a list by itself is just raw link data, although some of the links have attached descriptions. But it is the other lists that give value to this page. InvestorGuide has assembled resources for finding bank rates, describing electronic cash, reading news and articles, and more. Spend a few hours here, and your bookmark list will never be the same; it will be pumped up with destinations related to online banking.

Money *Magazine Introduction to Online Banking*
(www.money.com/money/features/banking/index.html)

This niche of the *Money* magazine site is basically a feature article about online banking. Distinct sections cover how cyber banking works, who benefits from online banking services, what it costs, what you need, what to expect.

MoneyCentral Banking
(moneyinsider.msn.com/banking/home.asp)

MoneyCentral is well known for its excellence at gathering information and presenting solutions. The banking portion of the portal covers both ends of the equation with original articles and reports about online banking and borrowed content from information leaders like Bankrate and Wingspan Bank. On the reference side, MoneyCentral Banking displays a nifty directory style that quickly gets you to an article or interactive tool related to your interest.

MoneyCentral is both an information and a service site. The online banking and bill-paying services offered here are licensed from other companies and may not be the best solutions for you. In particular, the bill-paying service, which is provided by TransPoint, is inexpensive but more limited in features than other choices.

**Business Week: *Dos and Don'ts of Cyberbanking*
(www.businessweek.com/1997/39/b3546039.htm)**

An article from *Business Week* with a futuristic slant, describing common-sense steps you can take to decrease risk when banking online.

**C|NET: *The Complete Guide to Online Banking*
(coverage.cnet.com/Content/Features/Dlife/Banking/
index.html)**

C|NET is a major new-media company delivering news and how-to information about all aspects of the cyber lifestyle. This introduction to online banking emphasizes how to integrate your banking activity with personal finance software programs. The site also delivers fairly detailed reviews and recommendations of online banking services. Uniquely, banking programs with major online services (America Online, CompuServe, Prodigy, and MSN) are described and illustrated.

ELECTRONIC CASH INSTITUTIONS

Electronic cash is a topic distinct from, and related to, online banking. As personal finances become ever more integrated with the online experience, the traditional distribution systems for cash seem awkward, slow, clumsy, and unsafe. "Electronic cash" refers to a broad and immature field in which institutions are attempting to find new payment methods for on-line products and services.

electronic cash   alternative forms of payment used on the Internet. Electronic cash (e-cash) is a new field and has yet to capture the public imagination, but some cutting-edge virtual banks are experimenting with electronic cash accounts and e-mailed money.

Some of the participating institutions are banks, but more often (and more excitingly) the companies creating workable systems are third-party technology companies positioned as intermediaries between online merchants and consumers.

E-commerce is the ripest application for cyber cash. As it stands now, shopping online is hampered by the relatively clumsy necessity of entering credit card information when purchasing. Not only does it take time, but many people fear for the safety of their card information.

Glimpsing the Future of Electronic Cash

E-commerce is mostly about using online interfaces to buy offline content—books, music CDs, stocks, cars, plane tickets. In other words, it is commerce governed by the economics of credit cards. Electronic cash may bring a whole new commercial sensibility to the Internet and its users.

What will we buy when electronic cash is as easy and prevalent as credit accounts? Virtual products will become viable for the first time, in a few categories:

✔ *Information.* Instead of spending $10 a month subscribing to an online magazine, you may pay 25 cents per article, or even fractions of a cent per word. Like phone service, you will pay for only what you use. Recently novelist Stephen King released his new book online.

✔ *Entertainment.* Music and books are already establishing residence online. New forms of cyberspace entertainment are being forged, including installment literature and animated series. Paying per view, per listen, and per read will create new ways of delivering culture.

✔ *Communication.* Phone service is moving onto the Internet, and billing for it will become even more precisely incremental with electronic cash. New technologies such as video chatting can best be purchased with flexible digital money.

✔ *Expertise.* The discovery of new ways to leverage their consulting and advice services may affect financial services. Instead of the traditionally expensive and all-encompassing consultation, for example, consumers may be willing to purchase small bits of advice with electronic payments.

A further issue is raised by the nature of some online products, particularly information. If an information site wants to charge for the display and download of a single article, the reasonable cost may be less than a dollar, which does not normally justify the use of a credit card. Some online content might even be priced in fractions of cents (much as some phone service is when incremented by the minute) if there were a way to do so.

Beyond all these significant but partly theoretical issues lies one concern that has online merchants truly hot under the collar, and that is that kids cannot shop independently online. There simply is no cash equivalent on the Internet. Without credit cards, teenagers, rampant offline consumers that they are, cannot buy a single thing online. Music providers feel this constraint more than most, since pop music is largely a youth product. Sites that offer free digital downloads of independently produced music (the legal sites that charge a dollar or so for each song) would benefit hugely by widespread adoption of electronic cash, and this fact explains why such sites are eager users of new payment systems.

Electronic cash systems sometimes resemble banks, although the providers are not financial institutions (and are not regulated as such). There are three main types of electronic cash:

1. *Barter.* Some systems bypass cash altogether by allowing users to accumulate credits, sort of like frequent flier miles. Credits may get obtained in various ways, such as visiting or doing business with affiliate sites. Then the credits can be spent at participating merchant sites.

2. *Cash deposit.* Analogous to banks, the cash deposit companies hold your money and act as a payment agent for online purchases.

3. *Credit.* Credit systems attach to accounts you already have, such as your phone service or Internet provider, and add any online purchases to your bill.

Whatever the particular system, all forms of electronic cash attempt to get past the difficulties with credit cards. The main advantage to credit cards, though, is hard to overcome—they are accepted almost everywhere. The system is mature and ubiquitous. That glaring fact notwithstanding, electronic cash has definite advantages:

✔ *Security.* You never have to enter your credit card information. Most systems place a small bit of data in your computer that enables merchant sites to recognize you, so you never expose personal information to the network.

✔ *Speed.* Ordering via electronic cash is usually much faster than using a credit card.

✔ *Low-cost purchases.* Cyber cash is infinitely divisible, unlike traditional cash. Digital payment systems open the way to less expensive, pay-per-item online information.

✔ *Kid-friendliness.* Barter and cash deposit systems have no age barriers. They open up online shopping to kids.

Some of the sites highlighted in this section are not up to full operation, and all of them are in the early stages of growth. The best ones provide a full solution to visitors, making it easy to sign up and listing a directory of participating merchants. It is important to remember that, for the time being at least, electronic cash works only with merchants that participate with whatever system you use. You may use several e-cash systems, to purchase from a wide selection of merchants.

All of the sites listed in this section are free; there are no annual fees or interest charges for using their services.

PayPal (www.paypal.com)

The growth of PayPal, one of the emerging success stories in the electronic payment field, has occurred largely due to its acceptance among folks who buy and sell stuff at auction sites. Online auctions are hugely popular, despite the lack of any easy payment system. Most people with something to sell accept cash or checks as payment, which on the Internet is downright anachronistic. An instant, person-to-person payment is needed, and PayPal has caught on. The system is rampant on eBay, which is by far the largest online auction space.

Anybody can join PayPal and use it on either side of the transaction equation—buyer or seller. You also can use it to send money to anyone with an e-mail address. Everybody involved must register at PayPal, but that is free and easy. Recipients of PayPal money can transfer the cash by direct deposit to a bank account or request a PayPal check. The beauty of the system is that the buying party funds the purchase with a credit card but needs to enter the card information just once, at the PayPal site. After that, any individual can receive payments from that account as if he or she was a merchant accepting a credit card payment.

Beenz (www.beenz.com/splash.html)

Beenz is a point-based credit system that does not use cash at all. Registered members join up at no charge, then acquire beenz at participating sites. Redeem beenz for goods and services at participating merchants. Those merchants include magazine subscription sites, pay-per-play games, and other recreational outlets. Beenz calls itself "the Web's currency," which is overstating the case considerably. But the system is fun.

1ClickCharge (www.1clickcharge.com)

1ClickCharge works with cash accounts. Users fund their accounts in the usual way, by sending a check, then draw on that account when shopping online. The company intends to facilitate micropayments for articles, music, and other inexpensive content. The system is off to a good start, accepted already by Hoover's, the famous company database site, and Zacks, the analyst information portal for investors. Other money sites using 1ClickCharge are Institutional Investor, BizWiz, and StrategyStreet.com.

Cybank (www.cybank.com)

Cybank envisions a cashless, paperless society. To that end, the company administers a cash-funded account system similar to 1ClickCharge. Several merchants have signed on at the shopping end, but no brand-leading stores.

CyberCash (www.cybercash.com)

CyberCash provides the back end of much of the credit card processing over the Internet. Accordingly, the company is well positioned to explore alternative methods of payment. This site is interesting as a vanguard of the future. The Digital Wallet product is fairly easy to set up, but fewer than 50 online merchants accept payments by this means. If you have a Web site of your own and a product to sell, you may want to visit the CyberCash site as a potential merchant.

Cybergold (www.cybergold.com)

This barter system awards points for participating in affiliated Web sites. The Cybergold then is redeemable at an impressive selection of participating merchants–ZDNet, CDWorld, MultiaMediaMart, Riffage, BuyMP3.com, BuyCollegeStuff, and Epitonic. Cybergold has strong affiliations with MP3 sites, which stand to benefit from alternative payment systems. (MP3 is a popular format for storing and exchanging music online.)

ECash (www.ecash.com)

ECash is a leader in field. The site's online demo demonstrates dramatically how easy the system is. However, you must open an account with a bank that support eCash. The bank then provides necessary software. The site fails to list participating banks and merchants.

ECharge (www.echarge.com)

ECharge has developed an innovative system of charging Internet purchases to your local phone bill. The idea is that since you have already established that line of credit, it can be leveraged to deliver more convenience when shopping online. Naturally, the phone company must agree to the deal, and participating merchants have to ramp up their end of the system. As it stands now, a complex purchase process involves disconnecting from the Internet and reconnecting through a special number. This system has an appeal but probably needs to become smoother and easier to use.

InternetCash (www.internetcash.com)

InternetCash is a promising system that would give independence to young shoppers and could be used by anyone, even given as a gift. First you buy a plastic card in a participating store. Then you register the card at the InternetCash site and spend the money at participating online stores. Simple, elegant. The problem is that almost no stores carry the InternetCash cards. The online merchant directory listed at the site is impressive, with lots of music merchants. If buying the cards becomes easier, this system could take off.

RocketCash (www.rocketcash.com)

RocketCash is a deposit account system marketed unabashedly at kids. Fund the account by sending a check or money order, then use that cash at participating online merchants. The range and prestige of the affiliated e-merchants is impressive. This is a popular system gaining momentum.

iPIN (www.ipin.com)

The iPIN system bears similarities to ECharge, the company that arranges online purchases to appear on your phone bill. iPIN puts charges on your Internet service provider bill. The service provider must participate, of course, and currently the system is available only in France. Some music merchants have signed on to accept iPIN payments.

C|NET's Guide to Electronic Cash (coverage.cnet.com/Content/Reviews/Compare/Ecash)

Billing electronic cash as "the future of money," C|NET takes a futuristic and optimistic approach to the subject. This tutorial covers basic how-to information and recommendations.

Chapter

3

Paying Bills Online

Chapter 2 touched on the convenience of online bill paying as a feature of virtual banking. This chapter covers the emerging bill-management industry in detail and spells out the possible impact on your financial life.

Bill-paying services offered by banks let you avoid the entire mailing process—the envelope, the stamp, the check-writing, the post office trip. By itself, that service can seem revolutionary. This chapter discusses *third-party* bill-paying services offered by companies not connected with your bank. (The three parties are you, your bank, and your bill-paying service.)

third-party companies companies that act as intermediaries providing specialized services. One prominent example is online bill paying. Virtual banks provide that service, but dedicated third-party services are taking some of that business.

No Need for an Online Bank

The question naturally arises: Do you need an online banking account to use online bill payment? Not at all. Any checking account works fine as a conduit for the funds used to pay your bills.

Third-party bill paying adds another layer of convenience by shielding you from mailed bills altogether. These systems receive your bills on your behalf, notify you of what is due and when, and send the check (or *electronic payment*) on your behalf. The whole shebang is managed online through e-mail and Web interfaces.

electronic payments   near-instantaneous transfers of funds when paying a bill. Electronic payments are initiated by an online bank, bill-paying service, or individual, to only those companies that are equipped to accept such payments. A harbinger of the future, electronic payments are becoming more prevalent.

The services detailed in this chapter are best used by those with some experience on the Internet who are comfortable with virtual interactions and transactions. You do not need a degree in physics to operate online bill paying, but you do need trust in the online process and familiarity with online navigation. Many of these companies take over your bill reception and *bill presentment* completely, and veteran Internet citizens are likely to be more comfortable with them than newcomers.

bill presentment   refers to the method in which you receive your bills. Online banks that offer bill payment do not present your bills to you—you continue receiving them through the mail. But third-party bill-management systems actually receive your bills and *present* them to you in digital form, as scanned images.

THREE TYPES OF ONLINE BILL MANAGEMENT

As young as this service category is, three distinct types of online bill-paying services already exist:

1. *Full-service.* The most complete online solution to managing your bills involves giving the service control over reception and presentment of your bills and access to at least one of your deposit accounts (usually a checking account). The service receives your bills, scans them, notifies you of them, presents them to you in scanned form, and pays them for you with your funds.

2. *Half-service.* This hybrid type of service does not receive all your bills but does deal directly with companies that use *electronic bills.* Those companies that do not bill electronically continue sending paper bills to you, which you can pay through another bill-paying service or by mailing your own checks.

electronic bills   bills that avoid the printing and sending of paper statements, just as electronic payments circumvent the need for paper checks. Electronic bills are delivered directly and instantly to virtual bill-payment systems, where they are presented to you online for examination and payment. If you want a paper record of the statement, you can print the bill directly from your Web browser. Electronic bills usually are paid using electronic payments.

3. *Selective service.* Companies that deal only with billers that present electronic bills provide the most limited type of service. You continue to receive all other bills, which you must continue to pay. The bill-payment service makes electronic transfer payments, and no other kind.

Electronic Payments and Online Payments

The terms "electronic payments" and "online bill payments" are often confused—understandably, since all online transactions have an electronic element. With an online payment, generally an individual orders a payment service to send a check. The process is identical to traditional bill paying, except the individual is spared the chore of writing and sending the payment. Electronic payments are money transfers with no paper involved. They are almost instantaneous and are becoming more prevalent.

ADVANTAGES OF ONLINE BILL PAYMENTS

Of course, convenience is the touchstone of online bill paying, but that convenience kicks in primarily for those who have integrated online services into their lifestyle to some degree. If logging on to the Internet is a hassle, or if you are not online very often, you probably do not want to depend on your computer to present and pay your bills.

The convenience of online bill paying manifests itself in several ways:

✔ *Saving time.* Mailing a single check is no obstacle to having a good day, but the continual chore of receiving bills and getting the payments out the door is a drain on anyone's personal time. You may not realize how liberating online bill paying can be until you try it. There is also the psychological advantage of not receiving bills in your postal mail. (Now if only you could get the junk mail sent elsewhere.)

✔ *Flexibility.* Bill-management systems let you get quite specific about how your bills are handled and automate the process to a large extent. You can set up payment schedules for your regular bills while paying others sporadically, on demand. Adding and removing payees (or *billers*) is never a problem, and you can send one-time payments through the system. Many services allow you to draw funds from multiple checking and savings accounts.

biller   any organization that bills its customers. Typical billers include utility companies, credit card issuers, and mortgage lenders. The term is used in online bill-paying systems.

✔ *Never lose a bill.* Even with the best of intentions and a well-organized kitchen table, sometimes bills get lost. Not so with online bill presentment, unless the bill gets lost in the mail on the way to the third-party service. Forgetfulness is more difficult, since most bill-paying services remind you to pay bills a certain time before their *due date*. These systems can be a godsend to folks who suffer from chronic disorganization. For many, online bill management results in fewer late fees and less damage to their credit ratings.

✔ *Consolidation.* At their best, bill-management services present you not only with bills but with consolidated reports of your total billing situation. Rather than scrambling through your check registry to remember whether you paid the last phone bill, a single screen tells you the status of all your current bills, paid and outstanding.

> **due date**   date on which a bill payment must be received in order to avoid penalty or interest charges.

✔ *Manage bills on the road.* Putting your mailbox for bills on the Internet means you can reach into it from any connected computer in the world. If you take many extended trips, a bill-paying system could spell the end of poring through stacks of bills upon your return and missing payment dates because of your schedule. As long as you can access the Web, you can receive and pay your bills.

✔ *Download to finance programs.* The best online billing systems let you download your bill and payment records directly to popular stand-alone finance programs such as Quicken and Microsoft Money. This means you need to enter payment information only once, and it ends up not only at your bill-payer but also in the permanent financial records you keep in the computer. The information is downloaded when you are logged on; usually it takes just a couple of mouse clicks.

✔ *Independent of online banking.* When you use a bank's payment service, you limit your options somewhat. In most cases, the bank uses only a single account to pay the bills—the account to which the payment service is attached. Third-party bill paying operates with complete neutrality and does not care what account(s) you use. Accordingly, you can add and delete accounts at will (but leave about 10 days for that process, since the payment service must verify your account status). In many cases you can even use cash in an investment account to pay your bills online.

How Do You Pay the Payment Service?

The payment service pays your bills by using a link to your checking account. This service is not free. How do you pay the payment service? The same way—the monthly service fee is simply *debit*ed from your checking account.

> **debit**   deduction from the balance of a deposit account, such as a bank checking account. Debits can be withdrawals, check payments, finance charges, or any other action that reduces the cash balance of the account.

✔ *Final piece of the puzzle.* When used with virtual banking and online investing, both of which have been in place longer than online bill paying, you effectively transfer your entire daily financial management to the online realm. Whether this is a harbinger of a bright future or not depends on individual temperament; for many people the virtual management of finances is a great step forward.

DISADVANTAGES OF ONLINE BILL PAYMENTS

Paying bills online is not all gravy. Online bill paying is a young industry, and some kinks are still getting worked out. Furthermore, a few inherent inconveniences may, for some people, balance the conveniences detailed earlier. Enthusiastic adopters of these new systems do not mind putting up with a few rough spots in the road, if that road leads directly to the digital future.

Following are the hurdles involved using an online bill-management system.

It Is Not Free

Cost is probably the most obvious disadvantage to paying bills online. How the fees break down for you depends on how many bills you have. Most services charge no more than $9 per month for a certain number of payments, usually around 25. There is a small additional charge for each payment above the ceiling.

All these systems are more expensive than most bill-paying services offered through online banks, many of which are free (at least up to a certain number of payments). So your real decision is between free limited service from an online bank and fee-based flexible service from a third-party company.

Is Online Bill Paying Expensive?

Does $8 or $9 a month seem too expensive for the convenience of avoiding your checkbook? Consider this. If you have 25 bills each month, you would pay $8.25 in stamps the old-fashioned way. Using an Internet service buys you a lot of convenience for a few extra pennies per month. Fewer bills make the system seem more expensive, but some companies profiled in this chapter have less expensive plans.

Changing the Billing Addresses

Setup is a hassle, no doubt about it. And the better the service, the more intense the setup. The worst chore is changing the bill address on all bills you want the service to handle.

An additional complication is that some creditors may be reluctant to make the switch from a personal address to a corporate address, but this problem is definitely on the wane now that these online bill-paying services are catching on. Online bill paying works to the billers' advantage, not only yours, because the systems tend to reduce missed payment dates. Now that companies of all kinds are starting to realize the advantages, the process of changing billing addresses is becoming easier and more streamlined.

Helping You Make the Change

Changing your billing addresses is the hardest part of setting up an online payment program. Thank goodness the better services now help by contacting your billers and making the change for you. The service may even keep a database of hundreds of billers—credit card companies, utilities, mortgage companies, and so on—so all you need to do is click on your billers from the list and enter your account numbers. The service does the rest and soon begins receiving your bills.

Watch Your Mail!

When you sign on with an online bill-management system, you must switch your billing address for the bills you want the service to pay so they are sent to the payment service instead of to you. Well and good, but do not start disregarding your mail immediately. It can take a cycle or two for the bills to be routed to the new address. And make no mistake about it—you are responsible for paying the bill no matter where it is sent. At some point, for each of your bills, you will begin receiving e-mailed bill notifications (from the payment service) instead of mailed statements (from the biller). Then you know that the switch-over has been completed.

Different Billing and Shipping Addresses

Different billing and shipping addresses can present inconveniences and oc-casionally more serious difficulties. Shopping online is more complicated in such cases, because in all likelihood you would be paying your credit card bill through the *online payment* system. That means when ordering at an e-commerce site, you must enter your credit card billing address (no longer your home address) plus your delivery address (your home address). That complication is minor, especially if you tend to shop at just a few online shops and can store your information profile after entering it once.

online payment   any payment of a bill that originates or is ordered online. Online payments are not identical to electronic payments. Not every online payment is an electronic payment, but every electronic payment is an online payment. The other main type of online payment is a check created and mailed by an online bank or payment service.

Early adopters of online bill management have reported a more se-rious difficulty: problems getting shippers to deliver to an address other than the billing address. This problem may affect small business owners more than residential customers, and at any rate is rare and getting rarer.

Speed Issues

The Internet is commonly regarded as a speedy realm. People even refer to "Internet time" as if cyberspace existed in some alternate dimension. So it is natural to think that online bill paying would provide a faster way to get money to your creditors.

Online bill payments are indeed swift when they involve electronic payments—transfers from your checking account to the biller's system. But the truth is, most of the time folks do not deal with companies capable of receiving electronic payments. Online payments involve sending a check the old-fashioned way.

This merging of online dispatch with offline sluggishness raises speed issues. Unfortunately, using an online payment system may *slow down* your accustomed pace of paying bills. Most services require five business days' notice to deliver a payment by the due date. Of course, you can pay a bill at any time, before or after it is due. But bill-management services guarantee timely payment only if they receive your payment authorization (or if such authorization is built into an automated schedule) five business days before the due date.

No More Kiting!

Online payment services cramp the style of those who practice "kiting" checks—that is, sending a check before the funds are available in the checking account. This maneuver plays out successfully if the funds clear into the account before the biller receives the check and forwards it to your bank for payment. Logistics are on your side with traditional banking systems. Not so with online bill-payment systems, where funds are extracted from your account instantly for electronic payments. Even in the case of nonelectronic payments, the service may check your account for fund availability before sending the check, which foils the kite scheme.

Occasional Lost Payments

When mail is lost it is misplaced by the post office, so lost payments should not rightfully be blamed on the payment service. And if you shift some of your bills to electronic payments, lost mail becomes increasingly a nonissue.

Some customers report unsettling stories of payments that got lost before even leaving the payment agency. That particular problem can be compounded if the agency withdraws money from your account and lists the bill as paid on your account screen. In that case, you may remain oblivious to a missing payment for a cycle or two.

To be fair, people have reported most such problems about online banking systems, not dedicated online bill managers. Presumably, the dedicated companies have devoted resources to making their systems as foolproof as possible. But no system is ever completely without the occasional error. Bill-paying companies generally promise to work with the biller in straightening out the problem, providing whatever stored payment records are necessary. These services can issue a stop-payment order on any check lost in the mail, like a regular bank.

Future Industry Shifts

The online bill-paying industry is young and relatively immature. Will the company you are with now still exist in a year or two? If your current service merges with another—industry consolidation is always likely in emerging fields—will your favorite features remain available? These questions are unanswerable, and anyone enjoying the benefits of online bill paying should balance the convenience against future uncertainty.

Lack of Paper Files

Paper is reassuringly solid for many people, while for others it just clutters things up. Members of the latter group do not miss billing statements arriving in the mail. Members of the former group may not miss them, either, until tax time arrives, or when assessing the family budget. At those times nearly everyone might experience a pang of regret over the abandonment of the paper filing system of yesteryear.

The good news is that habitual use of your printer can result in more compact paper files than you had before. Printing the consolidated statement of all your billing activity every month or so yields a paper record that is more concise than your old system.

Digital Paper

Most online payment companies realize that users occasionally need account summaries. True to their electronic roots, these companies usually provide annual account records in digital format, packaged on a CD-ROM. You may never find a company willing to send you paper statements, but remember: You can always print stuff out, either monthly from the account site or from a CD-ROM database.

HOW ONLINE BILL MANAGEMENT WORKS

This section is a step-by-step rundown of the online bill-management process. Once you sign up with a payment agency, that company leads you through its particular variation on these steps. The text here is meant to give you a clearer idea of how it all works so you can make a better choice about whether to use services like this at all. Managing your bills online is a difficult decision to reverse, although some companies make it easier by offering to switch back your billing addresses at any time during an initial trial period.

Step 1: Signing Up

Signing up is an online process, naturally. You fill out an online form as if you were opening an online bank account, but the first stage requires less information. At this point the service wants to know who you are, where you live, and your e-mail address. You may be asked to supply demographic information, but it is usually optional. You also may choose your user name and password at this point.

Step 2: Activating Payment Privileges

The first form completes your registration at the payment site. You may receive an e-mail confirming your registration and documenting your password. The next step is to activate payment privileges, which is a little more complicated. You must fill out an *authorizataion form*, which specifies the account(s) from which payments will be taken.

authorization form form giving permission to access an account. Customers complete authorization forms when setting up online bill-management accounts, allowing the service company to access their checking account to pay bills.

You almost always must return this activation form to the company by postal mail, sometimes with a voided sample check. You can print out the form from the Web site, which saves time, but usually you cannot submit it electronically. In the future this awkward and time-consuming step may be eliminated.

Step 3: Register Your Billers

In this step you decide which bills to pay with this new system. You can build up your list of billers (sometimes called payees) gradually, using on-line forms to add new ones at any time. (See Figure 3.1.) If the payment service is going to present your bills as well as pay them, it is a hassle to remove billers from your list; doing so entails switching the billing address back to your home after having switched it to the service. (If you are not using a bill-presentment service, you still register billers. You do not need to change billing addresses.)

Under the best of circumstances, the agencies simplify the arduous process of converting billers to a new system. Some provide extensive lists of common billers and handle the address switch for you. Things to have handy at this stage: the account number and payment address of each biller you want to register.

Delayed Start

Count on about two weeks before you can begin paying your bills online. The delay is due to the account authorization process by which the payment service checks the existence of your checking account. The fact that the authorization form must be mailed to the service company ("snail-mailed," in Internet jargon) just adds to the delay.

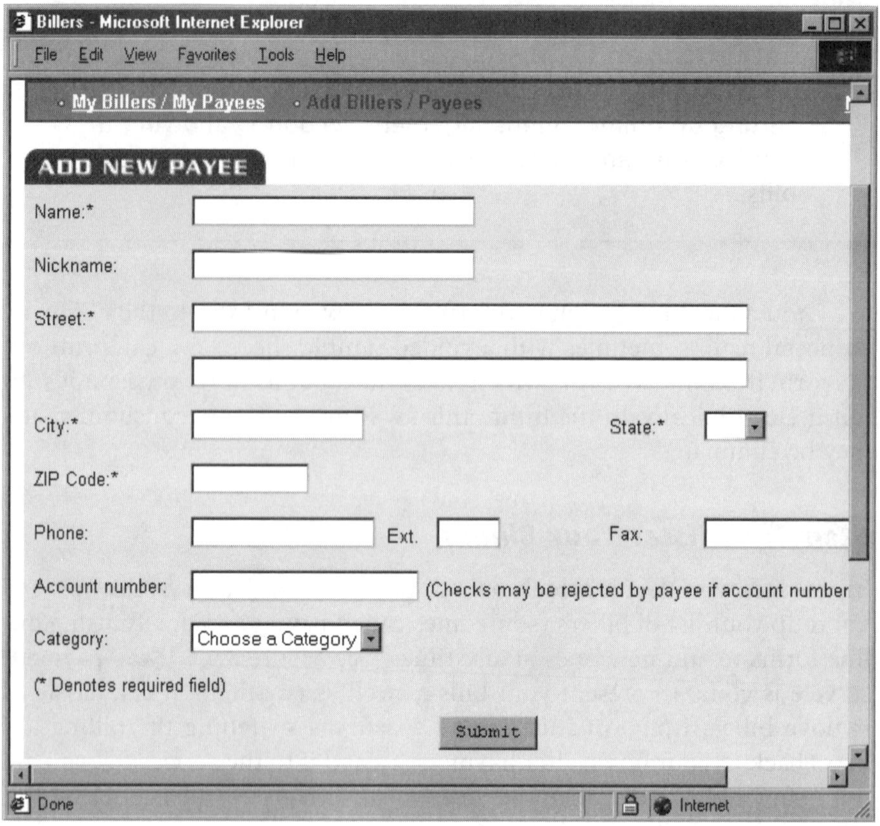

FIGURE 3.1 Adding a new payee to a bill-paying system. Each service has its own style of forms.

(Reprinted with permission of PayMyBills.com.)

If the payment agency does not handle the address switch for you, you must contact the biller yourself, by whatever method that company requires for an address change. Sorry, but there is no getting around it.

Step 4: Schedule Your Payments

Some bills, such as electricity, phone, and credit cards, must be paid manually, because they call for a different payment amount each month.

Other bills, such as rent, mortgage, and paying down a credit card no longer in use, can be scheduled for automatic payments. Automatic payments are the height of convenience, as you never have to think of them or take further action—except to make sure your checking account has enough money.

If you use more than one account to pay bills (checking and savings is the most common scenario), this is the stage at which you assign each bill to its payment account. You can change those assignments at any time and also change the payment schedules.

Step 5: Your Bills Arrive Online

If you are using a full-service bill-presentment and payment service, the day finally arrives when you receive your first bill online. Most services notify you through e-mail of a bill's arrival. (See Figure 3.2.) When you visit the Web site and log on to your account, you can view a scanned version of the paper bill.

If you are not using a presentment service, you continue receiving bills at home. You then log on to your account and arrange to pay them, just as if you had received the bill online.

Step 6: You Receive Due-Date Notices

In addition to telling you when a bill arrives, payment services usually notify you a few days before a bill is due to be paid. (Usually this feature is not activated for those bills under an automatic payment schedule, because you do not need to take any action in those cases.)

Step 7: You Order a Payment

Whether the service presents your bills or you receive them at home, you still must log on to your Web account to order payments for those bills not governed by automatic schedules. The services make this step quite easy, usually minimizing the process to a few mouse clicks and number entries.

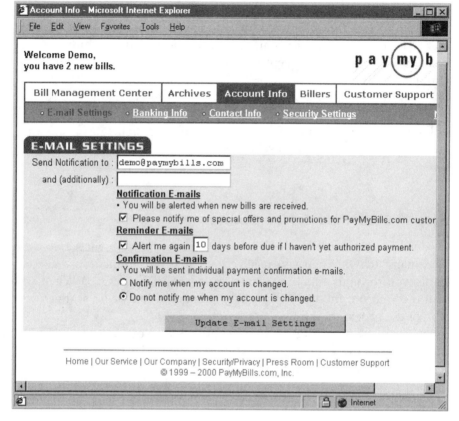

FIGURE 3.2 Setting up your e-mail notification system for bill receipt and payment date.

(Reprinted with permission of PayMyBills.com.)

Step 8: Service Pays the Bill

When you order a payment (or the date of a scheduled payment rolls around), the payment service creates a check and sends it. If an electronic payment has been arranged, the funds are transferred directly and almost instantly from your checking account to the biller's account.

In the case of check payments, the service may withdraw the money from your account immediately or wait until the payment check arrives back for clearing. In most cases the service company at least checks your account to verify funds before sending the check.

EVALUATING ONLINE BILL-PAYMENT SITES

Time to shop. As you cruise around the online bill-management sites—the ones featured later in this chapter and others you may find on your own—keep the following points in mind.

Trial Period

Competition for customers is heating up, and most companies let you try the service without charge for at least a month. Some offer a three-month or longer *trial period*. (Many also try to lure you in by running a sweepstakes.)

trial period   test period in which a financial service or subscription is provided at no charge. Online bill-payment services and virtual banks market trial periods aggressively. Also, investment subscription sites frequently offer no-charge trials of two weeks or a month.

Encryption

Network security is an issue when paying bills online and keeping all your records on the Internet. The strongest encryption currently available for commercial Web sites is 128-bit, which is supported by latest-version Web browsers. Check at the site to see what encryption level is used.

Customer Service

These bill-paying systems are meant to be trouble-free, largely automated solutions to paying bills. But you know what they say: The only trouble-free system is a nonexistent one. (Actually, nobody says that, but it is probably true.) Look around the site; if you cannot find a phone number or customer service e-mail address, chances are you will have nobody to call when things go wrong.

Using Web-Based E-mail for Bills

Bill-payment services use your e-mail address to notify you of the arrival of bills and to send you payment reminders. If you operate mostly from home, using your main e-mail address makes sense. But if you travel frequently and use online bill management to control your bills while on the road, it might make sense to use a Web-based e-mail account.

These free accounts, provided by Yahoo! Mail (mail.yahoo.com), Hotmail (www.hotmail.com), and many others, require only a basic Web connection for access. Since these e-mail services circumvent the need for a dedicated e-mail program as well as the need to configure that program to your main e-mail settings, they can take some hassle out of managing your finances when traveling. If you always travel with a laptop computer that has your usual e-mail program, you may not need Web-based e-mail.

Insurance

Almost all banks, online and offline, are covered by FDIC insurance. Bill-paying systems are not banks, strictly speaking, but they certainly are adjuncts to your bank. You may want to protect your account from unauthorized transactions. To that end, some companies retain account

Backing Out

More important than the temporary free service is a switch-back offer that some bill-presentment companies provide. The deal is that if you decide against continuing the service during the trial period, the company switches your billing addresses back to your home. Your creditors may wonder what the heck you are up to, but at least you will not have to do the chore yourself.

insurance; $100,000 per account is the usual coverage amount. Such coverage is completely free to customers.

Payment of Bill-Less Bills

The typical service profile allows a payment company to send a check from your account to anyone, from the plumbing company to your nephew. But watch out for services that do not allow payments to destinations not on a list of preaccepted billers. If all your regular bills are on that list, you may be lulled into thinking that you can send a check to anyone. Occasional checks to relatives are not a big deal—you can always write the check yourself, if you remember how—but it can be a problem if you rent an apartment from a local landlord and cannot set up automatic rent payments.

Receipts and Records

Virtually all payment services provide some kind of record keeping. Decide on what you want and see which firm offers it. Would you like to obtain paper statements? That is the hardest requirement to fill, and you will probably have to pay extra for it. Electronic payment receipts are often available. End-of-year records are important, so find out if the company supplies a digital version of everything that has passed through your account during the year—bills, payment orders, copies of checks, everything. Usually such files are compiled on CD-ROM, and customers often have to pay for that disk. (A $50 charge is typical.) Industry standards may change on this point, and the disks may become cheaper or free. Keep asking about it as you shop.

Archives

Two issues exist concerning record keeping. One, discussed above, involves the service's ability to provide an offline version of your account, either on paper or on disk. The other involves the site's capacity for archiving your documents in a retrievable location. All these companies maintain *archives* to a certain extent (see Figure 3.3), but that extent makes all the difference. The range is from one month back to two years back. Some keep your records in-house for at least seven

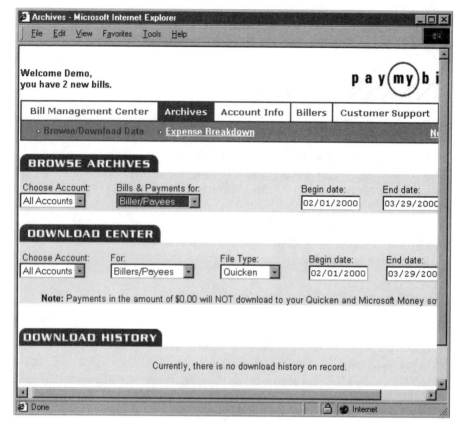

FIGURE 3.3 Accessing archived bills and payment records.
(Reprinted with permission of PayMyBills.com.)

archives previous content stored for future reference. Online bill-payment services archive their customers' bills and payment records. Online banks archive monthly account statements. Information sites archive past articles. In all these cases, customers may have varying access to the archived material.

years, against the possibility of a tax audit, and charge for copies of those records.

Disputes

Two types of dispute are possible when dealing with an online bill-paying service. You may have an argument with the service over the handling of a payment, or a biller may have an argument with you over the paying of a bill. The two concerns often overlap, as when you ordered a payment on time, but it did not get there. In that case, everyone is merrily arguing with everyone else. When shopping for a service, find out if it provides receipts and copies of bills during disputes with a biller. And find out if the service pays for providing those records or charges you. On a reassuring note, disputes are not common.

Multiple Payment Accounts

This chapter has, a number of times, referred to the nifty ability to juggle payment sources by registering more than one account with the bill-paying service. In theory, you can use almost any account as a payment conduit, using either checks or electronic transfers. With the proliferation of online brokerage accounts that provide basic checking, many people like to earmark different accounts for different bills. If you see yourself in this scenario, make sure your payment service can handle more than one account registration.

Electronic Bills and Payments

Electronic payments are fast, clean, safe, and in the coolest possible manner have one foot in the future. There may come a time when almost everyone routinely pays bills with instantaneous transfers and due dates include a time of day when the money must be there. We are inching toward this reality, and some payment agencies lead the way by accepting electronic billing and delivering electronic payments. Not all billers can cooperate. But look for the capacity on the service side if you want a taste of the future.

Degree of E-mail Communication

Standard thinking has it that when it comes to your finances, more communication from the bill-paying service is better than less. But some people consider the e-mail box to be even more sacred space than the postal mailbox and do not like miscellaneous clutter in the digital realm. Most bill-paying services notify you by e-mail when a bill comes in, even if the bill is scheduled for automatic payment. That is one communication you may not want. The service may remind you of payment-due dates in advance—again, crucial for some and an annoyance for others. Try to determine, by looking at demo screens and asking about the procedure, whether the degree of e-mail communication is configurable.

Conditional Payment Instructions

This item is one of the most helpful features when scheduling automatic payments. You can get a lot of mileage out of setting conditional payment requirements, if they are available. The concept works along the lines of the "if . . . then . . ." principle.

Say you have a credit card account with varying monthly charges. You may be able to set the payment site to pay automatically any balance up to $200 and to pay exactly $200 if the balance is higher. That way you never have to worry about missing a minimum payment; likewise, you do not have to worry about accidentally stripping your checking account with a full payment after a heavy buying month.

Of course, you can change the conditional settings at any time. Not all services allow conditional payment instructions.

Online Demo

Never mind the bells and whistles and the blinking come-ons. The best way to get customers is with a thorough, illustrative online *demo* of the service and its features. You cannot really judge an online service without seeing its screens. In particular, you want to get a glimpse of the payment scheduling screens and the list of recognized billers, if there is one. Do not worry if the demo does not show you a scanned bill—they all look pretty much the same. Likewise with the e-mail notifications—it does not matter what they look like. But the payment order screen and scheduling features should be displayed for your examination.

> **demo**   a demonstration. The term is applied to both software programs and on-screen illustrations of financial services. Demo versions of stock-tracking programs help users evaluate the products before buying. Demos of virtual bank account screens assist in evaluating virtual banking service.

On-Time Payment Guarantee

An on-time payment guarantee is the least a payment service can do—if it gets your payment there late, it should pay any late fees that accrue to your account. This guarantee is fairly common, and it is important. Any company that does not advertise such a guarantee may not be confident in its system. Now, part of the obligation is always in your hands; you must order payment (either manually or through automatic scheduling) a certain number of days before the due date. (As mentioned, the necessary safety period is usually five business days.) The guarantee, naturally enough, is void if you fail to order the payment on time.

> ### Small Business Features
>
> Some services cater to sole proprietors and other small business owners with two main features. First, they offer the ability to download account records to desktop accounting programs, which is helpful to many people who may or may not be in business for themselves. Second, the services may be able to customize outgoing checks, imprinting a company name on them. In that case, the payment service is almost like an accounting department outsourced by your business. These features, when available, sometimes are packaged into a small business plan with its own (usually higher) service rates.

Credit Card Shut-Out

Online bill-paying systems have developed into tools far more flexible than the online banking systems that spawned them. But one thing they still will not do is accommodate a desire to pay bills with a credit card. Only deposit accounts work with these systems. Manage your payment assignments carefully. If you always pay a certain bill with a credit card, simply leave it out of the online mix. If you have bills that you sometimes pay with credit cards, do not assign them an automatic payment schedule, or they could get paid from your checking account accidentally. Give those bills the manual treatment, and decide each month whether to order an online payment or use plastic.

Timing of the Debit

The tricky issue of timing of the debit is important but sometimes difficult to determine. When does the payment agency debit your account for any nonelectronic payment? (Electronic payments are debited immediately.) Online banks are notorious for debiting the account immediately, then holding your money until the payment check comes back to the bank for payment. The bank earns interest on the held money during those few days; you do not.

Pure Internet payment services are attempting to attract customers with service of a higher quality, so this practice is on the way out. You can expect to find one of the following systems in place:

✔ Your account is debited as soon as you make a payment order. This is the worst possible situation for you, because your money loses a few days of earning interest.

✔ Your account is debited a couple of days after the payment is ordered and the check sent out. This method is a reasonable compromise.

✔ Your account is debited when the check returns to be paid. This method is the most generous to you.

The industry is not unified on this point. If the site promotion does not explain the service's practice, ask customer service.

TOURING THE ONLINE BILL MANAGERS

This section profiles some of the most competitive online bill-payment sites. Most of these companies provide complete solutions, including bill presentment and payment.

StatusFactory (www.statusfactory.com)

A product of CyberBills, one of the leaders in the field, StatusFactory is an oddly named but popular and flexible payment service. The online demo does a good job conveying the process of online bill management, although it does not do justice to the well-organized payment order screens. That is a problem, but the service encourages you to try it out by offering to handle one bill, at no charge, for three months. It is an innovative trial feature, and if you do not like the service, you only have to change back one billing address.

A variety of service plans encourage customers to work into the system gradually. The Lite service costs just $3.50 a month for management of five billers, while the Standard plan is a more typical $8.95 for 30 bills. You can avoid the 75-cent charge for additional bills by signing on for the Premier service, which costs $29.95 a month.

The Premier service features emergency payments, in which Status-Factory ships a check with a courier service and charges you for the extra cost. Electronic retrieval of an old bill is free for 12 recoveries per year. All your account activity is stored on an end-of-year CD, free for Premier customers, $49.50 for everyone else.

PayMyBills (www.paymybills.com)

Clarity and communication are hallmarks of this cutting-edge plan. PayMy-Bills is a full-service presentment and payment solution. (See Figure 3.4.) It

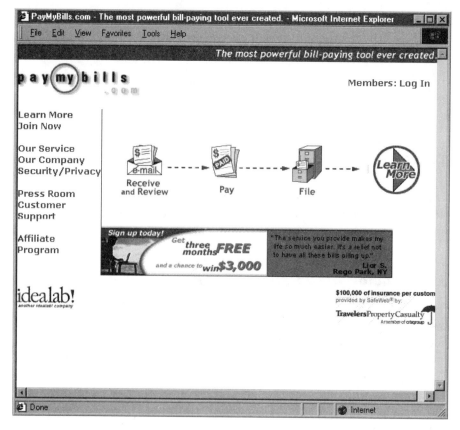

FIGURE 3.4 PayMyBills.com is a full-featured bill-management service. (Reprinted with permission of PayMyBills.com.)

sends prominent reminders when bills are due and displays exceptionally clear status reports that link to individual bills. One quirk is the use of Adobe Acrobat to display scanned bills—some users may have to download the Acrobat Reader. It is worth the trouble, though, as Acrobat is an easier format to print from than a browser.

The first three months are free. Then you pay the standard fee of $8.95 for 25 bills per month, plus 50 cents for each additional payment. PayMyBills handles the billing address switch for you, even for billers that do not appear on the company's list.

This service goes the extra mile in just about every department. You get e-mail reminders for auto-pay bills. The setup screens are models of clarity, making heavy use of drop-down menus to arrange payment schedules and payment account sources. Best of all are the summary pages that consolidate your billing activity into colored pie charts. A one-year archive is always accessible, and the company stores everything in-house for eight years. E-mail and telephone customer support are strong points.

Each PayMyBills account is insured by Travelers Property Casual for $100,000 per account. The site features an interactive multimedia demo.

Paytrust (www.paytrust.com)

PayTrust matches PayMyBills with a three-month trial period. Business owners may be attracted by the Small Business Edition plan, although it is a bit pricey at $19.95 per month plus 75 cents for every transaction.

One elegant feature integrates your bank balance with your PayTrust statement, so you always know if you have enough money to pay a bill, without making a separate trip to your bank site (or looking in your checkbook). However (and this is a big condition), you need to do your banking at one of Paytrust's affiliate banks for this feature to work.

Accounts are downloadable to Quicken and Microsoft Money. The site presents a variety of demos at different graphic levels to suit every modem. Telephone support is available 24 hours a day.

TransPoint (www.transpoint.com)

TransPoint is one of the best-known bill-payment systems, a leader of the field. Codeveloped by Microsoft and First Data Corporation, TransPoint is not a full presentment service. You continue receiving your paper bills, which TransPoint can pay for you. At the same time, TransPoint can receive bills from any biller sending electronic bills, and pay them.

Other limitations apply. You cannot open joint accounts. The Standard service covers only the list of 750 predetermined billers; you must subscribe to the Premium service to add other billing destinations. Thus you are forced to get the Premium service if you want TransPoint to write a check to a landlord; fortunately, both plans are priced below industry standards. The first six months of the Standard plan are free, while Premium gives a still-ample three free months.

Yahoo! Bill Pay (bills.yahoo.com)

Yahoo!, the giant online service portal, gets into the bill-paying act with its own Bill Pay service. Like everything else in Yahoo!, Bill Pay has a populist attitude and a stripped-down, functional look. If you like using Yahoo! and are familiar with its uniform design, you will feel right at home with the bill presentment and payment pages.

The first three months are free. After the trial period expires, you can choose a low-fee, pay-as-you-go plan with a minimum monthly charge of $2 and a fee of 40 cents per bill or an underpriced standard plan for $7 a month, which covers 25 payments.

Chapter

4

Finding an Online Bank

Chapter 2 discussed what online banking is and how to research it as a new type of financial service. Chapter 3 is dedicated to online bill paying as a financial service in its own right. This chapter rounds out the online banking trilogy by exploring how to shop for an online bank and by touring several of the major virtual institutions.

SHOPPING FOR FEATURES

Perhaps you have decided to take the plunge and sign on with an online bank. The future beckons. If you are unsure about whether to wade into the digital waters or stick with your current bank's online services, this section sheds light on considerations that may lure you toward virtual banks or send you scurrying away from them. At the very least, this shopping section can give you a detailed idea of the pros and cons of purely virtual banking.

The thought of starting to use a virtual bank can be intimidating. Everyone is familiar with traditional banking, but the Internet presents a learning curve. Be aware of the following considerations when looking at banking sites.

Do Not Be Distracted by the Site

A beautiful Web site is a lovely thing to behold, but do not rely on your aesthetic sensibilities too much when shopping for an Internet bank. Getting the features you need and good returns on your money are probably more important. Every virtual bank tries to make a good impression from the first click; some succeed better than others. Dig beneath the front page to find whether a virtual bank truly will serve your needs. Remember that an online bank differs from an online broker in that you will not spend as much time there, so the on-screen environment is not as important.

Clear Online Statements

Many online banks provide demo screens of their interfaces. Pay particular attention to the examples of online statements. (See Figure 4.1.) You

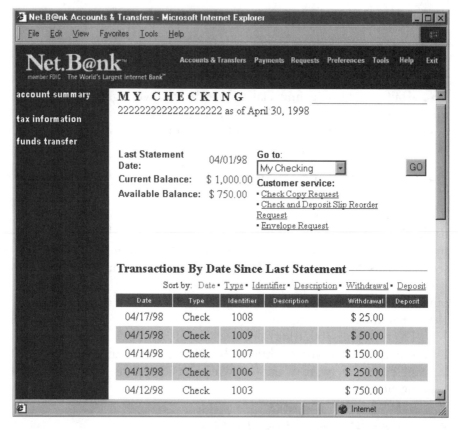

FIGURE 4.1 Ideally, your online banking account screen should be easy to understand.

(Reprinted with permission of NetBank.)

will spend a lot of time with these online statements, and it is important that they be clear and easy to use.

Look at how the statements are organized. Many on-screen statements are clearer and more intuitively understandable than their traditional paper counterparts. You should feel comfortable with the accounting layout pretty quickly.

Bank statements account for many types of activity—withdrawals, deposits, checks clearing, interest payments. The best online statements let you sort the display by type of event, so that all cleared checks are grouped together at the top of the statement, for example. In the best cases, you can search for certain transactions (cleared checks, deposits, ATM withdrawals) within a certain date range. That kind of flexibility is surprisingly useful sometimes.

Does the bank send a monthly statement in the mail? The site may not answer that question. If you want a paper statement, contact the bank to ask if it's supplied, but remember that you can print out the on-screen statement at any time.

Make sure that the bank archives statements and that you can look at previous months. All banks keep records; the question is how easily you can view them. Again, remember that it is a good idea to print statements from your computer once a month.

How Current Is the Statement?

One question that may or may not be important to your particular banking situation is how often the statement is updated. Daily updates are the bottom-line standard; anything less frequent is positively regressive these days. Even better are real-time statements that update whenever a deposit or ATM withdrawal occurs. Such high-level interactivity may not be crucial to your needs, and many virtual banks do not divulge the update frequency of their statements. If you must have an answer to this question, contact the bank by phone or e-mail to ask.

Online Bill Paying at Virtual Banks

This crucial service is explored in Chapter 3, which covers full-service, independent bill-paying programs. When shopping for an online bank account, it is important to realize that although almost all virtual banks offer bill-paying services, the quality varies. Here are some features to keep in mind.

✔ *Cost.* First of all, how much does the service cost? Some banks offer online bill paying free of charge, for unlimited use. Others charge a monthly fee for a certain number of payments. Or the system may charge a small fee for each payment. Obviously, the cheaper it is, the better.

✔ *Ease of setup.* The hardest part of online bill paying is setting it up, which involves entering account information for all bills you want to pay this way. Look for demo screens that illustrate the online forms used for entering biller (payee) information. Some banks step you through several screens, while others consolidate each biller's information on a single form—much easier.

✔ *Use of shortened names.* In addition to the account number and biller address, the form should allow you to give the biller entry a nickname (such as "phone bill" instead of the phone company's name) and a category—utility, for example, or credit card.

✔ *Preset list of billers.* One nifty feature that may appear in the demo is a preset list of billers—credit card companies, department stores, well-known retailers, and so on. If you find your biller on that list, you do not have to look up and enter the payment address. You still must put in your account number, though.

✔ *Ability to view payment history.* In the demo section, look for a way to view your payment history. Ideally, the system allows you to determine a date range and specific biller, so you can view at a glance the payment history of a certain bill.

✔ *Ability to skip or modify payments.* Most people's online payment systems include a mix of regular, unvarying payments (mortgage, rent) and on-demand payments of varying amounts (credit card, utilities). The bank's system should allow you an easy way to skip a regular payment or modify its amount.

✔ *Stop-payment feature.* This feature is nice to have.

Some virtual banks go much further in providing bill-paying service, even including receiving your bills for you. Chapter 3 describes cutting-edge online bill paying more completely.

Deposit Problem

Now we turn to the biggest speed bump on the path to virtual banking: getting money into the darn account. All banks accept checks in the mail as deposits, but some virtual institutions try harder.

Look for the ability to accept wireless transfers from other institutions. This service usually requires additional paperwork (real paper, not online forms), but you have to do it only once. After it is set up, you can make online requests for funds to be transferred from your traditional checking account to your virtual account. The money usually appears the next day.

The problem with wireless transfers is evident—you must keep two checking accounts: one for deposits and one to receive the transfer. The awkward arrangement can be well worth the trouble, though, if your virtual bank gives you high yields and irresistible convenience features. (Remember: Do not attempt the transfer until your deposited check has cleared.)

If you receive your income from a company that can make direct deposits of your paycheck (or if you are receiving direct-deposit Social Security payments), look for a virtual bank that accepts direct deposits. Depositing income checks directly is a good solution most of the time, but what happens when you receive a gift check or want to deposit cash? Then it is back to the post office.

For the time being, the deposit problem is intractable. No solution works in all situations. At some point you may need a walk-in, drive-through, ATM-deposit-capable, old-fashioned bank account for deposits. From that account, it is not too hard to get your deposits into your virtual account.

Withdrawal Problem

Deposits are not the only sore point among virtual bankers. Most people commonly use automated teller machines (ATMs) to withdraw cash from checking and savings accounts. Virtual banks do have ATM compatibility; the problem is with ATM fees.

Traditional banks own their own ATM networks and generally do not charge their own customers for using the network machines. You pay a fee for using another bank's ATM system. Well, when you bank virtually, every machine belongs to another network. Virtual banks, nonphysical institutions that they are, do not own ATM networks. (This fact may change in time.) When there are no "home" ATMs, every withdrawal costs money.

Virtual banks get around this problem by offering *ATM rebates*. The rebate can be a monthly dollar allowance or a per-withdrawal reimbursement. Per-transaction arrangements usually are better. When examining the policy look, for a service that allows at least four withdrawals per month—most people can live on one "home" ATM visit per week. Make sure the bank allots $1.50 per transaction, which is the standard ATM fee.

ATM rebates   rebates used by virtual banks to make up for the fact that the cyber banks usually do not own ATM networks. Because of that lack, virtual bank customers are subject to withdrawal fees at every machine they use. Many virtual banks pay back the equivalent of one withdrawal fee a week, thereby footing the bill for a reasonable amount of ATM use.

At the very least, any self-respecting ATM-rebate scheme pays back at least $4.00 per month in fees.

Interest and Yields

Virtual banks shine their brightest in the area of money yield. Whereas traditional banks have long paid some interest on deposited money, Internet institutions raise the stakes considerably. Virtual banks utterly blast the average checking yields at traditional banks, setting new standards of conservative money growth. In many cases the savings yields are higher at the Internet banks, too.

Historically, checking accounts offer the lowest interest yield in the financial universe, short of putting cash under the mattress. Virtual banks expand the earning power of checking deposits by as much as five times the national average.

Savings accounts (including specialty investment deposit accounts such as money market and CD accounts) traditionally yield higher returns than checking accounts. Again, virtual banks attempt to lure your business with rates that lead or exceed national averages.

When window-shopping banks at their sites, look for tables that compare the bank's interest rates with other banks (see Figure 4.2) or, even better, with national averages.

The high rate of interest on checking accounts offered by many virtual banks narrows the traditional interest spread between checking and savings. The thin yield difference may render the money market and CD rates less important. But still, find the best savings yields you can—check out all rates when exploring a bank site.

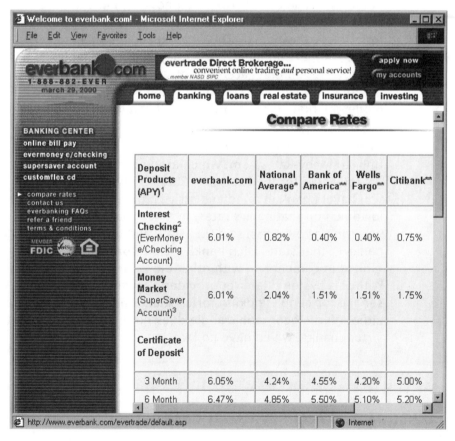

Deposit Products (APY)[1]	everbank.com	National Average*	Bank of America**	Wells Fargo**	Citibank**
Interest Checking[2] (EverMoney e/Checking Account)	6.01%	0.82%	0.40%	0.40%	0.75%
Money Market (SuperSaver Account)[3]	6.01%	2.04%	1.51%	1.51%	1.75%
Certificate of Deposit[4]					
3 Month	6.05%	4.24%	4.55%	4.20%	5.00%
6 Month	6.47%	4.85%	5.50%	5.10%	5.20%

FIGURE 4.2 Online banks show off their superb rate yields in comparative tables.

(Copyright everbank.com.)

Knowing the Rates

Virtual banks like to advertise their high yields on money market and CD accounts and often trumpet comparisons to national averages and even other banks. These tables make for good shopping, but can you trust the comparisons? Two sites place the research into your own hands and put the yield wars into broad perspective.

✔ **Money-Rates.com** (www.money-rates.com)
More than the comparison tables, Money-Rates.com is a veritable hub of information about interest on deposited money. Have you ever wondered how the annual percentage yield (APY) is figured, and why it differs from the interest yield? This site explains it all. But back to the comparison tables. At Money-Rate.com, tables identify high-interest accounts at various institutions, ordered by yield rate. Looking for the best CD rate or money market account? You can tell at a glance who has the best products.

✔ **RateNet** (www.ratenet.com)
Unlike Money-Rates.com, which assumes that you will go anywhere for the best rate, RateNet supposes that you have a bank in mind and strives to deliver the lowdown on that bank's rates. In a geographic directory, you can narrow down to a U.S. state and view all the banks in that state. Each bank's yield information is ranked in comparison with other banks in the state. With this system, RateNet provides a terrific comparison service for people looking for click-and-mortar service, although the geographic angle does not help locate virtual banks, which have no location.

Do Not Be Distracted by Credit Cards

Most banks—virtual and click-and-mortar—have credit cards. Virtual banks sometimes attempt to attract interest and business by linking their credit card products with checking and savings accounts. You may or may not eventually acquire the credit card offered by your virtual bank, but do not be lured too much by its hype while shopping.

There is no particular reason to use a credit card from your checking institution. Do not think for a moment that any bank will cut you slack in the credit-approval department just because you have a checking account with that bank. If approval is not an issue, what is?

Some banks may tout the ease of paying your credit card bill with a simple online fund transfer, but the truth is that it is pretty easy to pay any bill online. Still, if instant payments are an important part of your financial management, pay close attention to the credit card offer of any virtual bank you visit.

Online applications for credit cards abound. You cannot surf the Web without being pestered by ads for them. Just about every major bank and plenty of minor ones are soliciting credit business on the Internet. So remember that the entire Web is the portal for credit card deals, not just a prospective bank.

Banking on the Stock Market

Of the three main types of money account—checking, savings, and investment—banks traditionally provide only the first two. Investment accounts historically have been administered by brokerage companies. That specialty still exists, and many dozens of dedicated online brokerage houses exist. But increasingly, banks are providing brokerage service to their customers.

In the still-maturing milieu of online finance, two conflicting trends are evident. On one hand, specialization is creating ever more defined virtual institutions. On the other hand, consolidation is catering to people who want to simplify their money management by housing all their accounts at one place, not complicate things by farming money out to two or three specialized institutions.

If you prefer the one-stop style of personal finance, look for a virtual bank that provides investment services. A bank may supply its own brokerage department, or, more often, it creates an affiliation with an existing brokerage. FleetBoston, for example (a click-and-mortar bank) affiliates with Quick & Reilly (a securities broker) to give its customers investment accounts.

Membership in FDIC

Most, but not all, banks, virtual and traditional, are members of the Federal Deposit Insurance Corporation (FDIC), a U.S. government company

Your Bank's Brokerage: Is It Good Enough?

Depending on your investment style, you might want to look closely at what the bank's brokerage arm has to offer. In many cases, investment services at a bank are rather plain and unsophisticated compared to those of a dedicated online broker. Simplicity may be right up your alley, but check for the basics that are important to you: a selection of mutual funds; the ability to set up an individual retirement account (IRA); and a reasonable commission schedule for buying and selling stocks. (See Chapter 11 for a detailed discussion of many criteria.)

If you are involved in specialized trading (i.e., stock and index options) or accounts that require administrative expertise (i.e., Keogh retirement plans), you might be better off with a dedicated brokerage company, even if you must sacrifice the convenience of keeping your accounts together. Of course, you can spin off some money into a dedicated online brokerage for trading or establishing a specialized account at any time. Just remember that transferring an investment account from one institution to another can be a lengthy and painful business. Plan your strategy and shop carefully.

that inspires confidence in the American banking system by protecting owners of checking and savings accounts. Look for the FDIC logo on the home page of any virtual bank site. If you do not see the logo there, look in the section that describes checking accounts. If you still do not see it, visit the FDIC site at the following link: www.fdic.gov.

This site lets you search for membership records by institution name. As an added benefit, the FDIC search engine delivers a considerable amount of information about the bank's assets, liabilities, number of depositors, branch offices—and all these data are accompanied by links to glossary entries explaining what is meant.

Evaluating Customer Service

The truth is, evaluating *customer service* of any bank before opening an account is difficult. That is true with traditional banks as well as virtual

When FDIC Does Not Apply

Virtual banks usually advertise their membership in the FDIC by placing FDIC logos on their pages. However, if you are examining (or have a joined) a virtual bank with brokerage services, you may notice bold-faced disclaimers on some pages stating that investment accounts are not FDIC-insured. Quite true—the Federal Deposit Insurance Corporation, true to its name, insures deposit accounts, not investment accounts. Do not be spooked by this; the rest of the bank is still an FDIC member, and your checking and savings accounts are covered. Almost all online brokerages insure their customers through the Securities Investor Protection Corporation (SIPC). In a virtual bank that covers all the bases, your banking accounts are FDIC-protected and your investment accounts are SIPC-protected.

ones, but at least with a walk-in bank you are dealing with living people right from the start. Plus, you can share the experience of friends concerning local banks. It is impossible to tell from a Web site how a bank will come through for you in a pinch.

customer service customer service on the Internet can be provided in digital formats such as e-mail and on-site chatting, or by traditional means such as the telephone. The financial sites usually provide two types of customer service: help with site navigation and help with financial products offered by the site. Online banks and stock brokers are famous for poor customer service compared to walk-in banks and brokerages.

Some virtual banks promote their fine, responsive, at-the-ready customer service. If we are to learn anything from the more evolved online brokerage industry, it is that such claims are barely worth the pixels they are printed with when not backed by a true commitment to human resources.

You can try engaging the bank's customer service department before opening an account. Find the contact information for the bank (look for a "Contact Us" link) and call or write with a couple of questions. (If you cannot find contact information at the site, that is a bad sign.) Consider not only how quickly your query is answered but how personally. Did you get a form-letter e-mail?

If a bank is not quick to answer your preliminary questions, there is no reason to expect superb responsiveness once it has captured your business.

Second-Level Services

The previous paragraphs cover basic services usually associated with the daily banking experience—depositing and withdrawing cash, paying bills, receiving interest. Sometimes other traditional banking functions, particularly lending, are part of the virtual equation.

Online lending is a work-in-progress. The field is being shaped. Virtual banks are attempting to grab a portion of the loan business from traditional banks while at the same time fending off assaults from the even newer independent Internet lenders. (See Chapter 7.)

Any virtual bank may advertise a loan department. Well and good—there is nothing wrong with checking out the terms, rates, and loan products. But do not be swayed too much toward one bank simply because of its loans. Remember that when it comes to loans, the Web is the portal, not the bank. The only reason to borrow from the company you bank with is that you can make installment payments by instantaneous transfer—a convenience, but not worth sacrificing loan terms for.

Choose a bank because of its banking features. Then borrow from that bank if you want, or surf your way to another deal. There is no proximity on the Internet—every lender is just a click away.

Insurance is another field that some virtual banks are dabbling in. In most cases, the bank site serves as an information portal for obtaining insurance quotes. Here, more than ever, do not be fooled into thinking that owning an account at the bank improves your ability to shop for or acquire insurance online. (See Chapters 5 and 6.)

Next-Generation Services

On the Internet, the time-honored definitions of banking are being stretched. It is not uncommon to find some forward-thinking virtual banks totally redefining banking. If you want to be positioned at the cut-

cyber cash   the cyber cash concept is designed to simplify the present credit card system and make payments more secure. Electronic currency schemes are a sort of Internet equivalent of smart cards, whereby an online account is funded with deposited cash, then used to pay for online merchandise.

ting edge of online personal finance, consider a bank that keeps one foot planted in the future. Two candidates for your perusal are:

1. *Net.Bank (www.netbank.com).* With innovative account access schemes (see your statements at the bank site or at Yahoo!), plus a remarkable online safe deposit box for secure document storage, Net.Bank is getting its share of attention

2. *X.com (www.x.com).* A virtual bank with headquarters located at Ground Zero of Silicon Valley? Must be a high-tech venture. Indeed, X.com is making waves with a virtual payment system for shopping at online auctions, e-mail moneygrams, and a mutual fund with rebates. The entire industry is watching X.com to see what it will think of next.

It is difficult to predict what new technologies and features will be important to the future of banking. But instant online payments for Internet shopping looks promising—there is certainly demand for such a service. There have already been several cyber cash and other initiatives, all of which failed to get off the ground as of year 2000. Online auction markets such as the enormously popular eBay (www.ebay.com) practically beg for a better payment system by which individuals can pay other individuals for purchases. Today virtual banks are working hard to develop an electronic person-to-person payment system.

TOURING VIRTUAL BANKS

The banks in this section are some of the major virtual institutions offering cutting-edge online services. This selection is extensive but not comprehensive and is meant as a companion while you get acquainted with online banking features described earlier in this chapter.

The descriptions in this section convey a general sense of each institution's angle into the marketplace and strong points and detail some specific features. Remember, the details can change. A bank's general positioning in the marketplace can change, too, but not as quickly. Explore any bank site on your own before opening an account, using the considerations discussed earlier in this chapter.

First Internet Bank of Indiana (www.firstib.com)

Extra! Extra! First Internet Bank of Indiana (see Figure 4.3) did what online banks should have done right from the beginning—arranged for customers to make deposits through participating ATM networks. This bold stroke ameliorates the deposit problem like nothing else. For now, the initiative is limited. We can only hope it will spread to many ATM networks and many other online banks.

First Internet offers a modest range of services—checking, savings, loans, and credit cards—and does so with style and tight integration. Account screens update in real time, a seeming requirement for cyber banking that you do not find everywhere. The online bill-payment program supports electronic payments when available and places no limitations on whom you can pay by check. (Funds are debited from your account before the processing date, an unfortunate policy.)

Interest rates are middling at best. Money market yields are competitive, but checking account yields lag behind those of other virtual banks. (Of course, checking yields are far ahead of traditional banks.) A surprising maintenance fee for basic checking puts a fly in the ointment; you can avoid it by keeping a minimum balance or scheduling regular cash transfers into the account.

First Internet works with E-Loan to provide search engines and online quotes for mortgages and personal loans.

The Upshot: Customer buzz is generally positive but not superlative. The bank executes its products well but could spiff up its features, not to mention its aging site. Customer service enjoys a reputation for being helpful but is not available on the phone during weekends. Overall, a solid and experienced online bank.

X.com (www.x.com)

X.com is a cutting-edge cyber bank with one foot planted firmly in the future. The service opened with basic checking and Visa services. X.com quickly attracted a user base that launched it ahead of rivals in the com-

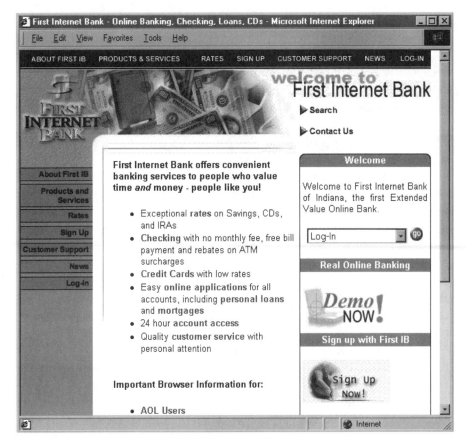

FIGURE 4.3 First Internet Bank of Indiana is a dedicated cyber institution with excellent account services and average rates.

(Copyright First Internet Bank of Indiana.)

petitive scramble for customers. One compelling attraction merges banking with investment: X.com offers three no-load, no-minimum mutual funds, one of which actually matches a small percentage of your investment. Now *that's* service!

X.com's banking services are provided by First Western National Bank, an FDIC-insured institution. X.com is essentially a technology company, located in Silicon Valley and partnered with a bank, which explains its innovative spirit.

It is the gonzo futuristic approach that draws in the early adopters. X.com is pushing its person-to-person payment system, and customers like it. This feature lets users exchange money through e-mail. Just before this book went to print, X.com announced a merger with PayPal, another leader in the electronic payment field (see Chapter 2), which further strengthens X.com's position in an exciting new kind of banking. X.com considers itself a Western Union of money.

X.com offers basic checking and CD accounts, with rates that compare to, but do not lead, other cyber banks. Checking account yields are far above traditional banks if you keep at least $1,000 in the account. Visa debit cards come with the accounts.

The three aforementioned mutual funds are Standard & Poor's 500 index fund, a bond fund, and a money market fund. Only the S&P 500 fund dishes back that matching percentage, but none of them charges any kind of sales, distribution, or redemption fees, and no minimum contributions are required. You can become an X.com customer with $10—$5 in checking and $5 in a fund.

The site describes account features well enough but fails to display any demos of the account screens. Also to the downside, no online bill paying was offered at the time of this book's printing, a glaring omission from an online bank.

The Upshot: X.com presents the highest of high tech, but not the highest interest rates by any means. This is a bank for early adopters who like virtual gadgets—in particular, person-to-person payments. Active online auction users are attracted to its electronic cash features, all the more so with the PayPal merger. But remember—person-to-person payment may become standard on the Internet within a few years regardless of what bank you use. X.com is a bank for those dedicated to the online lifestyle, but the lack of bill paying makes it more appropriate as a second bank.

NetBank (www.netbank.com)

From the name, you know this is a purely virtual bank. NetBank's site (see Figure 4.4) is clear and provides fast, uncluttered demo screens of account pages and features—quite a relief compared to the obfuscating shenanigans of some bank sites.

Two basic checking plans prevail here: NetValue Checking is absolutely free, and entitles you to a limited version of the online bill-paying feature. SuperValue Checking costs $4.50 a month, yielding a higher interest rate and giving unlimited online bill payments. Free checks and online reordering are provided.

FIGURE 4.4 NetBank is one of the more progressive online banks.
(Reprinted with permission of NetBank.)

NetBank has no ATM affiliations (most virtual banks do not) but does provide an on-site search engine for finding whatever local no-fee ATMs exist.

Considerately, NetBank mails paper statements to its customer every month. That is good service, but oddly, customer service over the phone is not available on Saturdays.

NetBank ties investment services into the mix with the help of brokerage company Uvest. Commission rates for stock and option trading are poor—well toward the upper end of tolerance for an online brokerage.

The Tips & Tools section of the site is available to all visitors and provides a few articles about money management.

The Upshot: NetBank makes it easy to get started with its simple and quick online application forms. Money market interest yields are an attractive feature, and checking interest is competitive with other online banks. While basic features are well executed, NetBank is not known for powerful integration of nonbanking perks, such as investing. This is a solid choice for virtual banking.

Security First Network Bank (www.sfnb.com)

One of a few institutions that claim to have been the first virtual bank, Security First Network Bank (SFNB) began online operation in 1995 and has established a strong online brand. The site gives a comprehensive rundown of account services. An animated demo graphically spells out how some tasks, such as online bill paying, are accomplished. Use the Welcome Kit portion of the site to see all the account screens. An online tutorial is embedded in the kit; it delivers useful information about online bill paying and other account features.

SFNB is committed to paperless banking and provides online images of cleared statements. Certificate of deposit accounts are opened with no certificates. In return for the virtual banking lifestyle, Security First issues some of the best available yield rates on checking and savings accounts. Two types of checking—Interest and Basic—are available, the main difference being a minimum deposit (only $100) required for the interest account. In both cases free online bill paying comes with the deal, with varying ceilings on the number of bills you can pay per month.

This cyber bank addresses the deposit problem aggressively, spelling out numerous methods of meeting the challenge. Scheduled, recurring transfers from another bank account are possible here, as are direct deposits of paychecks. Of course, checks are accepted, and the bank even maintains one walk-in office, in Atlanta.

SFNB is confident in its systems and puts out a reassuring aura. The bank's 100 percent security guarantee is spelled out in advance and covers hacking, human error (theirs, not yours), and misdirected online bill payments.

The Upshot: A good track record and very high checking/savings rates make Security First a reliable choice for online banking. Most of the basics are covered, and no minimums are required to get started with free (and interest-free) checking. However, no loans or brokerage services are offered. The site and the account screens could use a thorough update— this online bank is beginning to show its age.

Wingspan Bank (www.wingspanbank.com)

Wingspan Bank entered the online banking field with a noisy splash, using TV ads more than any other virtual bank. Wingspan is the virtual banking division of Bank One, and its intent has been to provide a complete range of personal finance solutions, from checking to lending, investing to insurance.

Wingspan has found it difficult to integrate its many services. At this writing, some obvious lacks were in evidence, such as the inability to pay bills online from more than one Wingspan account. The brokerage screens are basic to the point of being rudimentary. Bank and brokerage statements are updated daily, not in real time. The online buzz is that the bank experienced growing pains, but most people who make the effort to get the help they need are pleased with Wingspan's overall performance.

When visiting the site for the first time, a detailed frequently asked question (FAQ) page spells out the features of checking, bill paying, credit cards, money transfers, and system requirements for online banking. Very helpfully, an interactive ATM Locator finds cash machines affiliated with Wingspan by city, state, zip code, or street. (Even the affiliated ATMs charge Wingspan customers $1.00 per transaction.)

On the insurance side, Wingspan acts as a locator, using the InsWeb search engines to deliver online quotes for life, auto, homeowners, renters, and health coverage.

Interest yields? Wingspan's CD accounts are competitive; compared to other online banks, its checking rates are average. Current rates are listed at the site, but no comparisons with other banks are displayed.

The Upshot: Wingspan is an ambitious bank taking some time to work out the kinks. Even so, it has scored high marks among many users who discuss the bank on financial message boards. Many products are not integrated as tightly as they could be, so customers may be tempted to fulfill some elements of their finance needs (especially investing and credit cards) elsewhere.

everbank.com (www.everbank.com)

everbank.com's flashy online promotion (see Figure 4.5) throws several appealing features into a recipe for progressive virtual banking. Along the way, the site makes at least one claim that should be properly understood.

The loudly proclaimed no-fee ATM access means that everbank.com does not charge a fee when you use the provided Visa check card to withdraw cash from any ATM. All well and good, but that does not stop the

FIGURE 4.5   everbank.com is not shy about advertising its high account yields.

(Copyright everbank.com.)

host bank from charging your account, as they all do, so access is not precisely without fees. everbank.com rebates up to $4.00 per month in ATM fees—a better offer than none at all, but it does not cover one withdrawal fee per week at $1.50 per transaction.

The no-fee claim holds up better in the online bill-paying department. Checking and bill paying are paired in a free, unlimited-use setup. everbank.com deducts funds from your account two days after the scheduled payment date—a fair deal, better than at banks that debit the account on the due date. Furthermore, payments can be scheduled for that day's processing up to 11 P.M.—possibly the most relaxed deadline in the business.

Coupled with a general no-fee policy, everbank.com pays one of the highest checking account interest yields the industry has ever seen. Account screens for checking and bill paying are clear, if not exactly elegant.

everbank.com covers investing with the related but autonomous EverTrade service. EverTrade provides decent commission rates and, unlike many investment divisions of banks, looks and feels like a real broker.

The Upshot: everbank.com is gunning aggressively for your business, with a compelling mix of basic online banking features. Lack of integration hurts the investment side, protected as it is by a separate log-on path. So integration is not the point here, but exceptionally high yields and free account perks are.

Wells Fargo (www.wellsfargo.com)

A pioneer in online banking, Wells Fargo is a walk-in institution located in San Francisco that has extended its reach through aggressive online marketing and servicing. From its early roots as a limited click-and-mortar operation, Wells Fargo has evolved into a full-featured financial services operation providing deposit accounts, credit cards, loans, insurance, retirement accounts, and investing services.

Like most click-and-mortar banks, Wells Fargo has not completely disassociated from traditional bank practices, including the charging of fees. Of its four checking account plans, only one operates without a maintenance fee—and that one only if you maintain a certain level of direct-deposit activity. The other fees are waived when minimum balances (much higher than at most virtual banks) are met. The online bill-payment feature is free to customers keeping a combined $5,000 in their accounts, a rather stiff requirement.

Local customers have no ATM problem with Wells Fargo, but remote users certainly do. The bank charges its own fee when you use another ATM network machine, in addition to whatever the machine's bank charges you. Rebates? Not offered at the time of this writing.

Wells Fargo bundles investment services into the banking experience but buries the commission fee schedule deep in the site. There is a good reason for hiding it, as trading commissions are at the upper end of online brokerage. Most online investors would do better getting a separate broker, forgoing the advantage of housing all accounts at one institution.

The Upshot: Wells Fargo has a lot of users and a big online buzz. As a pure Internet banking experience, Wells Fargo executes well but encumbers its service with fees that do not go down easily with cutting-edge users. This bank has years of experience in the online realm, but if you want to move aggressively into the future, choose a less expensive virtual bank.

CompuBank (www.compubank.com)

CompuBank is a highly rated virtual institution that concentrates its efforts on deposit products. If it is more important to do a few things well than many things not so well, CompuBank is making the right choices.

The usual range of checking and savings accounts are available here—no-interest checking, interest-yielding checking, basic savings, money market, and certificates of deposit. Check out the Products page; no clearer rundown of service, minimums, and features could be desired.

You get interest on your checking account by maintaining a $1,000 minimum, and even the no-interest account requires an opening deposit of $100. Interest yields are better than traditional banks and significantly less that some virtual banks. The first round of paper checks is free, and additional customized checks can be ordered online. Statements are archived for 12 months—that duration is the industry standard.

Regarding the ATM fee problem, CompuBank generously refunds up to four transaction fees of $1.50 each, every month. The site features a search page for fee-free ATM networks in most states.

CompuBank is all about banking. The fact that it ignores the current trend of financial service integration might be a good idea—many virtual banks do not integrate investing, insurance, and lending well. CompuBank narrows its focus to checking, savings, and bill paying, and while its interest yields do not create headline news, it executes its products well.

The Upshot: Clarity, focus, and a laserlike commitment to quality banking service make CompuBank a fine choice in virtual banking for those who do not care about integrated financial services. The bank enjoys very positive buzz on the boards, although some people complain that the advertised 24-hour customer service slacks off at night.

DirectBanking (www.directbanking.com)

DirectBanking is an online bank venture spun off from Salem Five, a local bank network in Massachussetts. The online services department was renamed and established as a distinct institution. The site explains accounts and features very well but fails to show the account management screens.

One reason for that omission is the system of multiple interfaces used by DirectBanking.

To an unusual degree, DirectBanking caters to the individual's computing setup. Customers can register for PC HomeBanking, which uses special software to connect directly with the bank, or Internet Home-Banking, which uses a Web interface. Telephone HomeBanking is also available, and you can access accounts through Quicken, the home accounting program.

Checking and savings accounts hold forth with few surprises. The interest-bearing checking account requires a minimum balance. Interest rates escalate according to the account balance, an aspect that is a little unusual for an online bank. The rates are modest at lower balance levels, then kick in more impressively when you keep $5,000 in a checking account or $10,000 in a money market account. Investment accounts are linked to Clippership Financial Services, operating as a separate site. There is little attempt at integrating investing and banking, beyond cross-linking the two sites.

The Upshot: DirectBanking gets points for a clear site that performs well, especially for its interface flexibility. The choice between PC banking and Internet banking, by itself, makes this bank a winner for anyone who would rather avoid the Internet when managing finances. This is no bank to attempt integrated services, though, and the relatively low interest yields on low-balance accounts is discouraging. Customer opinion is volatile, with mixed reviews posted to the discussion boards.

BankDirect (www.bankdirect.com)

BankDirect spells out its features and advantages in a no-nonsense site that does not make you search through a labyrinth of screens to find important information. And nothing about online banking is more important than the account yields, which at BankDirect are outstanding. Clearly, this institution is trying to lure customers with solid growth opportunities rather than slick interface design.

Check out the bill-paying demo for a look at BankDirect's screen interface style. It is all plain and stripped down.

This service zips through the basics with little fanfare—low opening requirements, no fees unless you let an account become completely inactive for three months, an ATM card, and rebates for four ATM transactions ($1.50 each) per month. Exceptionally high money market rates become effective with a $500 minimum.

The Upshot: It is not pretty, but it works. And those interest yields!

This is a bank for those who care more about clear money management and high rates than attractive screens. User feedback repeatedly mentions poor customer service through e-mail but otherwise is uniformly positive.

Claritybank (www.claritybank.com)

Claritybank was not quite open as this book went to press, but keep your eye on this puppy. It should be open as you read these words, with what is advertised as a comprehensive array of financial services offered over the Web and through portable wireless devices. This system may appeal more to business users than others, but everyone has got to love the site's opening-screen animation.

E*Trade and Telebank (www.etrade.com)

As this book went to press, online stock broker E*Trade had completed the purchase of Internet bank Telebank, creating intriguing possibilities for the future. After closing this deal, E*Trade went to the marketplace again and announced its intent to acquire 8,500 ATMs. (That acquisition was not finalized by this book's deadline.)

If Telebank, to be renamed E*Trade Bank, becomes the third-largest operator of ATM machines, as the purchase would make it, the deposit problem that plagues most virtual banks would be largely ameliorated. That by itself is big news. Even more fascinating would be the integration of investing, banking, and ATM account access. The day might come when a customer can walk to a local ATM, get some cash, and place a stock order at the same machine.

Using Internet Insurance Resources

O f the many online financial services covered in this book, general insurance resources represent the most immature field. Oh, there are plenty of insurance brokers, as described in Chapter 6. But when it comes to news and data sites *about* insurance, the pickings get slim and difficult to find.

Online life is better for insurance professionals, because there are more trade resources than consumer resources. In some cases the professional sites are of interest to consumers, and this chapter lists a handful of them.

CONSUMER RESOURCES

The first part of this chapter gathers the best of the scattered consumer information sites into a single directory—something that is missing on the Web itself.

Insure.com (www.insure.com)

"We inform. You decide." That's the motto of this comprehensive online magazine covering insurance from the consumer's viewpoint. Feature articles are informative about the in-depth issues of insurance protection, while daily news coverage spotlights the corporate and regulatory developments affecting individual providers. Each major type of insurance—life, business, health, home, auto—has its own department with complete news sections. In each department, be sure to scroll down to the bottom of the page for a fine assortment of how-to information about virtually every insurance topic you can think of.

Association of Online Insurance Agents (www.cyberapp.com)

Oddly, this site is not a directory of online agents at all but of brick-and-mortar agencies sorted by state.

A.M. Best Company (www.ambest.com)

This insurance company ranking service appears, albeit invisibly, all over the Web's insurance space. That's because A.M. Best is the premier ranking service for the insurance industry. A.M. Best ratings are based on the financial stability of insurance companies and their capacity to meet their financial obligations on behalf of customers. Some brokers (see Chapter 6) deal only with insurance firms that A.M. Best ranks highly.

This site describes the A.M. Best ratings methodology and lets visitors search for insurance companies based on rating categories. It is a good adjunct to finding insurance, whether through an online broker or not.

Individual.com (www.individual.com)

Individual.com lived a long previous life as Newspage.com, one of the foremost publishers of wire service reports on the Web. Now, in its new incarnation, Individual.com still provides news in several technology and business categories. Go to the Bus. & Finance link and click the Insurance subcategory. There you will find groups of news headlines and stories under Insurance Brokerage, Insurance Industry Overview, Life Insurance, Annuities, and many other topical divisions. It is one of the best and quickest ways to keep up with industry news.

Insurance Information Institute (www.iii.org)

The Insurance Information Institute (III) is a nonprofit information resource about all aspects of insurance and safety issues. (See Figure 5.1).

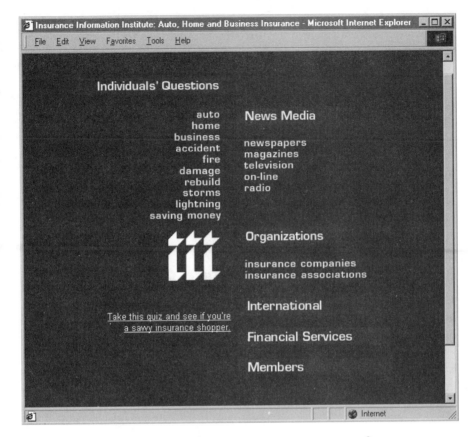

FIGURE 5.1 The Insurance Information Institute—a nonprofit resource.
(Reprinted with permission of Insurance Information Institute.)

At this site you can read educational material about how to buy, how to save money, and how to protect property and live more safely.

The III is an astounding source of industry statistics. Click the News Media link for a directory of information that will make you an insurance-issues expert at the next cocktail party.

MoneyCentral Insurance
(moneyinsider.msn.com/Insure/home.asp)

Part of Microsoft MoneyCentral, this site is an outstanding information portal and decision center. As comprehensive as every other portion of MoneyCentral, these pages deliver articles, interactive tools, industry news, and insurance quotes. Not in the brokerage business per se, MoneyCentral Insurance relies on other companies for its quotes—you would do better visiting the sites described in Chapter 6 when shopping for coverage. At this site, stick to the articles, news, and reference features.

The Quick Reference area is beautifully presented. Topics covered include Auto, Disability, Health, Home, Life, and others. You can choose Q&A, Tools & Articles, or Related Sites to answer questions, read up on insurance subjects, or link to other sites. Insurance news is international in scope, taken from multiple providers such as the *Financial Times*, the *New York Times*, and A.M. Best, the insurance rating company.

L.A. Times: *Insurance 101* (*www.latimes.com/business/insure101*)

This portion of the *L.A. Times's* Business section is a special report on life insurance. Ten lessons explore issues of need, insurance products, basics of whole life policies and annuities, how to cash out "without dying" (always preferable), and how to use insurance in estate planning. Geared for the quick learner and written with the clear journalistic style that made this business section one of the most read online, this virtual textbook is a keeper.

SafeTnet (www.safetnet.com)

SafeTnet is a uniquely organized launching pad for finding Internet insurance resources. Set up as a series of questions in about a dozen insurance-related topics, the site is a directory of other Web sites, many of which are overlooked in similar directories. Pull down the left-hand menu to select an insurance type or topic, then select one of the displayed links. The following page lists Web resources.

Foundation for Taxpayer & Consumer Rights: Insurance (www.consumerwatchdog.org/insurance)

This consumer watchdog site covers legislation related to insurance and provides all kinds of fact sheets. Newsy and current, this online publication might turn you into an insurance activist.

What Is Health Insurance (www.wmplus.com/licwal/whatis.htm)

One of the best single-page tutorials on health insurance. This quick lesson explains what health insurance covers, who provides it, types of policies, and government-sponsored health plans, and answers common questions. The site is provided by a California insurance company.

InsuranceQuote.net (www.insurancequote.net)

This site differs somewhat from the insurance brokers to be discussed in Chapter 6. InsuranceQuote is a more comprehensive clearinghouse than a typical *online insurance* broker, and links visitors to other companies without tying itself into the deal as an affiliate. The result is a good state-by-state resource of all types of insurance coverage. Do not let the site's retro design and gigantic letters dissuade you. The home page may look goofy, but underneath lurks good information. Scroll to the bottom of the home page for the state directory.

online insurance a fairly complex and quickly evolving field in which consumers can search out, compare, and apply for certain types of insurance policies. Life insurance is best represented on the Internet, but health and property insurance is available, as well. Some insurance carriers sell policies directly over the Web, but most of the action is through Internet-based insurance brokers.

Internet Insurance Directory (www.insdir.com)

Like InsuranceQuote.net, the Internet Insurance Directory is a bad-looking site with good information. A global directory to insurance companies (online and offline), the site's strongest database is the state-by-state directory. Start by selecting a state from a list or a map; from that state's directory page, select a type of insurance.

Impressively, the site reveals complete contact information for the insurance companies. Not as impressively, it forces you to browse by insurance type, rather than cross-referencing companies with types of coverage offered. The table display of InsuranceQuote.net is more effective in this regard, because you can see at a glance which companies provide certain types of coverage. But InsuranceQuote.net does not provide full contact information; it merely links you to the carrier's site.

State Departments of Insurance (www.insure.com/links/doi.html)

From Insure.com (and if you have not been there yet, go now), this page is your one-stop directory to the Web sites for all state insurance departments. Use your state's site if you want to begin a complaint process or check on local regulations.

You also might want to look at Insurance Connections!, a state-by-state guide to insurance regulation offices (www.connectyou.com/ic/states.htm).

Benefit Mall (www.benefitmall.com/Index.asp)

Benefit Mall is the complete insurance guide for owners of small businesses looking for company plans. The site, which is not comprehensive, covers primarily those companies it has affiliate relationships with. While you can compare plans and benefits (free of charge), perhaps the best value here is the educational material. It is a good destination if you are contemplating taking on employees or looking to switch from your current plan. The material presented here is value-oriented and aims to save small businesses money in the long run by pointing them to productive insurance choices.

Coalition Against Insurance Fraud (www.insurancefraud.com)

This independent, nonprofit organization keeps members and visitors informed about fraud news and legislative facts. A weekly newsletter is available through e-mail.

PickInsurance.com (www.pickinsurance.com)

This information resource was just getting started as this book went to press. (See Figure 5.2.) Keep your eye on it as an information resource and recommendation center. In the meantime, several useful lists of links are up in the Information & Resources category.

The site provides a selection of search engines for finding providers and even files of consumer complaints filed at state agencies. The Law-

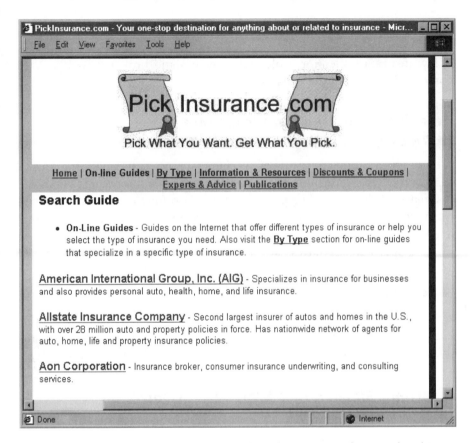

FIGURE 5.2 PickInsurance is about—what else?—researching and picking insurance.

(Reprinted with permission of PickInsurance.com.)

suit Library section tracks which companies are undergoing litigation, and why.

You could spend a month at this site and not absorb it all. No matter what your level of experience, no matter what type of insurance you are after, you will come away from this destination knowing a lot more than when you entered it. From one-month auto policies to the complications of health insurance for pregnant women, from laptop computer coverage to the consequences of lying about tobacco use on a life insurance application, Insure.com dishes the goods. And it is all packaged in the best way—easy on the eyes, simple to navigate, fast-loading pages. A definite keeper for the bookmark list.

TRADE ORGANIZATIONS

A few insurance sites for professional agents and brokers provide some content of interest at the consumer level.

American Council of Life Insurance (www.gsa.gov/staff/pa/cic/acli/page2.htm)

A trade organization consisting of 500 life insurance companies, the American Council of Life Insurance (ACLI) produces this tutorial site about life insurance. Written simply and clearly, this is a primer on how to approach this type of insurance protection. Not a navigation site by any means, this lesson reads like a short book, one page after another with no detours off to the side. It is a breath of fresh air in the clutter of hype about life insurance.

American Insurance Association (www.aiadc.org)

This trade organization produces a Web site for the insurance trade, and it is of interest to consumers who like to keep track of developments in the industry. Read the press releases every day and be the life of your next party.

Insurance Marketplace Standards Association (www.imsaethics.org)

A trade organization promoting ethical standards in the life insurance industry, the Web site of the Insurance Marketplace Standards Association (IMSA) has a surprisingly good glossary. The rest is of interest mostly to professionals.

Council of Insurance Agents and Brokers (www.ciab.com)

A stylish trade site with interesting Industry Affairs, Legislative, and International sections that are open and free to visitors.

TOOLS AND CALCULATORS

While tools and calculators abound in the fields of investing, credit, and online banking, there are not many sites dedicated to insurance calculations and data. Following are two sites that contain fine interactive tools related to insurance and a third destination that provides an exceptional insurance glossary. For more standard, shorter glossaries, try one of the many brokerage sites described in Chapter 6.

Consumer Reports Home Insurance Worksheet (www.consumerreports.org/Special/Samples/Reports/ hominswk.htm)

Use this calculator to figure how much home insurance you need. The form invites you into the unpleasant but worthwhile task of estimating how much it would cost to replace your home in case of utter disaster. You need to know your total square footage to complete this form. You also must know, or be able to estimate, current construction costs per square foot.

Life and Health Insurance Foundation for Education (www.life-line.org)

Life-line.org is a nonprofit consumer service that educates visitors about life, health, and disability insurance and helps them assess the value of appropriate coverage. Using editorial content divided into short, easy-to-digest chapters, the site is unintimidating. Each section contains one or two calculators for determining necessary coverage amounts. A fine glossary is presented in a pop-up window for use as you use the site.

Complete Glossary of Insurance Coverage Explanations (www.lcgroup.com/explanations)

The unfortunate color scheme of this site should not put you off from recognizing it as an underrated gem. This glossary is notable for its unusual entries and extensive explanations. Incredibly detailed glossary entries, such as Boiler and Machinery Coverage, lead to detailed definitions, some of which include calculations and multiple examples.

Chapter 6

Finding Online Insurance Brokers

On the Internet, insurance is sold by two main types of companies:

1. *Online insurance brokers.* These sites maintain affiliations with a number of insurance providers (carriers) and deliver quotes of competitive policies that match your needs.

2. *Insurance carriers with Web sites.* Some of the providers themselves peddle policies over the Web, using the medium to display quotes or provide an interface for contacting human agents.

The key difference between a broker and an *insurance carrier* is that the broker compares policies and quotes belonging to multiple providers. Carriers (for the most part, though there are exceptions) display information about only their own products.

insurance carrier a company that provides insurance coverage directly to consumers, as distinct from an insurance broker, which acts as an agent between consumers and many carriers.

Brokerage sites tend to be a little more technology-heavy than carrier sites, which often have the upper hand in site design and navigational ease.

Insuring Spot

Specialized and unusual insurance policies are hard to find in the thicket of life insurance sites, but you can do so. This chapter points to a few specialty coverage types:

✔ Pet insurance.

✔ Disability (such policies are usually part of a workplace package).

✔ Small business (for business owners).

But this distinction is subjective, liable to change at any time from site to site, and is really a matter of taste. This chapter details many of the strengths and weaknesses of insurance sites in general and several specific ones.

The online realm features most of the same basic insurance types as the brick-and-mortar realm:

✔ *Health.* Individual and group health quotes can be searched on-line. Brokers deal with health maintenance organization (*HMO*), Preferred Provider Organization (*PPO*), and point-of-service (*POS*) plans. Some brokerage sites list accident insurance, as an explicit species of

HMO   health maintenance organization. A group insurance plan affiliated with a network of hospitals and doctors. Customers stay with the healthcare network and trade monthly premiums for low-cost healthcare.

PPO   Preferred Provider Organization. A network of healthcare providers that provide services for a flat rate to covered members of an insurance plan.

POS   point of service. A health plan that gives customers a choice of using a network of healthcare providers (at low cost) or a doctor outside the network (at higher cost).

coverage. Traveling (international) health coverage is hard to find, but this chapter points out one brokerage that includes such coverage.

✔ *Life.* Life insurance is, by far, the most common type of coverage presented by brokerage sites. Almost all brokerages compare term life insurance policies, and many carrier sites focus on them.

✔ *Auto.* Auto insurance takes the lead among types of vehicle insurance. Motorcycle and boat insurance sometimes can be located in the brokerage sites.

✔ *Residential.* Homeowners' insurance rubs elbows with renters' insurance and specialized condo owners' policies. Of the top four coverage types, residential insurance gets the least attention among the online brokers.

EVALUATING ONLINE INSURANCE BROKERS

Use the following sections to fix your bearings before browsing through the brokerage reviews later in this chapter.

Breadth of Products

Many types of insurance exist, and a full-service broker should cover most, if not all, of the bases. Life insurance is the centerpiece at most brokers. Health insurance is increasingly found at these sites. Auto and home insurance round out the basic offerings.

Unusual types of insurance appear on the most comprehensive sites: motorcycle insurance, health insurance for pets, renter's insurance, and dental plans.

Multiple Providers

In the earliest days of online insurance brokers, you would go through a lengthy application process to find out the broker represented only one company that applied to your situation, or even none. That disappointment still can happen. You want a broker with a wide assortment of carrier affiliations.

Some sites flaunt their affiliations by showing their logos on every page. All those graphics may slow down the site performance, but at least you know the brokerage is drawing on multiple resources. If it seems like the results you are getting are not sufficient, try another broker.

Consumer Education

Insurance is complicated business. Guidance in the form of articles, industry updates, and glossaries can be useful. Online insurance brokers are

What State Are You In?

Visitors living in certain states may be blocked from receiving quotes at sites that do not affiliate with many carriers. Insurance companies are bound by various state regulations governing their business and may or may not offer nationwide coverage for health, auto, and life insurance. When a brokerage site fails to provide 50-state coverage in a certain area, it sometimes asks you what state you are from at the start of any form-filling process. That courtesy stops you before you spend time with a long form.

relatively undeveloped in this area compared to online stock brokers. A few are getting up to speed, but it is also worth remembering that the Web at large provides all kinds of information—you are not restricted to the brokerage site.

Ease of Use

User-friendliness is key. There is nothing like difficult site navigation to drag down the experience of shopping for insurance online. Insurance broker sites all have questionnaires and application forms. The ease with which you are led through the forms determines your frustration level.

There is also the question of how easily you can find your way back to hub pages from the middle or end of a form. Some application forms are presented in a *tunnel* configuration—the process bores away from the main site as if digging an escape tunnel. Returning to the main site requires using your Back button as if crawling backward through that same tunnel. A better layout has the main navigation landmarks accompany you through the application process.

tunnel   linear progression of Web pages that takes you far from a site's starting point. Tunnels are navigational inconveniences seen in many online application forms.

Besides untunneled forms, user-friendliness is manifested in smooth delivery of price quotes and seamless connection to carriers. Most broker-

Using New Browser Windows

Online forms and insurance quote applications can be monsters—screen after screen of fill-ins. Once you get embroiled in one of those forms, it can be difficult to find your way back to the point at which you started. (Some sites make it easier than others.) A useful tip is to keep your forms in separate browser windows. When you get to a link or button that says "Click here to apply" (or similar words), right-click on the button. Then when the select menu appears, select Open in New Window. (This tip works in both the Navigator and Internet Explorer browsers.) A new browser window pops up with the button destination (the first page of a form) displayed. You can proceed through the application, including submitting it, then return to the first browser window to pick up your session where you left off.

ages contract with third-party companies that provide the software engines that drive the display of forms and quotes. The brokerage may or may not integrate that engine into the site in a way that is coherent and friendly to you.

Personalization

Personalization is an important feature at an online insurance broker and is demonstrated primarily by giving you the ability to save and retrieve your unique information. With personalization, you can abandon a long questionnaire if something pulls you away from the computer and return later to complete the form. Also, it is handy to save a completed application, then retrieve it at a later date to revise certain aspects of it as your situation changes, shopping again for a new insurance quote.

Another great advantage of personalization, if it is implemented well, is the ability to enter personal information once, then apply it globally to any questionnaire or application you fill out at that site. (Your information does not transfer to other brokerages.) The site automatically handles filling in portions of forms that require your basic personal information; then you can concentrate on filling in the fields that require information specific to the type of insurance you seek.

Personalization should always be password-protected. You will be

personalization an important feature of some financial service sites, by which you can save and retrieve your unique information. The most common type of personalization occurs when you open an account and can view your account screens. Beyond simple account access, personalization is applied at research sites and insurance brokers, sometimes by allowing visitors to save incomplete applications for later completion.

asked to create a user name (sometimes your e-mail address) and a unique password. You need both to retrieve your saved information.

Form Assistance

Those dreaded forms. Not only can they seem endless, but they sometimes ask esoteric and baffling questions. What is a stop-loss on health insurance copays? What is level-term life insurance? What is a melanoma?

Eventually, everyone learns the ins and outs of whatever insurance he or she has, but familiarity with details during the application process is too much to ask. The best online forms contain embedded links next to words and concepts that might be obscure. (See Figure 6.1.) These links either take you to an explanatory page, or—better yet—pop up a window that explains the term.

Some of these insurance sites take customer assistance a step further by providing "live" help, via telephone or *on-site chatting*. Those solutions, well intended though they are, sometimes require more effort than they are worth. A simple pop-up window with form-filling advice works best. Sites that employ on-site chatting can identify when you are online (but cannot identify who you are) and often pop a window open on your screen, inviting you to chat with a specialist. Whether that specialist really knows anything beyond simple site navigation is another matter.

Customer Assistance

Navigating the site is one task. Filling in the forms is a whole other challenge. Both require occasional assistance. Then there are the questions about the insurance itself. Certainly, you would think, the most important

FIGURE 6.1 Some forms provide linked assistance. This life insurance history at InsWeb links each medical condition to a descriptive page.

(Copyright 2000 InsWeb Corporation. All Rights Reserved. InsWeb provides an online service available at www.insweb.com.)

on-site chatting mobile and nimble technology that can be applied to a single site. It often is associated with chat rooms. On-site chatting lets you "talk" with a customer service representative through typing, without logging off the Internet or using your phone.

Testing Customer Service

You can test the customer service at an insurance site simply by using it. Here are a few all-purpose questions to use. One good question to ask, either by using an on-site chatting feature or on the phone, is whether a certain type of insurance is available in your state. The question is not too much of a brain squeeze, yet it requires a good working knowledge of the site's products.

customer service mandate would be to provide help about the insurance products represented at the site.

Unfortunately, online brokers sometimes fail in comparison with human brokers on just this point. Of course, Web brokers represent so many companies, types of insurance, and specific products that it is somewhat understandable that they may not be up to speed on all of them.

Still, online insurance brokers are distinguished from each other by this important criterion: how responsive they are to queries about insurance products and insurance issues. The site comparisons later in this chapter touch on this criterion in more detail.

Decision Tools

The best online insurance sites include interactive tools for helping you reach decisions. In the forefront of these tools are on-screen calculators that assist in determining how much money you may need in certain situations, the financial advantages of refinancing a home, and other matters related to insurance coverage.

Generally, carrier sites are better equipped with decision tools than broker sites. Since carriers offer only one brand of insurance, they must work harder to keep you at their sites; thus they offer all kinds of interactive tools. Some brokerage sites are almost as comprehensive, however.

Just the Quotes, Please

Few results are more frustrating, after spending 20 minutes filling out a detailed quote form, than a nonquoted offer to contact a human agent. There is nothing wrong with speaking to a human agent, of course, but when you fill in an involved quote form, you expect an online quote at the end of it all. That reasonable expectation is thwarted more often that you might guess.

Sites cannot guarantee quote delivery, for a few reasons. First, every visitor's personal situation is different. Second, sometimes the forms are filled out wrong (although the best sites interrupt you if you enter wrong or confusing information). Finally, insurance carriers vary in their ability to provide online quotes, so if your information and needs direct your quote application to a certain provider, you may not get the *instant quote* you want.

instant quote   a quick price display in response to a submitted form. Used by online insurance brokers and mortgage brokers, instant quotes give visitors a fast and detailed view of the type of insurance or loan products that might fit their situation. Instant quotes come early in the shopping and application process when buying insurance or a mortgage online.

With all this uncertainty, some sites position themselves as quote delivery machines, and others are satisfied with directing you to agents.

Secure Forms

Quote applications require entering quite a bit of personal information. Privacy issues may not be important when it comes to auto insurance or pet-health insurance, but you must divulge more intimate details when filling out forms for health and life insurance.

Security is a more burning issue for some people than others, but there is no reason for an insurance broker site *not* to provide secure Web pages when displaying forms. The small padlock in the lower corner of your browser indicates that the page is encrypted. If privacy is an important issue, make sure you are using the most recent browser version that your computer can run.

Privacy Statement

Privacy is related to, but distinct from, security. *Security* protects your personal information from being spied on or intercepted by network snoops. Privacy policies determine the extent to which a brokerage can share your information.

privacy   refers to a Web site's policy regarding how it handles your personal information. Privacy and security are the two issues that determine how safe it is to engage in online personal finance. Most responsible Web-based financial services publish privacy and security statements that detail what measures are taken to keep your personal information private.

security   refers to the integrity of network connections and the impenetrability of information traveling over the network. Security is an important issue in online personal finance, because many Internet services require input of personal information. Security measures like encryption make that information difficult to intercept and decode.

You may not want any sharing at all. As an empowered, Net-enabled shopper, it is up to you to pick your carrier, and you may not want to be solicited by a company that has purchased your name and demographic from a brokerage site. Alternatively, this whole privacy issue may not be important to you. Bring on the solicitations—the more information, the better!

At any rate, the site should spell out its policy. The best privacy statements are linked prominently from the front page and are written in plain English that anyone (well, anyone who speaks English) can understand. The most comprehensive privacy policies do not allow even the brokerage site to retrieve or view your information—the online forms you fill out are machine-driven, unseen by human eyes.

Simple and Detailed Forms

After filling in a few quote application forms, you may be delighted to see the brief, cursory applications featured at some sites. How luxurious to enter a minimum of information and get a quote displayed in seconds!

Privacy Trends

Because privacy advocacy groups have been consumer watchdogs on the Internet for several years, most online companies have become sensitive to the privacy rights of their visitors. Accordingly, these days most privacy statements promise that your identifying information (name, address, phone number, e-mail address) will not be given away or sold to other companies. Your financial information should definitely never be sold, and virtually all privacy statements promise that it will not be.

In all cases, the personal information you enter at an insurance brokerage site is shared with providers as necessary in order to service your requirements. By using these sites, you generally are agreeing to give certain information to affiliated financial service companies; usually, however, you are protected from receiving solicitations unrelated to servicing your application.

All well and good, but there is no avoiding detailed forms in the long run. Ultra-quick quotes seem less desirable when that quote changes later on. The speedy systems are good, though, for getting your bearings with a ballpark quote. The best brokerage sites offer an option to delve into a detailed form. Many carrier sites provide both quick and detailed paths through the form process.

TOURING THE ONLINE INSURANCE BROKERS

The insurance brokerage sites in this section have risen to the top of the field by providing smart interfaces, breadth of products, and efficient service. These selected companies are not the only brokers doing business online. Visit Gomez.com (www.gomez.com, discussed in Chapter 1) to track the larger field.

InsWeb (www.insweb.com)

The unquestioned brand leader among online insurance brokers, the awkwardly named InsWeb (see Figure 6.2) provides a good one-stop shop-

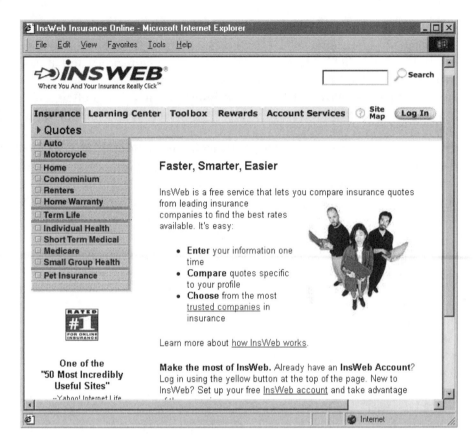

FIGURE 6.2 InsWeb provides one of the finest insurance destinations on the Web.

(Copyright 2000 InsWeb Corporation. All Rights Reserved. InsWeb provides an online service available at www.insweb.com.)

ping experience. The site does not indicate up-front which insurance carriers it represents, but its affiliations are broad, and InsWeb deals in many types of insurance. In addition to the basics—life, auto, health, and home—InsWeb passes the weird-coverage test by brokering condo insurance, pet policies, motorcycle insurance, and renter's coverage.

The InsWeb site is distinguished by an attractive interface and clear navigation. True, the forms are "tunneled," leading you far from the main site during lengthy applications. (Use a separate browser window when filling out forms.) But the progress bar on each form page, graphically illustrating how near you are to completion, almost makes up for the tunnels.

Although coverage at InsWeb is good, certain scenarios still return the dreaded "quote unavailable" message. If InsWeb is to maintain its leadership in this field, visitors can expect to see more regional affiliations that cover now-bare states. However, coverage does not mean you will get an online quote—InsWeb defers you to human agents all too often. (The availability of online quotes depends on the carrier most of the time; the site would display quotes if it could.)

On the convenience side, InsWeb encourages repeat visits by saving your information and automatically entering it into forms. You also can save incomplete forms for later completion. However, this automation could be implemented in a more global way, rather than forcing visitors to log onto the site again for each type of insurance.

InsWeb gets extra points for a privacy statement that is not only clear and detailed but actually gives an education about privacy issues in general. Speaking of education, the articles included in this site make it an insurance information portal. The glossary, categorized by insurance type, deserves a special note of praise.

In the tools department, InsWeb makes a strong effort to provide interactive assistance. Several calculators, quick estimators (they deliver a quote range—often all you need at first), quizzes, and aids for determining information requirements are available. There's even a Body Mass Index calculator (see Figure 6.3) for health information forms.

Hint: This site offers so much that it can be difficult to locate everything. Click the Site Map link from the home page. The resulting outline of links lays out all the tools, articles, insurance types, and other features.

The Upshot: InsWeb is an essential landmark in the online insurance brokerage landscape. Even if the site is not the easiest to use, the range of coverage and tools make it worth a small learning curve.

Quotesmith (www.quotesmith.com)

Customer service is a strong point at Quotesmith. A bright banner displaying the company's toll-free number and office hours is sometimes displayed, and helpful operators truly are standing by.

Quotesmith appeals to bargain hunters by offering rebates if the site fails to obtain the lowest possible premium (from top-rated insurance carriers according to A.M. Best, a carrier-rating service).

The site also emphasizes speed and lives up to its hype beautifully. Quote application forms are consolidated, with many information fields squeezed onto a single page. Further, scrollable menus are used for selecting information choices (date of birth, coverage amount, etc.), and this

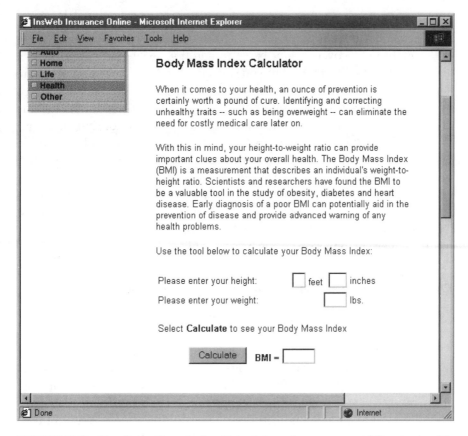

FIGURE 6.3 The Body Mass Index Calculator—how can you fill out a health insurance application without it?

(Copyright 2000 InsWeb Corporation. All Rights Reserved. InsWeb provides an online service available at www.insweb.com.)

method tends to reduce mistakes made when people are forced to enter data manually. And finally, helpful Q&A links assist in filling out these forms. The whole arrangement lends itself to speed and accuracy.

Quotesmith is proud of its many affiliations, and the quote delivery page is one of the broadest in the business. It is not unusual to receive over two dozen quotes for life insurance, each with the carrier's rating, links to policy details, links to formal applications, premium amounts (of course), and total payments for the term.

Navigation at this site leans to function over prettiness, which is fine—you are not looking for eye candy when shopping for insurance.

Quote applications are short thanks to the form-field consolidation, and links at the bottoms of pages return you to home base at any time.

Quotesmith covers many bases in addition to life, auto, and health. There is no home insurance, but you can shop for dental coverage, Medicare supplements, annuities, and worker's compensation (for small-business owners). When asked for a quote it cannot cover, Quotesmith pushes the visitor directly to QuickenInsurance, an affiliate broker. Rude, but effective.

The Upshot: Life insurance is Quotesmith's strongest suit by far. If life insurance is your primary or only interest, you would be well off to start here and gain a perspective on what is available to fit your situation. Excellent site performance and efficient designs make working with Quotesmith a pleasure, especially for those who dislike lengthy online sessions. Do not look for interactive tools helping you make insurance decisions, but the eager customer service is heartwarming.

QuickenInsurance (www.quickeninsurance.com)

QuickenInsurance brings to the table a decent range of self-help tools and a broad portfolio of coverage products.

Life, home, health, and auto insurance are placed front and center, with long-term care, disability, and small-business products around the edges.

The quote application for term life coverage is a grueling, multipage affair, but the payoff is worth it. The quote page is a beautiful display comparing premiums, renewing features, convertibility, waivers, and options. Further, the page separates products with online applications from agent-only products. If a company fails to provide online quotes (Allstate is famous for this), that option is separated from the other two. The quote page is more detailed than the comparable page at Quotesmith.

Visitors have a choice of using nonsecure (unencrypted) Web pages for quote applications—that choice speeds things along if privacy is not an issue and helps anyone logging into the site from behind a corporate firewall.

During the form process, Advice buttons next to each field explain why the information is needed. That kind of hand-holding is reassuring, even if the information displayed cannot always properly be regarded as "advice." Before each form, a Things to Consider section provides good information.

The Upshot: QuickenInsurance is graphically on the heavy side, making site navigation sluggish. The expanded forms yield item-by-item help and information, justifying the task of working through several pages. The excellent range of carrier affiliations makes this a hard site to get frustrated by—chances are, no matter what you are looking for and wherever you may live, you will get a quote here.

IntelliQuote (www.intelliquote.com)

Life insurance is the main course at IntelliQuote. (See Figure 6.4.) Visitors looking for health and auto coverage are linked to eHealthInsurance, an affiliated broker, and Progressive, an affiliated carrier.

For term life insurance, there is no better or more dedicated place to start. The front page gets right down to business with a quick-quote form. Unlike the lengthy questionnaires at some other sites, this one asks for age, smoking status, and coverage amounts, then displays a list of carriers and estimated premiums.

A fine selection of highly rated carriers distinguishes the IntelliQuote experience. After the quick form, IntelliQuote keeps you within

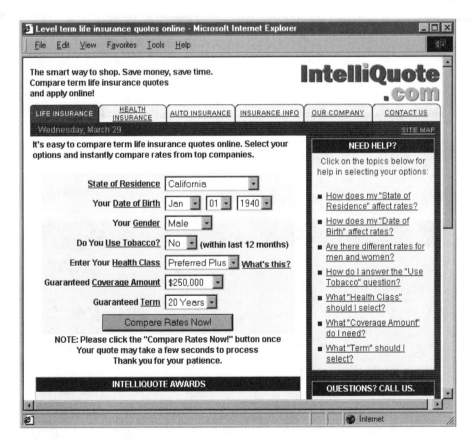

FIGURE 6.4 IntelliQuote does not waste any time, putting its quote request form right on the home page.

(Reprinted with permission of IntelliQuote.com.)

the site to fill in another fairly simple online application, which, once submitted, results in some personal contact by phone. The instant quote page (see Figure 6.5) is clear and contains links to specific insurance policy details.

IntelliQuote does not provide as much initial information about carrier matches as QuickenInsurance but more than makes up for it with the number of carriers represented.

From the front page, click the Insurance Info tab for a selection of articles, calculators, glossaries, and fact sheets about life insurance. The resources at this site match or surpass the life insurance sections at any of the other brokers.

The Upshot: Fast and focused, IntelliQuote gets you on the life insurance track without a wasted minute. It is educational, user-friendly, and

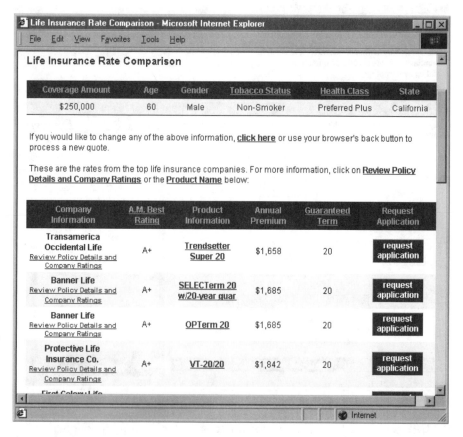

FIGURE 6.5 The instant quote page at IntelliQuote.

(Reprinted with permission of IntelliQuote.com.)

serious about term life insurance. If you are looking for health or auto coverage, better to go elsewhere. If you want property coverage, you have no choice—you must go elsewhere.

QuickQuote (www.quickquote.com)

QuickQuote presents the slickest brokerage interface (see Figure 6.6), but not necessarily the most useful to your needs. Concentrating on term life insurance, other coverage types lag behind. But there are a few unusual products here that you do not normally find at insurance sites.

Visitors are first greeted with a multimedia presentation complete

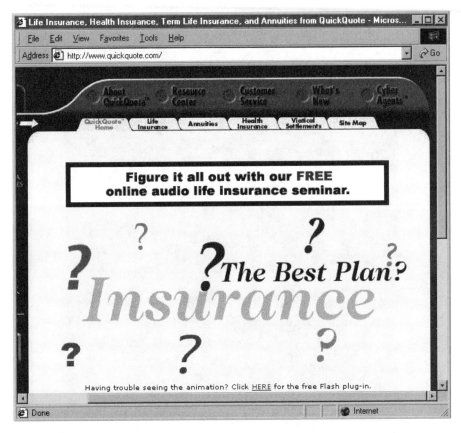

FIGURE 6.6 QuickQuote presents an animated audio-visual display every time you enter the site.

(Reprinted with permission of QuickQuote.com.)

with audio, and the site continues to favor a high-graphics style in its main pages—it is all very pretty, but rather beside the point.

Of greater value is the fairly detailed yet consolidated term life insurance quote questionnaire that fits onto a single page. (See Figure 6.7.) Drop-down menus and selection buttons help complete the form without inaccuracies, and it is on to the quotes.

The initial life insurance quote page is on the sparse side, but supplementary links flesh it out with policy details. You can view the lowest possible quote according to broad eligibility requirements, which is very useful for orienting yourself. In addition, you can view *all* possible quotes within those broad parameters.

Life insurance is the central focus at QuickQuote; health and disability insurance are a lower priority. However, dental coverage, student plans, and

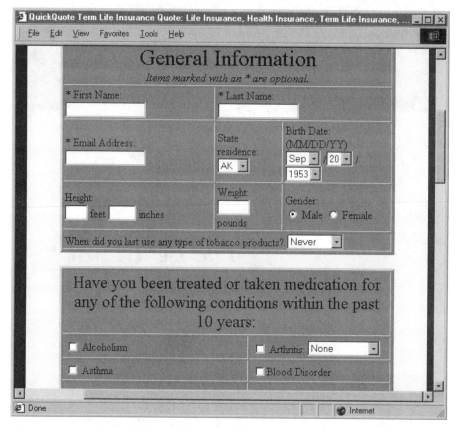

Figure 6.7 Part of the life insurance quote request at QuickQuote.
(Reprinted with permission of QuickQuote.com.)

international short-term health products add distinction to the site. If you are interested in any of those unusual niches, link right over to QuickQuote.

The Upshot: Too opulent in design for its own good, but pleasing to the eye nonetheless. While QuickQuote has value if you are shopping for life insurance, it probably is not as useful as IntelliQuote. It is indispensable for students and travelers seeking international coverage. Try to disregard the relentless self-promotions on QuickQuote's pages.

AccuQuote (www.accuquote.com)

The site does not look like much at first glance (see Figure 6.8), and indeed, AccuQuote is not a high-tech interface for instant delivery of

FIGURE 6.8 AccuQuote does not look like much, but it is an interface for human expertise.

quotes. Positioning itself far from the impersonality of many online insurance brokers, AccuQuote uses the site as an introduction only, not a final solution. The ultimate goal is to build a relationship of trust between you and AccuQuote experts.

Life insurance is the only product at AccuQuote, and the company takes an educational approach. Believing that the least expensive coverage is not necessarily the best plan for an individual, AccuQuote is on a mission to inform and assist. But the educational coverage on-site is far from objective or detached; most of the fact sheets and articles deal with the AccuQuote experience, not with generic issues of term life coverage.

The online quote questionnaire is of medium length but offers little assistance or data checking. It is not difficult to enter inaccuracies inadvertently. Since the form does not result in "quick quotes," you may not be aware of the mistakes for a long time. If all goes well, AccuQuote absorbs your information and contacts you by e-mail or telephone. So begins a more personalized shopping process than offered at most brokerages.

AccuQuote is a full-service broker that handles all aspects of the shopping, application, and buying experience. The customer service department is knowledgeable and eager. This core service-oriented approach distinguishes AccuQuote and makes up for inadequacies of the site.

The Upshot: AccuQuote is for those who desire a personalized experience when shopping for life insurance. This company radiates care for its customers.

eHealthInsurance (www.ehealthinsurance.com)

The standard for online health insurance brokerage (see Figure 6.9), the eHealthInsurance background technology and search engine are used by many other brokers to provide their visitors with health quotes.

Speed and clarity shine at this site. Unlike some other complex processes, eHealthInsurance gets you to a quote page within a minute or two, thanks to an extremely compressed questionnaire. (See Figure 6.10.) A broad range of results is provided, and user must do further research.

Customer service, available by e-mail or phone, goes beyond site navigation to include all kinds of health insurance issues. A basic page of frequently asked questions gives some good information, and the glossary is helpful.

The Upshot: The first and possibly only site to visit for health insurance information.

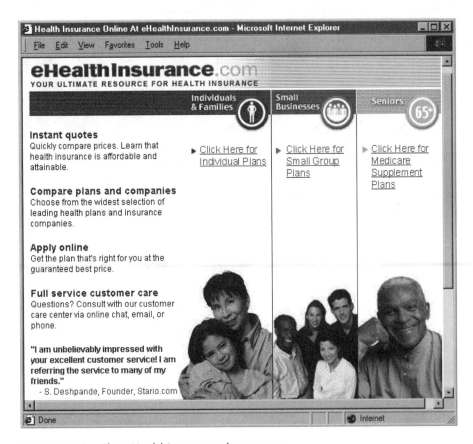

FIGURE 6.9 The eHealthInsurance home page.
(Reprinted with permission of eHealthInsurance.com.)

1st Quote Network (www.1stquote.com)

Using an extremely fast-moving site, 1st Quote Network delivers term life insurance quotes after a surprisingly short form. Do not be surprised if the quotes change after you supply the carrier with more information. This site's search engine delivers life insurance only, nudging visitors to eHealthInsurance for health quotes and Progressive for auto quotes.

The company provides one of the best online privacy statements. The customer service contact options include live online chatting.

The Upshot: A good place to compare many quotes for life insurance. Visitors will not find their time wasted at this sleek interface. For interactive tools, or for health and auto insurance, best to go elsewhere.

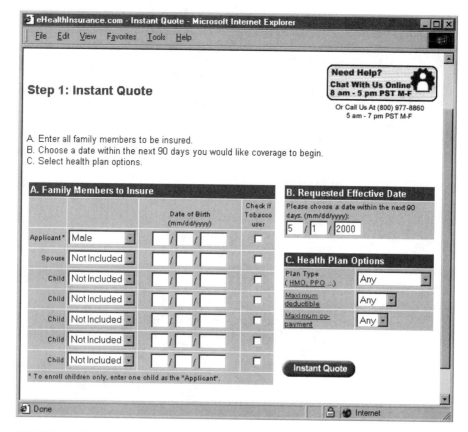

FIGURE 6.10 The compact instant quote form at eHealthInsurance is a pleasure to use.

(Reprinted with permission of eHealthInsurance.com.)

Esurance (www.esurance.com)

A somewhat graphics-heavy site, Esurance provides auto insurance. Although the site is slow to load, phone and chat service are provided, and you can save quotes and personal information for return visits. Coverage was available in only eight states at the time of this book's deadline, but Esurance promises nationwide coverage.

HealthAxis (www.healthaxis.com)

This beautifully designed site delivers health insurance quotes and connects visitors with agents for more information. Just before this book was published, the site's service for certain states and types of coverage was still spotty, but it promised that more comprehensive service was imminent. On the upside, HealthAxis *is* comprehensive in its breakdown of health insurance types, including major medical, dental, vision coverage, student health, short-term medical, and prescription plans.

Ebix (www.ebix.com)

Ebix is an interesting online quote delivery system that operates like Priceline.com, the well-known e-commerce site that allow visitors to suggest their own price for goods and services. Ebix presents a good deal of insurance information and lets you view other requests and quotes. You are invited to fill out a personal questionnaire related to the type of insurance you need and submit it with a suggested premium price. Within three days you may receive quotes competitive with your suggestion.

If Ebix has a downfall, it is that the process is not clearly explained, demo screens notwithstanding. There is a learning curve in any site that goes against the grain, and naming your own price for insurance definitely cuts against the swath. Still, it is worth a visit, if only for the excellent glossary.

SURFING THE CARRIERS

Online insurance brokers are useful for canvassing general availability of coverage from a variety of insurance carriers. Many of the large carriers have their own sites and make persuasive attempts to get you shopping there, where there are no competing products.

Carrier sites tend to have a few advantages over broker sites:

✔ *More interactive resources.* Calculators and educational materials are more common and professionally prepared.

✔ *More coverage detail.* You usually can find out more about products that interest you from carrier sites than from broker sites.

✔ *Better customer service.* Carriers have been in the customer service business a long time; often they outshine online brokers when it comes to assistance, online and offline.

These improvements over the brokerage experience come at a price—primarily the lack of breadth in product offerings. You have to visit several carrier sites to accumulate as much information as you can in a single brokerage site.

Following are several insurance companies whose sites provide effective introductions to their respective companies.

American International Group (www.aigdirect.com)

This is a clear site with a wealth of resources, tools, and calculators. Auto, residential, home, accident, and health insurance are offered. It is a little weak in the online quoting department for some products.

State Farm (www.statefarm.com)

A good site for insurance newcomers, with lots of information. State Farm is generally weak at delivering online quotes, both to brokerage sites and within its own pages. The process defaults to a human agent. On the plus side, you can personalize the site to match your needs.

Electric Insurance Company (www.electricinsurance.com)

Vehicle and home insurance only are offered from this company, and it does not cover all states. However, Electric Insurance helpfully bumps you over to the Progressive site if it cannot meet your needs. Motorcycle and boat coverage can be arranged here in addition to auto insurance.

Progressive Insurance (www.progressive.com)

The prominent auto insurance company on the Web, Progressive is used by many brokers to provide auto quotes. Why not get them from the source? The site delivers instant quotes and sells policies online. Progressive is known for good after-sales follow-up, including billing, at-site filing of claims, and coverage information. Before buying, you must fill in detailed forms and authorize a credit check. To its enormous credit, Progressive compares its rates with other carriers.

E-Term (www.eterm.com)

E-Term is the online division of Zurich Kemper TeleLife, a term life insurance provider. This site delivers lightning-quick quotes. The short quote form on the home page is convenient but ties up navigation when you try to use your browser's Back button from the quote page. A minor inconvenience.

Prudential (www.prudential.com)

The Prudential insurance site is part of a larger online financial services package. Here you can find instant quotes on life insurance and delayed e-mail quotes on auto insurance. Or you can make an appointment with an agent.

Amica (www.amica.com)

One of the most empowered of the online carrier sites, Amica lets its customers file a claim interactively or add a vehicle to auto coverage. However, you can get online quotes only for life insurance, not for auto and residential. (You must wait for an agent to call you about auto or home insurance.) This is a beautiful, clear, efficient site.

Liberty Mutual (www.libertymutual.com)

Liberty Mutual produces an extensive billboard for the company's products; however, online quotes are not available. Go here for general information and to play with its multitude of interactive tools and quizzes. No health insurance is offered.

SecureLife (www.securelife.com)

The site's simple, almost childlike design gets you to the quote page fast and presents detailed results. SecureLife deals with life insurance only and pushes visitors to eHealthInsurance for health quotes. A glossary and life insurance calculator are helpful.

GEICO (www.geico.com)

Skip this site if you live in Massachusetts or New Jersey. Otherwise, try GEICO for car insurance only. You can view online quotes or generate an instant callback on the phone. If you buy from GEICO, the site provides account access and payments.

Veterinary Pet Insurance (www.veterinarypetinsurance.com)

This company not only provides insurance for your pets' health but does a good job explaining the concept and detailing how the benefits work. Two plans are offered.

Premier Pet Insurance (www.ppins.com)

This provider of pet insurance offers three plans with favorable features but makes the visitor work too hard in getting a price quote.

Chapter 7

Borrowing
Money Online

Just as life insurance coverage dominates online insurance, so mortgages dominate online lending. (See Chapter 8.) Even so, you can find an auto loan through the Internet and even some personal loans and business financing. This chapter covers the nonmortgage areas of online lending as well as Web resources for debt relief and consolidation.

GENERAL LENDING

When it comes to securing a loan online, brokers are the way to go. *Direct lenders* are way behind in putting up Web sites and offering their products electronically in any coherent fashion.

Online loan brokers deal with the following products:

> **direct lender** a bank or other institution that lends money directly to consumers. On the Web, direct lenders are distinguished from loan brokers, who match loan applications with products offered by many lenders. Direct lenders, as a group, lag behind brokers in establishing Internet sites.

✔ *Personal loans.* Debt consolidation is the most common reason to secure a personal loan. Home improvement is another motivation, but that type of borrowing usually falls in the category of home improvement loans. When applying for a loan to consolidate your debts (and lower the interest rate you are paying), sometimes you are required to list those debts.

✔ *Auto loans.* Car financing is often part of the general-loan broker mix. In addition, specialized auto-loan brokers have sprung up; they are covered later in this chapter.

✔ *Home loans.* Mortgages, *home equity loans*, and refinancing are the three main areas of home loans. Chapter 8 covers online mortgages in detail. Mortgage brokers are fairly evolved on the Internet and are preferable to using a general loan broker for home loans.

✔ *Credit cards.* Lines of credit are not the same as cash loans. Chapter 9 describes online credit cards—how to find and apply for them. Given the wealth of dedicated resources in this area, it does not make much sense to use a loan broker to obtain a credit card.

home equity loan   loan backed by ownership of real estate. Home equity loans can be used for just about any purpose, from home improvements to vacations.

The following sites provide general lending services (beyond just mortgages) to some degree.

E-Loan (www.eloan.com)

E-Loan (see Figure 7.1) is the brand leader among Internet loan companies. To an extent, E-Loan put online lending on the map. The company was started in 1996 (an ancient era for a Web venture), spun off from a brick-and-mortar loan broker. E-Loan purchased CarFinance.com in 1999 and writes auto loans through that subsidiary. Small business loans are executed through an affiliation with LiveCapital.com.

Mortgages and mortgage refinancing comprise E-Loan's biggest business. In addition to the auto-loan and small-business divisions, E-Loan also supplies credit cards—but from just one provider, Aria Visa. If you

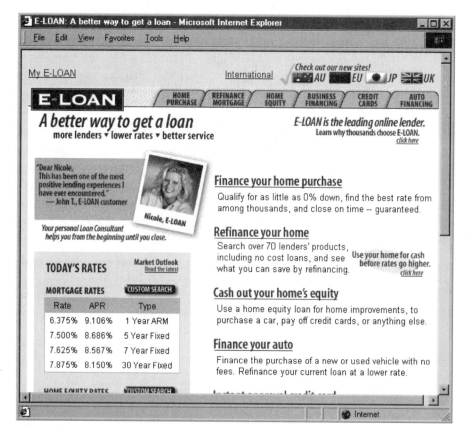

FIGURE 7.1   E-Loan helped establish online lending in the public mind-set.

(Reprinted with permission of E-Loan.)

are scanning the marketplace for a new credit card, E-Loan is not a resource worth your time.

E-Loan's outstanding execution and user-friendliness has earned it loyal customers and good reviews.

Creditland (www.creditland.com)

Creditland is an outstanding loan broker affiliated with leading lenders. The affiliate page of the site lists American Express, First Union, Bank of America, AutoDirect, American Pacific Bank, and others.

Yahoo! Loan Center (loan.yahoo.com)

The Loan Center at information portal Yahoo! is neat, efficient, and on the slim side. Working primarily with E-Loan for mortgage information and GiggoCar for auto-loan information, Yahoo! Loan Center does a nice job packaging information and application pages. The lack of other affiliations hurts the site, but Yahoo! is known for growing its relationships and aggregating content from other sites, sometimes in huge proportions. Currently the site is more information-oriented than product-oriented. Keep your eye on the Loan Center's growth.

In the meantime, two features stand out here:

✔ *Mortgage rates.* Check them by metropolitan area of state, updated continually, and consolidated in a friendly format.

✔ *Credit reports.* You can order yours from this site. A single report (delivered instantly on-screen) costs $7.95, and a consolidated version of all your reports from the three major agencies (delivered by postal mail) costs $29.95.

A short qualifying process helps determine which products and lenders you might match with. After qualifying, Creditland helps you apply directly to the lender.

This site is exceptionally clear, containing resources, interactive tools, glossaries, and rate monitors.

GetSmart (www.getsmart.com)

GetSmart alternately bills itself as the "financial marketplace" and the "borrower's marketplace." Either way, it is obvious that this service has its hands in a lot of pots. GetSmart brokers mortgages, credit cards, debt consolidation, student loans, CDs and savings, and consumer loans. The site can be proud of one of the most diverse portfolios of loan products on the Web.

There is quite a bit of application overlap here, meaning that you fill out the same form for several types of loan. In most cases you must provide your personal contact information—street address and phone number—or the application does not submit.

GetSmart does not provide online responses to applications, instant quotes, e-mail preapproval, or any of the interactive response perks other brokers do. Instead, your application is forwarded to appropriate lenders, who then contact you. This process makes GetSmart less of a purely virtual experience than most other brokers and may put off customers who do not want to be approached by an unknown number of lenders with their advertising materials.

Debt consolidation loans are for homeowners only. The credit card section (as at E-Loan) is dominated by Aria Visa and is not a worthwhile credit shopping experience.

Lending Tree (www.lendingtree.com)

This attractive, useful, easily navigated site makes good use of pop-up windows and drop-down menus. It is hard to get lost at Lending Tree.

Ease of use and friendly service is emphasized here. There is no broker fee when your loan is placed, and loan offers are delivered online with no unsolicited callbacks. (Are you listening, GetSmart?) Lending Tree provides home, auto, and personal loans, plus a credit card search engine. Nationwide coverage is promised, but the fact is that geographic coverage is not comprehensive across all products and types of loans. Debt consolidation loan applications are provided to homeowners and nonowners alike.

The site stores your personal information and uses it to fill in subsequent forms during future visits. No registration is required for this service—the site tracks your information by your Social Security number and last name.

LOAN RATE MONITORS

The following two sites do a good job tracking rates for various types of loans.

Bankrate.com (www.bankrate.com)

Bankrate is discussed in Chapter 1 as a fine first-stop destination for information about all kinds of personal finance online. The site fits into this section thanks to its several loan sections—auto loans, home equity, and personal loans. These resources stay up to the minute on all aspects of the national lending scene, with articles and rate tables. The Personal Loans section is one of the few online databases for personal loan rates itemized by locality. You can drill down to your state and/or town to discover what you would pay for a free-standing personal loan.

The Auto Loans area presents a daily rate monitor, with a nifty ticker symbol indicating what direction rates are moving in. (See Figure 7.2.) Again, in this area, you can narrow down to your locality for explicit rate information. The Home Equity portion of Bankrate has the same monitors and a terrific assortment of articles.

BanxQuote (www.banx.com)

This is one of the handiest sites around for keeping your finger on the pulse of loan rates. Using a friendly system of multiple drop-down selec-

---

LiveCapital.com

Small business owners can do no better when seeking institutional financing than to visit LiveCapital.com, a loan broker for business. LiveCapital is affiliated with some of the top lenders in the field, including Wells Fargo Bank, American Express, U.S. Banks, PNC Bank, Provident Bank, and others.

The site is clearly presented and offers term loans, lines of credit, corporate credit cards, and business leases. LiveCapital does not perform its own application processing, and the process shuts down in the evenings and on weekends. A single application suffices for all types of loans—the procedure gets more specific later. If you are applying within business hours, LiveCapital usually gets a prequalification back to you within a few minutes and then helps you with a more formal application to the lender.

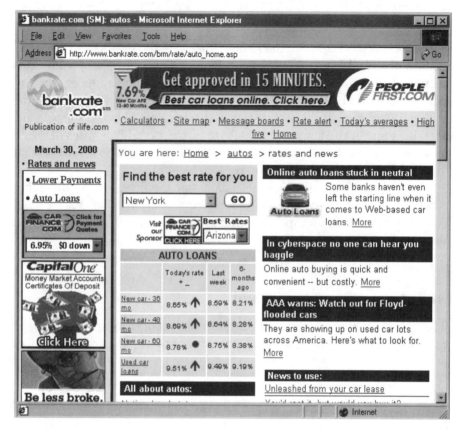

FIGURE 7.2 Bankrate.com shows in which direction auto loan rates are moving.

(Reprinted with permission of Bankrate.com, a publication of iLife.com, Inc.)

tion menus, BanxQuote makes it easy to choose a product type. The search engine operates quickly, so within seconds you can be gazing at a list of regional lenders offering your selected type of loan product, with their rates and terms presented in a table format.

Loans of all types are represented here: mortgages, credit cards, unsecured loans, auto financing, and more. The menus contain surprises, such as relevant calculators. The menus even track global economic indicators and key stock market numbers.

BanxQuote is an underrated site that everyone should know about.

AUTO LOANS

Cars are big on the Internet. When e-commerce began taking off, nobody thought that eventually it would apply to big-ticket items, such as automobiles. But frustration with the in-person experience of brick-and-mortar dealerships helped drive (so to speak) an emerging marketplace of online car buyers.

Along with buying automobiles, car buyers shop online for financing. Generally, purchasing and financing are kept separate on the Internet. The two distinct tasks are merged only to the following limited degrees:

✔ Car-buying sites that incorporate financing tools from lenders. These lenders run their own sites, and it usually makes sense to go there for complete financial service.

✔ Finance sites that offer car-buying research tools, such as Giggo.com, described in the following section. These tools allow you to compare car models and get a feel for prices but not actually buy.

This section describes auto lending sites, not car-buying sites. On the Internet, auto financing companies can be divided into three groups:

1. *Lenders.* These companies fund auto purchases directly. Their sites provide online applications, and approvals are sometimes very fast, almost instantaneous.

2. *Brokers.* Auto financing brokers operate like online insurance brokers. These sites provide online applications and match your needs with a lender. Approval is sometimes fast. Once approved, you can shop anywhere.

3. *Brokers with dealer affiliations.* These auto financing brokers work with car dealer networks. Generally, their sites provide less automated service. Approval takes longer and sometimes is accompanied by personal contact on the phone. Once approved, you can shop at an affiliated car dealer.

What About Online Auto Leasing?

The quick answer is that there is not much online activity in this department. Even the online dealers do not generally offer leases. For the most part, car leasing is the domain of brick-and-mortar dealers who provide leasing alternatives on their own inventory. Online lenders and brokers are essentially in competition with the lease contracts offered by dealers. If you are hoping to lease a car, the best help you will get online is in the form of calculators that assist in deciding the lease/buy question. When it comes to the lease contract, you need to hit the road and talk to local dealers.

When shopping for auto financing on the Web, in the following sites and others you may find on your own, keep the following considerations in mind.

What Types of Auto Loans Are Offered?

You may be in the market for a new car purchase, in which case the situation is uncomplicated. But several other types of vehicle financing exist. Not all online lenders and brokers cover all kinds of loan products. Following are the types to look out for:

- ✔ New car loans.
- ✔ Used car loans, which may have unique application requirements.
- ✔ Motorcycle loans, which sometimes carry different rates from car loans.
- ✔ Lease buyouts, in which a leased vehicle is purchased from the dealer with finance assistance.
- ✔ Refinancing, in which current loans are improved to save money.
- ✔ Person-to-person loans, which provide financing assistance when buying a car from a private owner.

Rates

In the online auto-loan field, interest rates often beat national averages. This online advantage is similar to the interest-rate whipping that on-line banks give their traditional counterparts. Look for comparison tables that demonstrate the savings you can expect by signing on with a lender.

Keep in mind that excellent rates go to borrowers with excellent credit ratings. Many people with troubled credit histories buy cars and obtain financing, and the Internet is a good place to find such deals. But the price you pay for previous credit trouble is an interest rate a point or two above the national average.

Fees and Costs

Application fees and closing costs are nothing new in the financing industry, but these conventions are quickly being eroded from the online auto-loan marketplace. Isn't competition grand? Look for lenders that advertise no application fee and no closing costs. These perks generally are reserved for prime borrowing situations, though, so if you're a subprime candidate, you may be forced to pay fees.

Application Turnaround Time

Instant gratification is encouraged when shopping for online financial services. Auto loans are no different. Direct lenders can turn around an online application within minutes, in some cases. That means you receive some kind of response—approval, you hope, but at least an acknowledgment—on your computer within the time it takes to make a cup of tea. Approval arrives either in your browser window or via e-mail.

Loan brokers can take longer to respond. The delay is due to an extra step. Brokers must not only evaluate your application but match it against many products offered by their affiliated lenders.

Either way, the postapproval process should move along quickly, too. Best of all is when the lender express-mails a blank check or authorizing paperwork. If you get those papers the next day, you could drive home in a new car that night, and the entire process of financing and buying can be accomplished in 24 hours. While perhaps the process is no quicker than buying and financing at a dealer, it probably is quite a bit cheaper.

Payment Window

Some lenders offer a delayed start to your payment schedule. There is no putting off the inevitable forever, but that extra time gives a nice feeling. In some cases it may be necessary—for example, if you are waiting for a tax refund. In those cases, look for this feature advertised at the site, or call customer service and ask for it.

Customer Service

In the customer service department for auto loans, interactive online help is not as prevalent as it is in the mortgage sites. (See Chapter 8.) Most customer service help is delivered over the phone and through e-mail. Other than that limitation, you want the same qualities in this niche of the financial services world as elsewhere: accessibility and helpfulness.

Typically, car-loan brokers have better technology for customer assistance, but direct lenders are more knowledgeable. (The preceding sentence is a generalization that may be disproved at any particular site.) Since the Internet is a 24-hour, 7-day shopping environment, look for telephone service and application processing around the clock. But be forewarned: Those speedy application turnarounds often turn sluggish during the weekends.

TOURING THE AUTO-FINANCE LENDERS

This section concentrates on pointing out and describing a handful of the most promising online auto-finance lenders and brokers in a still-emerging industry.

Giggo.com (www.giggo.com)

You cannot buy a car at Giggo.com, but you can do nearly everything else associated with getting a set of wheels under you. This magnificent portal is a good place to start for comparing models, researching all kinds of car-shopping issues, and applying for a loan. Whether you're a nervous beginner at car-shopping or an old hand on the verge of making a purchase, Giggo.com probably can help with some part of the process.

Education gets a big emphasis here. Every page of this site is infested with links that spin off into definitions and fact sheets. Articles and Q&A sessions illuminate the entire shopping experience—for both the car and the loan. As with buying a home, buying a car is a two-part experience:

getting the vehicle and paying for it. Giggo.com helps knit the two to-gether, although you must buy the vehicle elsewhere.

If nothing else, check out the Compare New Cars section, which al-lows you to perform a sticker-price comparison of up to four car models, revealing invoice prices as well as dealer prices, and recommends a target price. Take *that* to your local dealer (along with a "giggocheck" that au-thorizes the loan) when shopping.

Giggo.com generally beats national average interest rates by a point or more, using the national averages posted at the site. You can see a state-by-state breakdown of loan rates that itemizes major banks operating in those states. Impressive. As this book was printed, Giggo.com did not of-fer refinancing, lease buyouts, or balloon loans.

The loan application process takes about 5 minutes to complete, and approval arrives via e-mail in about 30 minutes. (Unusual employment or credit situations may take longer, as is always the case with online appli-cations.) Once approved, the company express-mails a giggocheck overnight. You have 30 days to activate the loan.

PeopleFirst Finance (www.peoplefirst.com)

PeopleFirst was established in 1995 to provide more efficient car-loan ser-vice to people with good credit. The company requires an excellent and substantial credit record and lends a minimum of $7,500 (higher mini-mums in some states).

While this site is not nearly as informative and educational as Giggo.com, PeopleFirst offers a better range of loan products. Loan types include new car loans, motorcycle financing (in most states), used-car loans, refinancing, lease buyouts, and even person-to-person loans when buying a car privately. Rates are good and drop especially low when you sign on with the automated payment system. A $100 service guarantee holds for 30 days after a loan is approved.

PeopleFirst enjoys a sterling online reputation. Internet loan brokers often use its back-end software and loan products in their auto-financing departments. Subprime borrowers will be frustrated here, but anyone with good credit who does not need a lot of hand-holding or education can do no better.

Auto Loan Online (www.auto-loan.com)

Lovers of simplicity, come hither. Auto Loan Online cuts right to the chase with a minimum of flash, educational material, interactive gadgets, or anything besides a loan application form.

This company specializes in subprime borrowers who may be daunted by the prospect of walking into a bank to ask for a loan. The EZ Loan Calculator asks visitors to estimate the quality of their credit, fill in a few other fields, and dishes up a loan scenario. Interest rates are missing from the results, unfortunately, probably hiding higher rates sometimes charged to subprime borrowers.

The online application takes a little longer than the calculator. Once you submit it, you wait to be contacted—a definite disadvantage compared to online notification systems.

Auto Credit Finders (www.autocreditfinders.com)

An online auto loan broker, Auto Credit Finders does not waste time with editorial content, glossaries, or any of the information perks standard at such sites. It is straight to the application here. This company specializes in bad credit scenarios and prides itself on finding anybody a loan. Auto Credit Finders covers all 50 states, and applications are usually processed within two days.

Carlender.com (www.carlender.com)

Another no-nonsense lender, Carlender competes with PeopleFirst and Giggo.com. No miscellaneous features clog this site, which takes a methodical, step-by-step approach to walking customers through the loan application process.

Sporting a fairly broad range of products, Carlender finances new and used cars, refinancing, lease buyouts, and person-to-person purchases. Separate online applications exist for each type of loan. The application for new cars is unusually demanding, displaying required fields for the car make and model. You must provide a Vehicle Identification Number for used-car buys. This type of lending is less open-ended than at Giggo.com.

At the time of this book's deadline, Carlender administered loans in only 12 states. This limitation has been the company's big drawback, but 50-state coverage may be in place by the time you read this. Carlender is developing a nearly instant approval process. Rates are very competitive with other online lenders.

Ugly Duckling (www.uglyduckling.com)

A used-car specialist, Ugly Duckling operates a dual business as dealer and lender. The company works with used-car dealers that you specify but has no objection to selling you a car from its own inventory. Ugly

Duckling operates a chain of dealerships in eight states. Troubled credit and no credit do not intimidate Ugly Duckling as a lender.

A standard online application takes your information, submits it, and alerts an Ugly Duckling loan officer to contact you. Online notification is not an option.

Household Automotive Financing (www.householdauto.com)

Household Finance lends for new and used vehicles and offers *refinancing* of current loans. With an emphasis on speed and simplicity, this company leads visitors through a fairly detailed application process. If all goes well, a check could be in the mail the following day, although the site fails to specify exact turnaround times.

refinancing replacing one loan with a new, more favorable loan. Refinancing takes advantage of interest rates that are lower than they were when the first loan was taken. In most cases, the new lender pays off the first loan and lets the customer repay the money at a better rate.

Household Automotive Financing invites applications with troubled credit but at the same time spells out some minimum salary requirements, and all applicants must be up to date on all current financial obligations.

Big Three

The traditional "Big Three" American car builders provide financing on their own cars, with online interfaces. Each furnishes online applications and a small range of financing plans.

- ✔ *GMAC* (www.gmac-into.com). Express Credit with GM dealers; hybrid buy/lease arrangements.
- ✔ *Ford* (www.fordcredit.com). Financing and on-site account management.
- ✔ *Chrysler* (www.chryslerfinancial.com). Car model comparisons and calculators; applications for buying or leasing.

DEBT CONSOLIDATION

Debt consolidation is a thriving field on the Internet that resembles a big pot of soup with many ingredients. Debt consolidation is a healthy business because of two complementary facts:

1. Many consumers are in debt trouble thanks to overuse of credit cards.
2. Creditors wish to avoid losing all hope of repayment if the consumer declares bankruptcy.

debt consolidation   debt counseling and renegotiating are both bundled into this term. To add further confusion, there are two types of real debt consolidation: loans and renegotiations. Loans provide consumers a way to refinance several ongoing bills at once and are used in cases where credit may be troubled but is not seriously delinquent. Renegotiation is used in dire scenarios to avoid personal bankruptcy.

Basically, then, debt consolidation is bankruptcy evasion, which can be a win-win solution for both the consumer and his or her creditors. Consumers can put an end to the stress of receiving creditor phone calls and consolidate their various debts into one negotiated payment. Creditors can stop spending their resources pursuing the debt and be confident that they will receive at least a compromise payment.

Sorting through the thicket of competing sites, debt consolidation as a distinct field is comprised of the following core services:

✔ *Credit counseling.* Not consolidation services, strictly speaking, credit counselors are usually nonprofit companies that seek to educate consumers into more productive paths than bankruptcy.

✔ *Credit negotiators.* By far the biggest niche of debt consolidation, credit negotiators treat dire consumer debt scenarios through negotiation with creditors. In the best cases, the result of such negotiation is lowered interest rates, elimination of delinquent late fees, and a new repayment schedule for the consumer.

✔ *Loan companies.* Much less common than negotiators, some companies lend consumers money to work their way out of debt. The loan consolidates many creditors into just one.

In order to qualify for debt consolidation service that goes beyond mere counseling, most companies require at least a certain amount (typically about $2,000) of debt. And that debt must be *unsecured debt*. Debt consolidation clients must be at least 18 years old and have a minimum income (in the neighborhood of $1,000 a month). The only other requirement is a willingness to pay one's debts and avoid personal bankruptcy.

unsecured debt   debt not backed by any collateral, such as a security deposit, an automobile, or a house. Generally, unsecured debt refers to consumer credit card debt.

Here is how debt consolidation through negotiation typically works:

1. At a debt consolidation site, you fill out an online application. The application form asks for details about all the debts you want to consolidate.
2. The consolidation company contacts you either by e-mail or on the phone to discuss the specifics of your situation and how the company might be able to help.
3. You make an agreement with the consolidation company and authorize it to negotiate with creditors on your behalf. A signed (on paper) agreement is usually required, and sometimes a first payment.
4. The consolidation company notifies all your creditors that you have entered a debt consolidation program. Immediately, all creditor phone calls to you stop.
5. The consolidation company negotiates new repayment terms with creditors, resulting in a single payment plan for you.
6. Every month, you send a check to the consolidation company, which disburses the money to creditors.
7. When the program is complete, the consolidation company may obtain letters from your creditors acknowledging that your debts are closed.

E-Debt Consolidation (www.e-debtconsolidation.com)

This company provides negotiated debt reduction for consumers with at least $5,000 in delinquencies. E-Debt Consolidation claims an impressive list of creditors who recognize them and work with renegotiations every day. A free analysis consultation is offered. The company charges a fee, bundled into the negotiated monthly payment.

Debt Consolidation Online
(www.debt-consolidation-online.com)

This company is strong on information and dissuasion, warning visitors of the long-term disabling consequences of bankruptcy. Not a negotiator, Debt Consolidation Online is a broker for debt consolidation loans. Visitors are helped by the plainness of the site, which does not throw a lot of distractions or ads on its pages.

Federal Debt Consolidation Services
(www.federaldebtservice.com)

Federal Debt Consolidation Services claims to suppress finance charges, interest rates, and late fees. It works with a wide assortment of creditors, including Visa, MasterCard, Sears, MBNA, American Express, and others. In the detailed online application, you list all your debts. Applications by fax and postal mail are also supported.

Washington D.C. (www.wdcfinancial.com)

This debt renegotiator presents an attractive and encouraging site. The FAQ page is too brief, though, and the online application does not provide enough fields to enter creditor information easily.

American Debt Consolidation (www.godebtfree.com)

This is a sympathetic, informative, and clear site with a good online application form. American Debt Consolidation advertises to reduce repay-

---

Who Pays the Debt Consolidating Company?

The company may charge a fee to you or to your creditors, but ultimately the specifics are invisible as far as you are concerned. Either way, your monthly payments are lowered and simplified.

Gather Your Facts and Avoid the Malls

When making your online application to a debt consolidation company, have all your creditor information at your fingertips. That includes credit card statements with the creditors' names and addresses, account numbers, and total balance due.

The question naturally arises: Can you continue using your credit cards during the consolidated repayment? The answer is usually no. In fact, if the debt situation has progressed far enough into delinquency, the accounts may already be frozen. Regardless, many debt consolidators require that you cut up your cards and may instruct the providers to freeze your account.

ment interest rates to between 5 and 10 percent. Interestingly, the company distributes creditor payments by wire transfer and claims that this convenience makes creditors eager to negotiate.

Federated Financial Services (ww.debt-hospital.net)

This site is distinguished by an extensive discussion of the Fair Collection Practices Act and how it may apply to a visitor's situation. A multipage application form is more difficult to wrestle with than some others.

Consumer Credit Counseling Service (www.cccsintl.org)

This site is full of information and educational material. The service offers counseling but is not an intermediary for negotiating debt reduction. An on-site questionnaire helps determine nascent credit trouble.

Consumer Counseling Centers of America (www.consumercounseling.org)

This consumer advocacy group interprets the Fair Credit Reporting Act and helps visitors understand their rights and obligations. As an intermediary, the Consumer Counseling Centers of America help dispute credit reporting errors and problematic debt collection practices. Legal aid referral is available.

National Foundation for Consumer Credit (www.nfcc.org)

This classy nonprofit site is the Internet presence of a network of credit counseling offices around the United States. Some limited online service is available, but the National Foundation for Consumer Credit (NFCC) is basically a physical service. The site is informative and distractingly slick.

Debt Counselors of America (www.dca.org)

Debt Counselors of America (DCA) was the first Internet-based debt counseling service and is an information portal of debt management and repair. Here you find an unparalleled range of self-help resources—mailing lists, publications, an online bookstore, and current news. Online chatting with the Crisis Relief Team is a progressive feature. DCA offers a debt consolidation plan called One-Pay.

OTHER RESOURCES

- ✔ *Avoid Bankruptcy* (www.avoid-bankruptcy.net/index.htm)
- ✔ *Credit Counseling Centers of America* (www.cccamerica.org)
- ✔ *Debt Consolidation Loans* (www.debtconsolidationloans.org)
- ✔ *Debt Specialist Network* (www.debt-specialist.com)
- ✔ *Family Debt Arbitration & Counseling Services* (www.familydebt.org)
- ✔ *Free Debt Consolidation* (www.debtconsolidation.com)
- ✔ *Personal Credit Counseling* (www.helpwithdebt.com)

Chapter

8

Online Mortgages

The real estate industry, like many others, has been shaken up by the Internet. Real estate agents find themselves threatened by the Web's power to market properties more efficiently than any one person or office can. On the financial service side of the home-buying equation, mortgage companies find themselves in an increasingly competitive environment filled with interactive sites that facilitate the borrowing process.

Lenders who approach the Internet as an opportunity, not a threat, are thriving under these new conditions. Online *mortgage brokers* expand the borrowing business from a local industry to a national one. Some mortgage lenders are going online directly, producing their own Web sites to attract new customers.

mortgage broker   agency that matches home buyers with lenders. Mortgage brokers have flocked online. Online mortgage broker sites let visitors apply for preapproval online, then send the necessary paper forms to complete the application.

But Internet database technology favors brokerage sites that can search for loans on behalf of prospective home buyers across multiple lenders and mortgage products. Accordingly, the consumer trend in the online mortgage business is toward multilender mortgage brokers. And several large sites are filling the niche, with their services becoming more sophisticated all the time.

HOW ONLINE MORTGAGE BROKERS WORK

Different Internet mortgage brokers may have different processes by which they lead customers to loans, but a basic template is characteristic of all of them. When shopping for a mortgage online, you can expect to find variations of the following features.

Shop Online

Most brokerage sites provide loan shopping tools such as *rate monitors*, calculators, and various comparison tools that help you get your bearings and decide what type of mortgage you need. Filling out on-screen forms delivers instant quotes—displays that feature every aspect of the loan, including amortization tables. At this point you are not committed to anything and, in fact, may not have even entered your identifying information into the site yet. Shopping at this level is like kicking tires; you are just nosing around for basic rate, term, and availability information. (See Figure 8.1.)

rate monitor   online display of current interest rates. Rate monitors are found at insurance sites, loan sites, and bank sites as well as at information portals that track rates of all kinds.

Many online brokers urge visitors to prequalify at this stage. Often you can take this next step with your anonymity preserved. The *prequalification* form asks for basic financial information, does not involve a credit check, and is meant to give you a basic idea of what you can afford and what sort of loan application is likely to get approved. Prequalification never implies a commitment on either side.

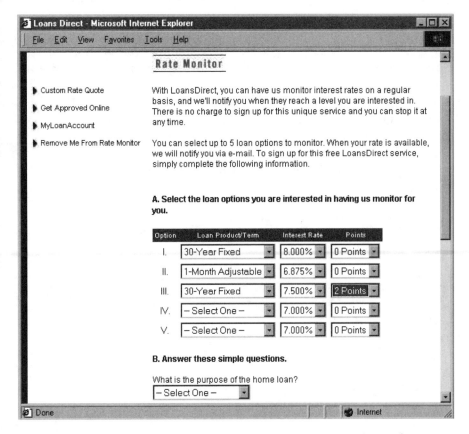

FIGURE 8.1   Some loan sites invite you to set rate criteria, then inform you by e-mail if one of your targets is met.
(Reprinted with permission of LoansDirect.)

prequalification   a preliminary step in the loan process, prequalification tells a prospective borrower that, according to the personal information submitted so far, a certain type of loan is likely to be approved. Prequalification is based on just the barest information, and is not usually verified with a credit check.

Apply Online

When you are ready to get serious, you fill out and submit your application online. In truth, this step is just the first part of the complete, formal application process. It is here that you abandon your anonymity and divulge more detailed and personal information, including your Social Security number. (The key to lost anonymity. Surrendering your Social Security number opens the door to a credit check.)

At most brokerages you do not need to have selected a home to buy at this stage, although you do need to know what state (and, in some cases, what county) your future home will be in. (See Figure 8.2.) The ap-

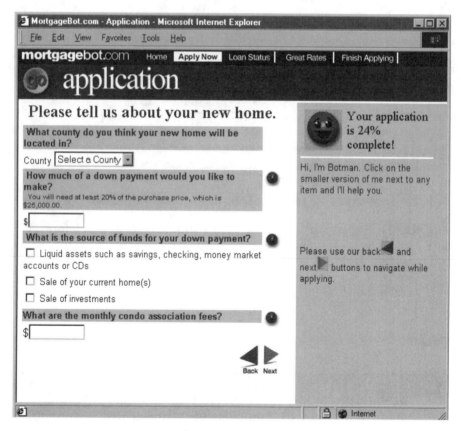

FIGURE 8.2 Part of the preapproval application at Mortgagebot.com. The small icons link to help pages, and the smiling face tells you how close to completion you are.

(Reprinted with permission of Mortgagebot.com.)

plication form could be a lengthy one, spread over several pages, taking as long as 15 or 20 minutes to fill in.

Many brokerages emphasize the speed with which they respond to your form. The goal of this stage is *preapproval*, which means that your application seems to be supported by sufficient financial resources. The broker may or may not perform a credit check at this point. Preapproval is not a commitment.

preapproval more definite than prequalification, but still not a firm deal, preapproval is part of the loan-approval process in which the prospective borrower's financial condition has been verified and the basic terms of a future loan have been agreed on.

Paper Documents

Once you are preapproved, the broker sends a lot of paper to you through the mail. Now the *real* application process begins. Some of the forms may be partially filled out on your behalf already, using information you submitted at the site. These documents spell out every detail of the loan product you specified online—term rates, payment amounts, and finance charges. A summary of estimated *closing* fees usually is included. You must slog through any number of disclosure forms, sign everything, and send the application back. Most brokers make it easy by including a return envelope.

closing consummation of a business or financial agreement. Most typically, closing refers to the final step in the home-buying and mortgaging process, at which all contractual documents are signed, the deed is handed over, and the mortgage check is delivered. Closing is almost ceremonial in its complexity, and is attended by buyer, seller, attorneys, and lenders.

Locking the Rate

It is important to remember that the interest rate you are applying for often is not locked in at this stage. You are applying for a *rate lock* for a certain period of time. When your final, paper-intensive application is approved, your rate will be locked and you can begin pursuing a closing date on a house.

> **rate lock**   guarantee of a certain interest rate, for a certain duration, when taking a loan. The lender guarantees low rates for short periods and higher rates for longer periods. Rate locks are important when negotiating a mortgage— ideally the lock period is long enough to close the real estate purchase but short enough to assure a low rate.

Tracking and Approval

After sending your documents back to the broker, you may be able to track the progress of your application at the broker site. Brokers who provide this service usually include a unique user name and password with the paper documents so you can log on to your account right away.

Approval usually is delivered online. Lenders have a lot to do for each home purchase they help finance, including getting various appraisals performed on the property. The best online brokerages promise "on-time" closings in which the lender gets everything done by your closing date and shows up with a check.

RESOURCES

This section spotlights sites whose resources go beyond matching home buyers with lenders. Some of the following services are, in part, mortgage brokers with specialties, such as subprime lending. Others are information portals to rates, lenders in your locality, and other aspects of the mortgage universe.

International Real Estate Digest (www.ired.com)

The audience for this interesting e-zine is 60 percent real estate professionals. It features articles about the global real estate industry. One recent piece covered the state of home-buying and mortgaging in Bulgaria.

Editorial content aside, the core feature of the site is a vast directory of real estate office Web sites around the world. Some 25,000 links are presented in a geographical directory that certainly is the most extensive on the Web.

Loanpage (www.loanpage.com)

Flashing banners give Loanpage's home page a cheap look, but ignore all that. This tremendous directory of lenders and brokers is a delight to use once you get under the surface.

Click the Mortgage Search tab to use the fine Java directory interface. You can select a point of search that is geographical (state, county, city, zip code, area code) or financial (loan length, loan type, brokerage type).

The Reference Desk packages a few tutorials, Q&A screens, and a dictionary of terms. The Private Mortgage Insurance section in the Reference Desk gives valuable information and international contacts for insurance companies that can lower your down payment.

Some chat rooms and calculators round out the site.

America Mortgage Online (www.amo-mortgage.com)

An outstanding mortgage information portal, America Mortgage Online provides the usual array of calculators (payment, affordability, amortizations), but the site's real distinction is in the Mortgage101 section. This treasure of information consists of 12 tutorials and over 150 articles covering applications, down payments, Federal Housing Authority (FHA) loans, mortgage insurance, refinancing, title insurance, and much more. The section on FHA programs is particularly informative.

American Mortgage Online is a search engine and directory of online mortgage brokers. Drill through the pages using a geographic model to find loan brokers who operate in your neck of the woods. The site provides generic on-screen application forms—they are long and detailed, so settle in for a spell. Unfortunately, there is no information about the lenders represented at the site, so visitors have little basis upon which to choose.

Mortgage Net (www.mortgage-net.com)

If you prefer a local touch to the relatively anonymous realm of cyberspace, Mortgage Net can help you find lenders and mortgage brokers near you. Using a state-by-state directory, you can zero in on a list of institutions in your state that specialize in purchase loans, imperfect credit situations, or home equity loans. Each listing is accompanied by a short descriptive paragraph and a link to the lender's Web site.

There's more. Mortgage Net has some of the best educational material around. The Mortgage Reference Desk is filled with plain-talk explanatory articles about many aspects of the borrowing process, and includes an on-screen dictionary.

In the Calculators and Mortgage Tools area, the Premium Java Calculator is definitely worth a bookmark by itself. This great tool uses interactive sliders instead of input fields to change variables such as interest rate, loan term, and loan amount. As you slide one variable around, the others adjust in real time. It is like a slide rule for mortgage budgeting and saves time over every other calculator on the Net. You have got to see this addictive little gadget to believe it.

MortgageQuotes.com (www.mortgagequotes.com)

Do not be put off by the scattered and too-colorful page design of this site. Excellent tools lurk beneath the amateurish aesthetics.

MortgageQuotes.com is a haven for home-shoppers with imperfect credit. All stigma attached to past repayment difficulties is erased in the rigorous quantifying spirit of this site. Credit self-assessment questionnaires help you determine exactly what your credit rating probably is from a mortgage lender's viewpoint and what to do about it. A geographic angle is included, so you get a specific idea of the rate you are likely to pay in your area.

Throughout the site, rate tables have embedded calculator links for figuring monthly payments. And those calculators! Of course they display monthly payment amounts, as any self-respecting online mortgage calculator should. Additionally, they highlight end-of-year totals. And the amortization tables are tricolor graphs that display the shifting relationships of balance, principal, and interest, year by year. Beautiful.

Homeowners.com (www.homeowners.com)

A multilingual site written in English, Spanish, and Chinese, Homeowners.com steps newcomers through the entire home-shopping process, from considering a purchase to filling out an online application. Three levels of research are provided here, accommodating casual and serious visitors. At the most casual level you can check daily rate tables. For more specific rates that apply to your situation, fill out the short quote form. Serious shoppers can initiate their mortgage hunt with a long application form.

The site is divided into two broad categories, addressing the home buyer and the homeowner. The latter section deals with home equity

Mystery of Amortization

Many online mortgage calculators give you a choice of displaying an amortization table along with the monthly payment data. What is that table, and why is it so much fun to look at? (Fun might be an overstatement.)

Amortization is the formula by which your monthly payments are balanced between principal and interest. Lenders, being the savvy institutions they are, want to get their hands on the interest first, just in case the worst should happen and you cannot pay back the whole loan. (There are other accounting advantages from the lender's viewpoint.) So at the beginning of the loan, your payments consist of mostly interest—very little principal is getting paid back during the first few years. Then, gradually, even though your monthly payments remain the same, the principal contributes increasingly to the balance. By the end you are paying almost all principal, because the interest has been mostly repaid.

While it may seem dreary to review a table showing how little you are repaying of the money you actually borrowed, there is a bright side. That silver lining is the tax deduction you receive on the interest payment, which is higher at the beginning of the loan. That side of the total equation puts money in one pocket as it removes it from another pocket. And tax considerations should always play a part in home-buying calculations.

loans and mortgage refinancing. In both areas a library section delivers a multitude of informative articles.

HSH Associates (www.hsh.com)

HSH promotes itself as the largest publisher of consumer loan information in the United States, and this site certainly pushes a lot of data to your screen. Daily updated statistics are available on a nationwide basis as well as for metropolitan areas. Lots of mortgage calculators are housed here. HSH is an information provider, not a mortgage broker, and does not accept referral fees or commissions. The site is objective and does not carry banner advertisements.

EVALUATING MORTGAGE BROKERS

Mortgage brokers have flooded online in a tsunami of financial services. The availability of information and the selection of lenders is terrific, but choosing a site at which to centralize your mortgage search is no piece of cake. This section helps untangle the mosaic of features and claims that scream out from mortgage broker sites. Keep these points in mind when surfing.

Rates and Closing Costs

Obviously, the interest rate you pay on your mortgage is one of the most important considerations. While various brokerage sites may scream about carrying the lowest rates, the truth is that the underlying industry is fairly consolidated in this department. Different lenders configure their products in various ways—and there is some divergence in rates according to whether *points* are paid, what state you live in, the type of loan, and other factors.

points cash increments of 1 percent of a loan amount, usually a mortgage. Points are variable items in the negotiation of mortgage terms, with each point usually worth 0.25 percent of interest rate on the loan. So paying 2 percent of the loan amount up front (2 points) can reduce the loan's interest rate by a 0.5 percent.

Certain considerations aside from the basic interest rate help distinguish brokers. *Closing costs* comprise one category of expense that differs from broker to broker. Look for disclosure of closing costs as part of the quote process—it is usually called up-front fee disclosure. An itemized estimate is helpful and inspires trust. All the better if the estimate is specific to your location, at the county level.

closing costs charges and fees associated with finalizing a real estate and mortgaging transaction. Most closing costs are charged by the mortgage lender and are used to pay for assessment services and to compensate the lending institution for its risk.

When it comes to the loan's interest rate, you may (rarely) be able to lock in a rate as part of the online process. Normally, the rate lock lasts for a certain time period—15 days, 30 days, and 2 months are typical. The longer the time period, the higher the rate, to cover the lender's risk. Being able to lock rates without a commitment to borrow is even better.

Closing Costs Revealed

Online mortgage quotes usually include so-called closing costs. These fees are always part of the home-buying budget. So what is in that mysterious bundle of fees associated with closing a home purchase? Following are several of the most typical closing costs:

✔ **Title insurance fee.** The title is your claim to property ownership, and insuring that claim protects both you and the lender from disputes to that claim. All titles are cleared before closing by a search through public records; this fee insures against potential claims that were not found. The title insurance fee is often the most costly ingredient in the closing costs.

✔ **Appraisal fee.** No matter what independent surveys of your prospective property are conducted, the lender orders its own appraisal and charges you for it. The lender contracts a local appraiser, familiar with local real estate values, to do the job. This fee often costs a few hundred dollars.

✔ **Underwriting fee.** Some lenders charge this fee as a sort of bonus that compensates them for the risk of lending you money. Nothing like a ringing endorsement, eh? The underwriting fee can cost some hundreds of dollars.

✔ **Settlement fee.** This charge goes to the lender's attorney. Isn't it fun paying your lender's bills?

✔ **Document preparation.** This fee pays for the documents prepared by the lender that you sign at the closing. The charge might be between $100 and $200.

(Continued)

✔ **Credit report.** You know what this is—it is your credit being reported. This step normally happens during the application process and may or may not be billed at that time. If so, some online brokers and lenders rebate the small cost ($30 to $50) at closing.

✔ **Tax service fee.** Another lender's expense pushed onto your plate, this one pays for a third-party company to verify property taxes. Normally $100 or less.

✔ **Recording fee.** This money goes to the local government, paying for the expense of placing your mortgage documents into the public record. The cost varies by locality but typically is about $100.

As you can see, most of the closing costs go straight into the lender's pocket, making closing day all the more joyful for the borrower.

Performance Guarantees

Mortgage brokerage sites sometimes offer two types of performance guarantees. One involves cost. Low-rate guarantees are fairly typical and not that hard to honor if a brokerage is affiliated with enough lenders. A guarantee of lowest possible closing costs, an increasingly common feature, indicates a broker's experience and confidence. Actually cashing in on such a guarantee is difficult, as it requires determining that lower closing costs would have been possible by some other method. A guaranteed dollar amount for final closing costs sometimes is locked in with the loan rate.

Another type of guarantee, a time guarantee, is more practical. Some brokers assure you that the lending deal will close within a certain time period (10 or 15 days) after they receive your fully completed documents. This closing is for the loan, not the home purchase.

Product Range

When dealing with an online mortgage broker, you want a selection of loan products. The Internet is the world's greatest information medium, after all, and you want an online agency that can match you with the absolutely perfect loan.

There are three main types of home loan:

1. *Home purchase.* Here the loan is used to buy a residence.
2. *Refinancing.* The loan is used to buy out a previous mortgage and improve its terms.
3. *Home equity.* The loan uses your home as collateral, and you use the funds for home improvement or some other purpose.

The number of lender affiliations a broker has determines, to a large extent, the range of products offered. (Some online brokers are themselves lenders and mix their own products into your search results.) Geographic coverage is also important; there really is no excuse for a broker not to cover any state in the United States. If you do not seem to be finding a satisfactory range of borrowing possibilities from the broker, move on. Do not commit too early on this point. The right loan awaits you somewhere.

Customer Service

Customer service is a sore point at financial service sites across the Web and across specific service types. Just as at online brokers and virtual banks, customer service at mortgage brokers plays a big part in the quality of your experience. Customer service may be even more important with mortgage companies than with other financial services, because this is an area of finance that you cannot do alone. You need help, and the broker better provide it.

You can get an idea of the quality of customer service through a detailed initial visit to the site. Invitations to contact give you a good feeling; it is bad news if you have trouble figuring out how to get help. Some mortgage brokers maintain an online staff available for real-time, interactive chatting. This service does not require any special software; it is built into the site. Internet-initiated callbacks are nice if you have an extra phone line—they work by your requesting a phone call from the site and receiving it within a few minutes.

Another aspect of the integration of online and offline services is the site's willingness to schedule property appraisals and in-home document signing. The latter is rare and probably unimportant to many people willing to shop for a mortgage online in the first place.

Follow-Up Customer Service

Most mortgage sites send a package of paper forms at some point in the application process, then follow up with phone calls. This process presents another way of evaluating customer service. Did the information packet arrive quickly? Are the information sheets within the packet clear? Is the person who follows up helpful and knowledgeable? Remember, there is nothing to stop you from applying at more than one mortgage site and letting the service quality determine which one you eventually use. The only drawback to multiple applications is filling in all those forms.

Database Flexibility

Online mortgage brokers display quotes in tables that indicate the various characteristics of the loan products, such as term, interest rate, and points. Sometimes you get a truckload of results to your questionnaire, and it is helpful to sort them according to those criteria. Grouping together all the loan products that require a percentage point of the loan in advance, for example, makes it easier to compare them.

Approval Process

When you start with an online mortgage broker, you like to see your way clear through the process, as if you were looking through a tunnel to the light on the other side. The feature to watch for is online status tracking. When a site provides this feature, you can follow the progress of your application by logging on to the site. Best of all is a detailed form of tracking with which you get a separate report on each submitted document. Obtaining a mortgage is never an instantaneous process. Online status tracking at least makes it less mysterious.

Another important part of a good approval process is instant prequalification. Qualifying for a mortgage is not the same as being approved, but it points you in the right direction for eventual approval. You get prequalified by filling out a short form that usually does not involve a credit check. As long as your answers are accurate and verifiable, the result is a sound indication of your prospects.

Decision Support Tools

Some mortgage sites are information portals, and others concentrate on the application and approval process. Which is better—lots of information or fewer distractions? Some of the decision support content brokers use to lure you in include:

- ✔ Educational articles, tutorials, and glossaries
- ✔ Mortgage calculators to help figure monthly payments (see Figure 8.3), interest rates, and terms
- ✔ Credit assessment forms that help determine what principal and rates you can afford

As useful as it is to have calculators and credit assessment tools at your disposal in a single site, information features by themselves should not influence your choice of a mortgage broker all that much. Remember, as is repeated often in these pages, the Web is the portal, not the site. This chapter details a number of sites with extraordinary information resources. Many mortgage brokerage sites also house handy tools, but that does not mean they have the best loan products for you.

The best bet is to treat information and financial service as two different criteria and use brokerages for what they are best at—securing a loan.

Despite the rule of separating information and brokerage services in your mind, there is one type of information service that you should watch for, and that is centralized comparison of loan features across multiple products. This feature lets you compare rates and costs of the different plans that your search brings up.

Subprime Lending

Not everyone has the grade-A borrowing status that most online mortgage brokers aim their services at. Many people do not realize that less-than-perfect credit does not necessarily stand in the way of buying and mortgaging property. If you are concerned about your credit status, and especially if you are unaware exactly where you stand in the lending universe, using a broker site with subprime tools and services is crucial—perhaps the most important feature of all.

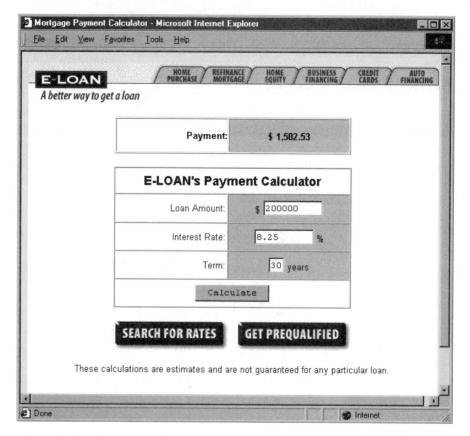

FIGURE 8.3 Payment calculators like this one at E-Loan help you figure out what you can afford.

(Reprinted with permission of E-Loan.)

Features that cater to subprime borrowing candidates include:

✔ *Credit assessment tools.* These questionnaires are usually fairly short, and ask you to detail any delinquencies, liens, late payment records, and bankruptcies in your fiscal picture in order to help you determine your status. The result is an estimated credit grade that resembles a school grade.

✔ *Solutions advice that matches your credit status.* It does not do much good to learn of your subprime credit status if you cannot move forward to a loan solution. Many lenders market specifically to individuals with credit troubles, providing higher-interest mortgages. All the better if these brokers provide strategic advice as well.

✔ *Educational material.* Information on how you can make the most of bad credit and ways to improve your credit are useful.

Buying property is one way of improving credit, and plenty of lenders are willing to work with many types of credit histories. Owning a home can improve an individual's financial picture in ways beyond credit rehabilitation, as, for example, by lowering monthly expenses (owning often is cheaper than renting) and by yielding tax benefits (mortgage interest is deductible).

Ease of Use

Prowling through mortgage broker sites usually involves viewing multiple pages and bouncing around from application forms to calculators to rate tables. The site should make it easy for you by providing consistent navigation features. If you find yourself getting lost or frustrated easily, try another site.

Page-loading speed is critical when dealing with online financial services. Pretty home pages are fine, but once you get into the site's information pages, you do not want graphics and heavy ads slowing you down. This consideration is less important with mortgage sites than with online investment brokers, because your relationship with a mortgage broker is close-ended in most cases. A cumbersome site is a nuisance only temporarily—until your loan goes through.

Stability is another quality to watch for—or, to be more accurate, *in*stability. Site crashes or glitches (look at the review of Mortgage.com in this chapter for a description of one such glitch) may shake your confidence in the security of your applications and forms.

Privacy Statement

Mortgage brokers universally use secure site pages for collecting information through their application forms. Data security is not an issue, but privacy—what the company does after it collects your information—is. The issue is more important at mortgage sites than in some other areas of financial service, because in applying for a home loan, you disclose a lot of personal information. (The only online application likely to be more personal is that for term life insurance.)

Third-party auditing of the site's privacy statement is becoming popular now as a way of reassuring visitors. At least, look for a public statement of the policy, and make sure it is not written in cryptic legalese.

Integration of Listings

Some brokerages aspire to be one-stop home-buying portals, displaying real estate broker listings, for-sale listings, neighborhood reports, and home sales data. A single site that provides the means to shop for and finance a home is impressive. But do not overvalue the presence of the real estate side of home shopping at a brokerage site. Home listings are a distinct realm of information, and they have no bearing on whether a broker can find the best loan for you. Real estate brokerage is not a financial service, and there is no reason to expect your lender to find your dream house—just to help you afford it.

Credit Reports and Rate Alerts

Two miscellaneous features are handy to have at a brokerage site. First, rate alerts notify you by e-mail when your desired rate is available. As this book was being published, mortgage rates were inching upward with no backsliding—a trend that discourages waiting for a better rate. Rate alerts really become useful when rates fluctuate up and down, and you want to lock in a certain interest level or lower. During those times, an online broker can help by monitoring the field for you and alerting you when your requirement is met.

Credit report access is another convenient brokerage feature. Some reporting agencies deliver online versions of individual credit reports, usually within minutes, for a fee. There is nothing like taking the guesswork out of assessing your creditworthiness.

TOURING MORTGAGE BROKERS

The sites in this section are big players in the online mortgage business. While there is no room to describe all the Internet brokers (some are simply listed at the end of the chapter), this selection should be enough to get you started. The descriptions paint a composite picture of what an online mortgage broker can do.

Do not forget Gomez! Gomez.com (www.gomez.com), a financial services rating service mentioned repeatedly in this book, presents a review section dedicated to online mortgage brokers.

Mortgagebot.com (www.mortgagebot.com)

Welcome to the future of mortgages. That's the site's catch-phrase, and Mortgagebot.com (see Figure 8.4) covers all the bases, going an extra mile or two in some cases. This company seems determined to keep its position as a state-of-the-art online mortgage broker.

One feature that puts Mortgagebot.com on the map for good is MortgageMarvel (see Figure 8.5), a multiple-broker comparison tool. There is nothing else like this thing, although imitations probably will emerge. Click the MortgageMarvel link first thing, and marvel at its self-less delivery of information. After answering a few questions about your proposed loan amount, type, and location, MortgageMarvel displays a

FIGURE 8.4 The home page of Mortgagebot.com, a streamlined mortgage broker.

(Reprinted with permission of Mortgagebot.com.)

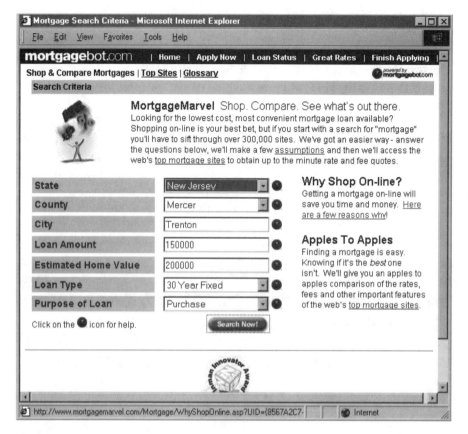

FIGURE 8.5 MortgageMarvel at Mortgagebot.com is a great tool that compares rates at several online mortgage brokers.

(Reprinted with permission of Mortgagebot.com.)

table of relevant products from several other online brokers. (At the time this book was completed, Mortgagebot.com was scanning data from six other online services, all reviewed in this section.) Mortgagebot.com products do not always offer the best terms in this comparison table.

Online approval and in-site application tracking are definite selling points. Rates often are locked for 60 days, and some approvals get delivered in 15 minutes. Most forms and tables contain strategically embedded links that display pop-up windows with definitions of terms.

Mortgagebot.com leaves no stone unturned. The privacy policy is explicit and prominently displayed. Rate, fee, and approval time guarantees are advertised, with $250 back at closing if the company closes late. Customer service has defined hours seven days a week and includes on-site chatting.

E-Loan (www.eloan.com)

The brand leader of online lenders maintains a full-service lending destination that specializes in mortgages. Plenty of calculators and interactive tools support the site's mission as a one-stop lending portal.

E-Loan eschews on-site glitz in favor of solid products and services. The company is especially strong in the relocation department but offers a compelling range of mortgage products across the board. E-Loan was founded in 1996 and, as such, has more experience than most virtual mortgage brokers.

The site's rate tables (see Figure 8.6), displayed in response to a bit of questioning about what you want to borrow and where the property is,

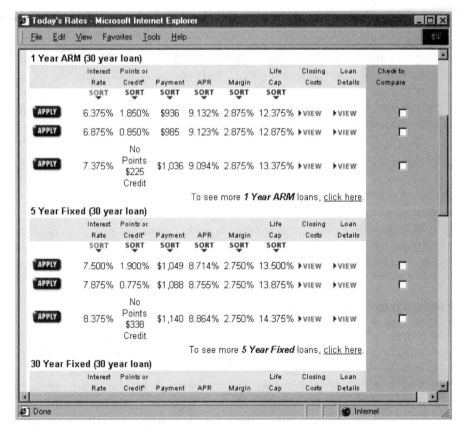

FIGURE 8.6 E-Loan's rate comparison tables let you link to loan details and compare two or more loans.

(Reprinted with permission of E-Loan.)

compare products from multiple lenders. Do not confuse this comparison with Mortgagebot's comparison of multiple brokers, which is a unique feature.

The site features a detailed privacy Q&A page, and its policy has been third-party audited. Customer service operates during defined hours seven days a week. Loan application materials are sent swiftly, without harassing telephone follow-up. At this book's deadline, no price, fee, or closing time guarantees were offered.

MortgageIT.com (www.mortgageit.com)

A relatively new online mortgage broker, MortgageIT was spun off from IPI Financial Services, a prominent traditional brokerage. The online venture leverages that background of experience to deliver good rates for many types of home loans.

Exceptionally fast response time conveys the impression of loan experts poised behind the site, eager to leap out and help. MortgageIT guarantees ($100) to call on the phone within an hour of a submitted online application. On-site customer service is likewise accommodating, using an interactive chat window that pops open when you first enter the site. Three of the four main top-page navigation buttons relate to customer service; MortgageIT is determined to providing a personalized experience.

In the privacy department, MortgageIT tracks visitor movements anonymously for technical reasons that are clearly disclosed. The rest of the privacy statement is short, sweet, and reassuring, with contact information for getting more details. A security statement provides an education in encryption and network issues.

The Resources section assembles a fairly typical range of calculators and interactive gadgets. One page everyone should visit is the LockIT tutorial on when and how to lock interest rates.

iOwn.com (www.iown.com)

The iOwn online mortgage broker is a good one-stop location (see Figure 8.7) that integrates real estate listings, educational materials, interactive tools, and—oh, yes—mortgage loan shopping.

Extremely clear definitions of terms that go beyond cursory glossary entries, and explanations of procedures, distinguish this service. Up-front fee disclosure and closing cost estimates dispel mystery in those two important areas.

The site's main comparison tool is RateShopper, which culls instant quotes from hundreds of sources, delivering any that relate to your local-

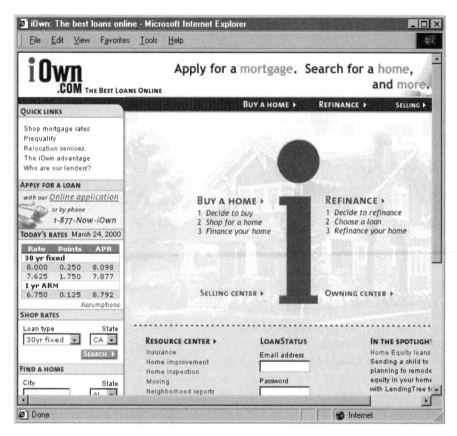

FIGURE 8.7 The iOwn.com home page.
© 1997–2000, iOwn, Inc.

ity and loan requirements. The system can deliver e-mail rate alerts if you ask it to. iOwn promises 24-hour response (48 hours on weekends) to application submissions.

On-site postapplication tracking is another strong suit here; Loan-Status allows document tracking and provides an evolving checklist of steps that still need to be completed. You are assisted throughout the application process by a personal loan consultant, and the service offers a $500 guarantee of an on-time closing.

On the real estate side, integrated home listings are nicely implemented but far from comprehensive. E-mail alerts of properties that meet your buying criteria are available, but frankly, you would do better at Realtor.com (www.realtor.com). Keep your home search separate from your mortgage search.

Homespace.com (www.homespace.com)

Homespace delivers visitors immediately to a secure-page environment, which slows navigation down a bit but demonstrates the site's commitment to network security. The privacy statement, by contrast, is a little glib, with no dedicated contact information.

One unusual service distinguishes Homespace among mortgage brokers: the Home Services section, which offers recommendations and savings on a variety of home-ownership services such as security systems, moving companies, and furniture repair. None of which bear much relation to obtaining financing, of course.

The Real Estate Services section sounds promising but is actually a bit mystifying. The site helps you find a real estate agent in 50 states and 350 metropolitan areas and offers discounts on commissions with affiliated agents. This service is far from comprehensive and does not explain how customers would save money on the buying side of a real estate transaction, which normally does not pay commissions at all. It is also unclear why choosing a real estate agent in this manner is preferable to walking into a local office. Finally, there is no disclosure of how affiliated agents are chosen. Avoid this service until it is improved.

Loan applications get a response within 48 hours—not bad, but far from best of breed in the responsiveness department. Customer service is available by phone, including instant callbacks from the Web site, but there is no on-site chatting.

InstaMortgage.com (www.instamortgage.com)

Guarantees and more guarantees. In a heatedly competitive field, price and timing guarantees are a noisy and perhaps effective way to lure customers into a site. InstaMortgage hawks its assurances from the first page: $250 guarantee on lenders' rates and a $250 guarantee if you do not get a loan decision in three hours.

Customer service? Telephone service is prominently advertised on the site pages, and the number delivers the caller to a voice menu that eventually delivers a real person. Calls are recorded, and the service is available during defined hours, seven days a week. On-site chatting is promoted but failed to work during repeated tests.

While InstaMortgage's service appear solid, the site presents navigation and stability problems. Visitors are encouraged to drill into the site in a linear fashion, which makes it easy to get lost. The home page is flashy but uninformative, failing to provide a coherent map of the terrain.

iQualify (www.iqualify.com)

This mortgage broker places an aggressive emphasis on speed. The site claims to process applications and deliver approvals within minutes of submitting an online application. The approval is not a rate lock but does include data from your credit report and a detailed explanation of what is needed to gain final approval.

The site displays instant rate quotes for a variety of products, but blindly; that is to say, you do not see whom the quote is from. Although that is a bit disconcerting, the site's easy navigation and friendly encouragement is alluring, and filling out the application does not take that long. iQualify breaks up the arduous form into several segments, each with its own reference to a checklist that reassuringly becomes more complete as you proceed. Rate locks last for 30 days in most cases.

iQualify does not spend any resources on educational material or calculators. It is all down to business here, with a no-nonsense, let's-get-the-job-done approach that is more heartening than brusque.

Loanz.com (www.loanz.com)

Loanz.com presents an interesting twist, even beyond its annoying fixation on the letter *z* (Today'z Rates, Home Buying Tipz). Primary among its innovations is a reverse auction feature by which visitors can name a loan rate and receive bids from lenders. Do not get too excited—this is not a groundbreaking device by which home buyers everywhere can attain outrageously low mortgage rates. The Name Your Rate service is merely an alternative way to butt through the jungle of quotes.

Say you want a loan of $150,000 and are eager to pay up-front points to lower your rate. Rather than surf through endless rate tables looking for a loan that meets your criteria, make an offer at Name Your Rate. (Drop-down menus help you make reasonable choices.) The bids you receive all will have features relevant to your needs.

Loanz.com has created a stand-alone software program called Powerhouse, freely available as a download from the site, that combines many of the interactive tools and calculators you find at broker sites. Powerhouse helps you figure a home-buying budget and strategy.

Instant quotes are not so instant at Loanz.com. After two screens of questions, the site offers to contact you by phone, fax, or e-mail, but no on-site quotes are to be found anywhere. This lack of information seems almost scandalous compared to the copius displays of rate comparisons found at other brokers. Loanz.com intends to provide a more personal experience, and there is certainly a wealth of educational content here.

Infoloan.com (www.infoloan.com)

Infoloan presents many of the typical interactive decision aids that you expect from a brokerage—including mortgage calculators and basic educational material. None of the basics is particularly distinguished, but neither are any lacking.

Perplexingly (and annoyingly), the live chat window pops open even outside of customer service hours. This useless feature creates a small active window that must be closed or buried before you can proceed.

This site's unique feature is the interactive Portfolio that can hold information about both properties and loans under consideration. This collection of data can be updated whenever you like, and keeping your personal information in there helps Infoloan get in touch with you. E-mail rate alerts can be set within this section.

Quicken Loans (quickenloans.quicken.com)

Quicken has put together a consolidated lending site with heavy emphasis on mortgages. This site offers a standard assortment of calculators and tools. Its rate tables are undistinguished technically—they cannot be sorted by loan criteria.

In the privacy department, Quicken discloses how it tags your hard drive and what it does with both anonymous and personal information. The site also describes its network security precautions.

Mortgage.com (www.mortgage.com)

An attractive and useful site, Mortgage.com certainly has the best name of the bunch. Concentrating on low rates and quality customer service, the site also presents very useful home-shopping information. A search engine for comparables—home-sale data by neighborhood—is excellent and is found through the "How much are homes selling for in my area" link on the home page. Many other interactive tools help home-shoppers at all levels.

OTHER MORTGAGE BROKERS AND DIRECT LENDERS

✔ *Alternative Lending Group* (www.alternativelending.com)

✔ *Capital Mortgage* (www.approved.com)

✔ *EhomeCredit* (www.ehomecredit.com)

✔ *Interloan* (www.interloan.com)

✔ *Keystroke.com* (www.keystroke.com)

✔ *LoanCity.com* (www.loancity.com)

✔ *LoanPlaza* (www.loanplaza.com)

✔ *LoansDirect* (www.loansdirect.com)

✔ *LoanSurfer* (www.loansurfer.com)

✔ *LoanWorks.com* (www.loanworks.com)

✔ *The Mortgage Exchange* (themortgageexchange.com/home.htm)

✔ *Mortgage Mart* (www.mortgagemart.com)

✔ *Mortgage Network* (www.themortgagenetwork.com)

✔ *Mortgageselect.com* (www.mortgageselect.com)

✔ *Nowlending.com* (www.nowlending.com)

Chapter

9

Online Credit Cards

T his is a good time to use the Internet to find credit cards, for a couple of reasons:

✔ *Choice.* There are more credit card choices than ever before. Interactive directories and search engines can help slash through the forest-thick growth of products, features, and conflicting hype.

✔ *Online access.* The credit card industry is continually evolving. Without the Internet, you would be forced to rely on magazines or random solicitations to be aware of your card and feature choices.

✔ *New features.* New Internet-only credit cards are raising the bar when it comes to online management features.

The online realm promotes all kinds of cards, not just the virtual type. In the fiercely competitive credit card field, banks and issuers are trying everything to get your attention and your borrowing business. Accordingly, almost all card companies and banks advertise their credit products and features online, and many put their application forms on the screen, too. You can even get approved online. (Fate is too kind to deliver credit rejections online—those usually come through the postal mail.)

Debit cards are promoted online, too, but remember that these convenient pieces of plastic are glorified ATM cards and connect directly to a deposit account (checking or savings). As such, their online promotions usually are associated with deposit accounts at online banks. Shopping for a debit card independent of a bank account does not make much sense.

> **debit card**   plastic cards, similar in appearance to credit cards, that deduct money from a checking account for purchases. Debit cards often are branded by prominent credit issuers, such as Visa or MasterCard, but in fact do not extend a line of credit to their owners. Users employ the cards in ATMs to get cash and in shops and restaurants to make cash purchases.

Virtual credit cards operate in essentially the same manner as traditional cards. In fact, at this stage of the field's evolution, you would be hard pressed to notice important differences between them at first glance. The difference between bank credit cards and virtual cards, in some cases, lies in the quality of online service rather than the nature of the service.

> **virtual credit card**   a card provided by an Internet-only company, not a traditional bank, that is made of plastic and used in the usual fashion. Online products like this let you manage and pay your account online.

BASIC ONLINE CREDIT CARD SERVICES

Managing a credit card account falls within the realm of banking. It makes sense, then, that online credit card services would bear a certain similarity to online banking services. The two primary online features of virtually all credit card accounts are:

1. On-screen account statements.
2. Online bill paying.

Look familiar? Those are the most important features of online banking as well.

Plastic Money Primer

Three basic kinds of money card are widely used in the United States, all of which are marketed online in one of two ways. Confusing? Here is how it all breaks down:

✔ *Credit cards.* The most prevalent type of consumer borrowing, credit cards represent an always-available line of credit and can be used for almost any kind of purchase. Users do not need to repay the card's balance immediately—hence the convenience and addictive quality of credit cards. These products are marketed aggressively on the Internet.

✔ *Charge cards.* Charge cards entitle the owner to a line of credit, just like credit cards, but all expenditures must be repaid monthly. Not nearly as many charge cards exist as the more popular and forgiving credit cards, and they are promoted with more discretion online.

✔ *Debit cards.* Debit cards are associated with bank deposit accounts (checking and savings accounts) and are used to extract cash from those accounts at ATMs. Some debit cards are branded by the main credit networks—Visa and MasterCard—and can be used in restaurants and shops like credit cards. Unlike credit cards, all debit card purchases are paid for instantly from the checking or savings account that funds the card. Because of the nature of debit cards, their online promotion is limited to virtual banks and click-and-mortars.

Credit cards may be secured or unsecured. The secured types require a security deposit and are effective products for restoring damaged personal credit. In most cases, the card's credit limit is equal to the security deposit, although some more lenient cards multiply the deposit to arrive at the spending limit.

Two types of credit card are marketed with abandon on the Net:

✔ *Reward cards.* These products reward spending with some kind of barter, such as frequent flier miles or points toward purchasing a car. The cards usually are branded by the rewarding agency, such as an airline or a car maker.

✔ ***Affinity cards.*** Affinity cards are like vanity license plates—they carry a brand the owner likes to be associated with but do not offer any financial reward related to that brand. Sports teams sometimes issue affinity cards.

Online Card Statements

For some people, the always-on access to credit card statements eliminates the need to hoard credit slips during the month. For others, there remain good reasons to keep those slips (checking against the statement and returning products are two that come to mind), but tabulating them by hand is no longer necessary to determine whether the current month's credit activities are within budget.

All online credit card statements feature the basics that you expect from a paper rundown of your account: current balance (what you owe); credit line (your total borrowing power); available credit (borrowing power minus current balance); and last payment amount. You also can expect to see an itemized list of transactions—all the stuff you have bought since the last statement closing date.

At best, online credit card statements update to include all charges as they happen. With a really good system, you could charge a thoroughly self-indulgent Irish wool sweater, then run home, fire up the computer, and view the damage on your statement.

At the very least (as with online bank statements), your virtual statement should update once a day. On the low end of the convenience scale are companies that update your account once per day but only on business days. With this system, if you go on a rampant buying spree Friday night, you cannot view the credit carnage until Monday morning.

Online credit card services vary in the degree to which they provide an archive of past statements. There are three main variations on a theme:

1. *Unlimited access.* Some cards give you unlimited access to your entire account history. This is obviously ideal and is most likely to be

Save Those Statements

No matter the quality of your online service, it is a good idea to save your paper statements. (Most online credit cards send paper statements and also provide online statements.) You may never need to refer to the mailed statements, but the day may come when you are very glad to have them. (The day, for example, when you need to know your card balance and your Internet service provider will not let you log onto the Internet.) Remember, too, that with a printer attached to your computer, you can always make a paper statement from a virtual one.

available when opening a new account with a virtual credit card. Traditional card issuers that have recently introduced online services may delay archiving past statements for on-screen access.

2. *Limited access.* Striking a middle ground, some companies stretch your account access back in time for a limited duration, such as three months.

3. *Current access only.* Bringing up the rear are companies that let you see only what is going on in the current statement cycle, with even last month's activity lost in the ether.

Paying Credit Card Bills Online

Most online credit card services allow you to arrange payment without writing and mailing a check. This is a great convenience in a couple of ways. You always can pay the traditional way—by receiving a statement and writing a check for at least the minimum amount due. But there are three major reasons why paying online is popular, all of which are related to speed:

1. Paying with a few mouse clicks is faster than licking envelopes.
2. The actual payment is accomplished quicker than the postal route. You may realize on Thursday that you want to clear some space on your card for a big weekend. Mailing a check will not do it, but certain types of online payment would.

3. Speed also plays a part when you have delayed paying the bill but want to avoid slipping beyond the interest-free grace period. When you're on the 23rd day of a 25-day grace period, the last thing you want is for the post office to take over.

Paying off your credit card online is a convenience, and there are three main ways of doing it. You can pay:

1. With another credit card.
2. Through your online banking system.
3. By allowing the card company access to your bank account.

The difference between the first two methods is crucial. While both give you advantages over the relatively awkward check-writing routine, only using another credit card accelerates the actual transfer of funds. As discussed in earlier chapters about online banking, virtual bill-paying systems use mailed checks—the advantage is that you do not have to write them. (Some bill-paying systems also make electronic-transfer payments, which are just as speedy as paying with another credit card.)

Some card issuers allow you to initiate bank transfers over the phone, and usually charge a fee each time you pay that way. This method

Using Your Bank's Credit Card

Most banks offer the same credit cards to their customers as to the rest of the world, with no special perks for people who maintain deposit accounts at the bank. (As mentioned already, even credit approval is generally no easier for customers.) However, there is one distinct advantage to owning a card issued by your bank—quick and easy bill payments. When banks offer online services, they generally bundle all related accounts together, so you can access a checking, savings, and credit card account in the same browser window. Transfers among those accounts are, in the best cases, simple and nearly instantaneous. Ideally, in that scenario, paying your credit card bill is a simple matter of a few mouse clicks to transfer funds from a deposit account to the credit account.

is just as fast as, but more expensive than, paying online with another credit card. Note that not all online credit cards implement bill paying by this method. Even rarer is the option of initiating a bank transfer from your online account.

The upshot is that if you have an online bill-paying system (through your bank or a third-party service), you can use it to pay any credit card in the world. If you use an online credit card, you may or may not be able to initiate payment from the credit card site, either by using another credit card or by approving a bank transfer.

NEW BREED OF CREDIT CARDS

In addition to online services (account access and bill paying) that many traditional cards provide, a new type of virtual card has emerged, packaged with new services that fit the wired lifestyle.

The idea of a virtual credit card is suspect, since the card itself is always physical. In this respect online cards are more familiar and traditional than virtual banks, mortgage companies, or investment brokers, all of which replace human services and physical buildings. What distinguishes virtual credit cards are their features and the fact that they are marketed exclusively online.

Virtual cards specialize in some or all of these characteristics:

✔ *E-commerce protection.* The truth is, any credit card protects its customers from fraud and merchant error, whether it occurs online or offline. The e-shopping protection advertised by virtual cards is mostly a marketing reassurance.

✔ *E-commerce paybacks.* This feature is not hype. Virtual cards, in an attempt to lure customers living the Internet lifestyle, affiliate with e-shops to give customers a rebate when they shop. Some of these cards present shopping directories at their sites to encourage shopping.

✔ *Advanced online service features.* Virtual cards are better positioned than traditional cards to provide sophisticated account displays, online payments, and future technology advances.

You may be getting the idea that virtual credit cards are not essentially different from traditional cards, and that impression has some truth to it. The online credit card revolution is more about access and choice than innovative features.

Unlike online investment brokers, who charge more favorable stock commissions, and virtual banks, which beat traditional banks at the interest game, online credit cards do not offer much more favorable interest rates than traditional cards. Traditional card issuers are very adept at playing the interest-rate game and have brought their acts online. So online card shopping involves appraising everything out there, traditional and virtual, and finding the best combination of features for your financial style.

FINDING CREDIT CARDS ONLINE

A few Web sites act as credit card directories, search engines, and information sources. Not as numerous as the information sites related to other financial services, these selected sites are all the more outstanding for the unusual services they provide.

CardTrak (www.cardtrak.com)

CardTrack is a deep and informative site that presents a mix of editorial content and card data. Here you can find monthly compilation lists of various types of credit cards, including low-rate, no-fee, platinum, secured, reward, affinity, and student cards. On the editorial side, you can learn a lot about the card industry by reading the oft-updated articles. Tutorials abound—even games. A credit card information and entertainment portal? If there can be such a thing, CardTrack must be it.

Credit Card Network (www.creditnet.com/home.html)

Credit Card Network supplies lists of certain kinds of specialty cards, including secured, low-teaser-rate, and low-fixed-rate cards. In addition, the site specializes in providing information on credit repair and building a good borrowing history. The site interfaces with a credit agency so visitors can order their credit reports, then provides information about interpreting those reports. If you want to be truly overwhelmed, call up the list of over 900 credit cards, unsorted.

Credit Card Menu (www.creditcardmenu.com)

This is a user-friendly site that makes card browsing easy and informative. The directory is distinguished by full descriptions of each listed card's features (see Figure 9.1), plus links to the detailed Terms and Conditions statement and the online applications. These features create a compelling

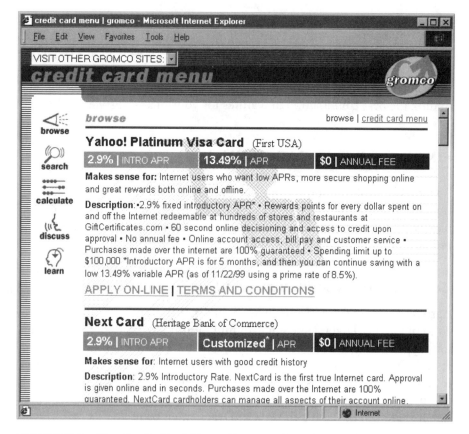

FIGURE 9.1   The Credit Card Menu directory describes each card and links to its application.

(Reprinted with permission of gromco, Inc.)

interface for exploring your options. However, the browsing directory is far from comprehensive. To be thorough, try the search engine, which allows you to select criteria. Message boards and educational material round out a clear site.

Credit Choice (www.creditchoice.com)

The beauty of this site is speed. Credit Choice is a lightning-quick database for finding cards of various types. Search for low-APR cards, special-interest affinity cards, online applications that provide immediate acceptance, and new-credit cards with low credit ceilings for students.

The site sometimes throws peculiar choices into each category, but the thumbnail descriptions and data information, plus the no-delay site design, make this resource a keeper.

EVALUATING ONLINE CREDIT CARDS

If you surf the Web at all, you almost cannot help shopping for credit cards, because the ads are so prevalent. You are bound to absorb some impressions of the energetically marketed cards. This section gives some advice about what to watch for in the many interesting deals being offered.

Interest Rates

This is the killer selling point. Everyone who owns a credit card and does not always maintain a zero monthly balance is motivated to find the best (lowest) interest rate. Card-issuing companies use low interest rates as hooks to lure customers, and the price wars among credit cards are most expressed as lowering (or vanishing) interest rates.

It's important to understand the distinction between the *teaser rate* and the *fixed rate*. The teaser rate is a temporary, very low interest rate that lasts for some duration—usually about six months. Then a fixed rate applies—this interest level is sometimes called a go-to rate. Teaser rates are, in some cases, 0 percent, an obvious attraction. Fixed rates for these competitive cards are usually much less than the 20-percent rates of yesteryear's cards. (Rates fluctuate all the time, but intense competition for customers has lowered rates across the board.)

teaser rate   initial interest rate charged to purchases made with a credit card. The teaser rate is sometimes as low as 0 percent and usually lasts from three to six months, after which a fixed rate begins.

fixed rate   permanent interest rate charged to credit card purchases after the teaser rate period has expired. Also known as the go-to rate.

A Hidden Feature about the Fixed Rate

Many people do not realize that the fixed rate, when it kicks in, will most likely apply to entire balance—even charges incurred during the introductory teaser-rate period. If you dislike this system, the remedy is to pay your bill in full every month, or find a card that distinguishes between initial-period charges and later charges. The online advertisements do not make this distinction for you. If this point is troublesome, contact the card issuer and ask explicitly whether the fixed rate applies to purchase balances incurred during the teaser-rate period.

Fees

Some credit cards charge an annual fee in addition to interest on your purchase balance. This practice is much more common with charge cards (where there is no revolving balance to charge interest on) than credit cards (where the balance need not be paid in full). But plenty of credit cards charge an annual fee, too.

These days, often there is no reason to pay that annual fee, because so many credit cards have eliminated it. No-fee cards do not hide their advantage under a cloak of secrecy; the fact is blared in Web banner ads.

Remember, though, that high interest rates are far more damaging to your pocketbook than most annual fees, especially if you carry a high balance each month. Do not leap at a no-fee card without taking everything into consideration and figuring what combination of features is really best. If you have a pristine credit rating, you can get low rates and no fees pretty easily, all online.

Grace Periods

Grace periods are important to banks and may or may not be important to you. They are no-interest periods of time, recurring every month, during which you can make interest-free payments. That is one shopping criterion right there. The longer period is obviously more convenient, especially if you customarily cut your payment rather close to the due date. (Online bill management, described in Chapter 3, can help eliminate late payments.)

Power of Negotiation

If you feel like you are paying high interest rates in a low-interest world, in some cases you can negotiate for a lower interest rate on your purchase balance. Call your card issuer or send an e-mail to the customer service department, asking about the possibility of establishing a lower rate. In this very competitive marketplace, many companies prefer changing the terms of your credit arrangement to losing your business. If you cannot finagle a better rate and have good credit, switch to another card.

grace period   period of 20 or 25 days within which no interest is charged to credit card purchases. If the full card balance is paid within the grace period each month, interest charges never accrue.

Another consideration involves how credit card companies manage the grace period, and this really is important. Some cards eliminate the interest-free grace period if the full balance was not paid in the previous month. In other words, the grace period exists on those cards only when you pay the whole bill every month, as if the credit card were a charge card. If you typically carry an unpaid credit balance, clarify this point before you sign on.

Great Offers

Too good to be true? You know what they say—it probably is not true. Read everything before getting any new credit card. This rule of thumb is especially cogent in the online realm, where advertising banners are brief and hype intensive. If an outstanding interest rate catches your eye, it may be accompanied by no grace period (a situation most people should avoid) or may not be fixed.

The danger of rushing too quickly into an unfavorable deal is heightened online, where applying and obtaining approval—and even transferring existing balances from other cards—is so easy and quick. From seeing a banner ad to altering your financial situation is a short step on the Internet, easily accomplished within a few minutes if you have a good credit background. So it is up to you to slow yourself down and get all the information you need before jumping in.

Count on Change

In the credit card world, change may be the only constant. Features that enticed you to open the account may be dropped with little fanfare. Issuers must disclose all changes to your credit terms, but not necessarily with eye-catching visibility.

The important point for online financiers is to avoid placing too much emphasis on the type of come-on features that seem so appealing in Internet ads. Travel discounts, buyer's protection, and other appealing features may be dropped at any time. However, reward cards that are affiliated with, and branded by, companies that pay you for using the card (with frequent flier miles, for example) are reliable. In that case, the card's entire existence is founded on the reward program, and it will not be yanked away.

Cash Advances

Most credit cards allow cash advances through ATMs and in walk-in banks. The terms for cash advances present a shopping consideration with the online cards, some of which are eliminating the traditionally higher interest rate associated with cash advances. Some interest rate will apply, of course, but not necessarily a higher rate than for purchases. Here are the plans to watch out for:

- ✔ *No grace period for cash advances and a higher rate.* This is the most unfavorable situation for you and is falling out of vogue among online credit cards.
- ✔ *Normal grace period and a higher interest rate.* There is nothing wrong with this plan if you pay back cash advances quickly.
- ✔ *Normal grace period and normal interest rates.* This is the best scenario, in which a cash advance is not distinguished as a special use of the credit card.

Terms of cash advances usually are buried in the fine print or impossible to find at all in online promotions. If this point is important to you, contact the card issuer and ask.

Debit Card Protection

Debit cards have a few of their own rules, distinct from the regulations governing credit and charge cards.

If you have a deposit account (checking or savings account) and a credit account at the same bank, you might be under an agreement that allows the bank to remove funds from the deposit account if the credit account becomes delinquent. This is one reason to separate your online checking and credit card accounts.

Debit cards—whether at traditional or virtual banks—do not carry the same government consumer protection as credit cards in cases of bad purchases and lost cards. Federal law does not mandate charge-backs, in which the card issuer reimburses your account for a bad purchase, with debit cards, as it does with credit cards.

Losing your card need not be damaging, but failing to report the loss makes the situation much worse. Two kinds of protection can limit your liability in case of a lost or stolen debit card:

1. *Federal protection.* The American government does not protect your bank assets if you fail to report a lost debit card within 60 days. But if you report the loss within 2 days, you cannot be held liable for more than $50. Report between 2 and 50 days, and federal law limits your liability to $500.

2. *Industry protocol.* The banking industry is more lenient than the government. A self-imposed industry protocol restricts your liability to zero if a lost debit card is reported in 2 days and to $50 if the lost card is reported after 2 days.

Industry protocols are a little on the vague side and are not enforced by law. It is always best to keep track of your debit card and report its loss quickly.

By the way, many people do not realize there are two types of debit card: signing and PIN. The signing card, which is more common, requires a signature when purchasing. The PIN style requires your personal identification number in place of a signature and makes the card hard to use if stolen.

CREDIT CARD SHAREWARE

Shareware is downloadable software that you can use for a certain period free of charge. If you decide to keep the program beyond the trial period, you must send a payment and register the program. (Some shareware programs stop working automatically when the try-out period expires.)

shareware   software that may be downloaded from the Internet and used, free of charge, for a predetermined trial period. After the trial the program must be purchased and registered or deleted from the computer. Financial shareware includes accounting programs and credit card management programs.

Many thousands of shareware programs exist, in all fields. Credit card assistants are a vibrant shareware niche. In addition to the Web-based interactive features that distinguish online credit card management, stand-alone programs can help keep track of your cards. Some programs provide budgeting tools and calculators. Others are debt analyzers (with forecasts of dire futures) and debt-reduction tools. Still others track interest and uncover how your money really is being spent.

You can generate a list of available programs by running simple search at Download.com, one of the Web's largest shareware distribution points:

1. Go to www.download.com (or another shareware site of your choosing).
2. Select the keyword entry form.
3. Type "credit card" as a keyword.

The resulting list of programs contains short descriptions, the date of release, and the number of downloads to date. The list is ordered in descending popularity—popular programs are usually popular for a good reason.

NOTES FROM THE CREDIT CARD FRONT

Understanding a bit about the quickly evolving credit card industry can help put rampant online marketing in perspective.

Financial services of all sorts are consolidating, as consumers flock to the high-profile brand names. Online services may help buck that trend by providing legitimate and exciting alternatives. In the credit card field, those virtual alternatives have not yet made a dent in the dominant position of traditional card issuers. At the beginning of 2000, the top 10 credit card issuers controlled 77 percent of the market:

1. Citibank
2. Bank One
3. MBNA
4. Discover
5. Chase Manhattan
6. American Express
7. Bank of America
8. Providian
9. Capital One
10. Fleet

Gold cards, once the status-bearing credit card type, are still issued, but their prestige has become tarnished. You do not see a lot of gold cards advertised on the Net. Platinum cards, the first evolutionary step beyond gold, are reaching saturation levels in the marketplace, with Visa and MasterCard stealing the spotlight from American Express. New titanium cards (what exotic metal will they think of next?), introduced by First USA and now offered by Capital One and Fleet, sport very attractive introductory and ongoing rates. At the time of this book's deadline, titanium cards were appearing in banner ads, and that trend probably will spread quickly.

Beginning in April 2000, Americans can charge tax payments (starting with 1999 taxes) using MasterCard and American Express cards. (Visa is not participating in the program's first year.) The taxpayer must pay the service charge that retailers normally absorb (2.5–3 percent). U.S. federal law prohibits the Internal Revenue Service from absorbing that fee.

Chapter 10

Using Online Investing Resources

Television ads for online stock brokers seem to promise fantastic riches to those willing to take an aggressive approach to the stock market. Meanwhile, newspapers run stories about the pernicious, addictive, destructive horrors of *day trading*. Where does the truth lie? Is *online investing* a promised land for the astute, or a realm of dissolution for the greedy? Is there a place for sensible investing online? And if so, is there an advantage to moving assets to Internet accounts?

day trading   the practice of buying and selling securities (usually stocks) rapidly in an attempt to capitalize on small price movements. Typically, day traders do not hold any stocks overnight. Day trading is a high-pressure and controversial method of investing. Day traders often work in offices set up to access the stock markets efficiently, but new online brokers and information services are encouraging some to operate from home.

Those are a lot of questions. Let's get down to business.

online investing to most people, "online investing" means online brokerage. But in fact online investing means taking advantage of any aspect of the investment information and service revolution. That could mean researching investments online while continuing to use an old-style broker. Online investing is characterized by a wealth of free information, inexpensive brokerage, and unprecedented access to the securities markets. All kinds of investing styles, from day trading to retirement planning, can be pursued online.

ONLINE INVESTING COMMUNITY

In January of 2000, according to one study, over 5 million investors maintained all or some of their assets in online accounts. (Some investors keep more than one brokerage account, so when measuring the industry it makes sense to count investors or their assets, not the accounts.) All projections predict multiplying growth as a wave of second-generation adopters discovers the value of managing their investments online.

Online investors come in almost every stripe—and some polka-dots (the day traders). *Mutual fund* connoisseurs, price-momentum traders, retirement builders—all kinds of investors realize the convenience and savings of online accounts. With investing, very much as with online banking, the benefits of online account access are hard to deny. In fact, online brokerage accounts multiply the standard convenience benefits, because to some extent they have replaced what many consider a dysfunctional brokerage system.

mutual fund professionally managed securities portfolio open to contributions by individual investors. Mutual funds are pooled investments, the most popular of which control billions of dollars in assets. Open-ended funds do not have a determined number of shares but create shares as investors buy into the portfolio. Closed-end funds do have a determined number of shares and trade very much like stocks.

Online Brokerage

Internet-based stock brokers are leading the online financial service revolution. Online brokerages (usually called online brokers) provide on-screen interfaces for buying and selling stocks, mutual funds, and other securities. Low fees, account convenience, and more direct access to the securities markets give online brokers an advantage over their brick-and-mortar cousins.

NEED FOR ONLINE INVESTING

The online investing phenomenon has been catalyzed, at least in part, by dissatisfaction with traditional methods of stock brokering. Before the World Wide Web made the Internet popular, the only way for most people to buy stock involved calling a *personal broker* and placing the order by telephone.

personal broker   a human broker, sometimes employed at an online brokerage. With the advent of online investing and automated virtual brokerages, personal brokers comprise a special service category. Many online brokerages provide personal brokers when customers do not want to use the online interface for some reason. Commission fees are usually higher when ordering through a personal broker.

There's nothing inherently wrong with flesh-and-blood brokerage, but human brokers generally charge hefty fees for the stock *transaction*. These fees, called *commissions*, represent one big point of differentiation between traditional brokers and online brokers.

transaction   sale or purchase. To investors, a transaction is a filled order to buy or sell a security.

> **commission** fee charged by every brokerage (online or offline) for the service of assisting in securities transactions. The most common commission at online brokers is the stock commission, charged when buying and again when selling stock. Broker commissions usually are charged on a per-transaction basis; less often they are charged as a per-share calculation or a percentage of assets.

It is not only high fees that bother online investors, and it is not only the reduction of those fees that has spelled improvement over the old brokerage system. In the old days, an investor's broker was the main source of information and advice about what was considered a relatively mysterious world of stocks. For the most part investors did not buy or sell stocks and funds without the help and advice of a broker.

The growth of online services, even before the World Wide Web, began to open new possibilities. E*Trade, a pioneer of Internet brokerages, provided online stock services through CompuServe and America Online when the Web was merely a concept. Furthermore, information about investing started being published online. The revolution had a toehold.

Once the Web came along, online investing rocketed in popularity along with online shopping, online music, and online everything else— but perhaps with special fervor because investors felt liberated by reduced commissions and the ability to effect stock transactions as if *they* were the brokers.

Other factors have contributed to the demand for online investing:

✔ *American bull market.* Nothing encourages investing like an optimistic, can't-lose sentiment, and the stock markets during most of the 1990s certainly encouraged that attitude.

✔ *Growth of the American investing class.* To some extent, investing accounts have replaced savings accounts. The maturation of the Baby Boomer generation and (to generalize) its affluent pouring of excess money into mutual funds made the stock market a major repository of retirement funds. Today's average person knows much more about stocks, funds, and investing strategies then people did 20 years ago. Investing is no longer an elite activity.

✔ *Online publishing.* Once a critical mass of readers was online, virtual publishers went bonkers (to use a technical term). Truckloads of stock data, commentary, daily news, opinion, advice, and all kinds of other investment information flooded into cyberspace. Seemingly overnight, anyone could be almost as well informed as a professional broker. And in the bull market, many amateur investors discovered they could be more successful than their professional advisers.

✔ *Rise of the Nasdaq.* This computer-networked stock exchange was formed in the early 1970s but did not gain prominence in the popular consciousness until the 1990s. The computerized nature of the market, plus the fact that it represented a large share of publicly traded technology companies, encouraged investment in the very technologies people were reading about in the papers every day.

✔ *Rise of the technology sector.* High-growth technology stocks have fueled the bull market to a large extent and certainly have riled it. Online investors are the very ones who know the most about the companies inventing, manufacturing, and distributing new technology. The early Internet adopters were the same people adopting high-tech stocks as investments. Suddenly it seemed that "the little guys" knew more about picking stocks than the pros, and high brokerage commissions seemed completely unacceptable.

These developments, and frustration with traditional brokers and the rise of Internet alternatives, converged to create a new universe for investors, one that continues to evolve at a breakneck clip. Investing, the sexiest and most lucrative of all financial services, is far more evolved on the Internet than are online banking, lending, insurance brokerage, real estate, and credit card shopping.

SUDDEN REVOLUTION

Online investing is epitomized by online brokerages. As with online banks, online stock brokers come in two flavors:

1. *Pure Internet brokers.* Branchless institutions that provide online interfaces to brokerage accounts and the tasks of buying and selling securities.

2. *Click-and-mortar brokers.* Traditional brokerages that have seen the light and introduced online services. For some years there was resistance among the old-guard brokers whose high-

commission business models were threatened by low-commission online services, but now most have joined the information age to some extent.

Over 150 online brokers of various shapes, sizes, and specialties exist today. Naturally, it is hard to distinguish among them. It is no day at the beach for the brokerages, either, as they compete with each other.

When online investing was first gaining traction and a few dozen brokers struggled for dominance, investors were treated to an all-out commission war. One by one the brokers cut their fees for buying and selling stocks, attempting to lure starry-eyed investors with bargain-basement trading. There was a giddy feeling in the air as commissions—which only a few years before had been locked in the stratosphere by traditional brokers—spiraled down to the single digits in some cases. You could hardly blame light-headed investors for their euphoria as they reduced their trading expenses (in the most drastic cases) from hundreds of dollars per *execution* to $10 or less.

execution   completed order to buy or sell securities. Using an online broker, you can buy or sell stocks; when your orders are confirmed as filled, the execution is complete. One of the ways online brokers are rated is by execution speed.

Inexpensive commissions are responsible not just for catalyzing the entire online investing movement but also for developing the trend of short-term trading. High commissions have a natural restraining effect on quick darts in and out of the markets. Cheap commissions almost oblige daring investors to buy and sell rather than to buy and hold.

The online investing revolution matured over time, and virtual brokers found new ways to distinguish themselves besides slashing rates. Specialty categories emerged to meet investor demand for certain types of accounts. Brokerages discovered that some people did not want to trade actively and would pay higher commission rates for more personal service. The evolution of online brokerage services continues unabated, and the categories of service continue to define themselves.

Chapter 11 describes brokerage types and details how to shop for the best online broker.

LEVELING THE PLAYING FIELD

What exactly is the investing revolution? There is certainly a lot of hype about it, but what does it mean? Are we talking about low stock commissions—and if so, does that really qualify as a revolution? Is the whole subject overblown?

The subject is not overblown, and the revolution is more substantial than mere pricing, although low commissions are an important feature. The online investing revolution packs a democratizing wallop that goes beyond broker fees. The big news of the last 10 years is not that stock trades are cheap but that individual investors have become empowered. As a group, consumer investors have wrested control of large portions of the investing landscape from the grasp of institutions.

A potent shift of power is in progress. Individual investors are sticking their hands into areas that once were the exclusive domain of institutional investors. The line between amateur and professional investing has become blurred. Not only are many home investors outperforming the pros, they are doing so with tools previously reserved for institutional offices.

A famous TV ad for an online brokerage portrayed an angry horde of investors breaking down the doors of a venerable stock exchange and storming into the building, as shards of glass rained down upon the heads of bewildered brokers inside. The commercial's violence captured the rebellious mood that has characterized investor empowerment in the Internet age.

The playing field continues to be leveled as individual investors are given increasing access to three elements of the investing domain:

1. *Markets.* Intermediaries that stand between investors and securities continue to be knocked out of the picture. Individuals investing from home computers now enjoy unprecedented access to markets without going through a phalanx of brokers. Low stock commissions are part of the equation, but speed and accuracy are just as important. Increasingly, investors are plugged directly in to the securities markets.

2. *Information.* Institutional-quality information includes real-time stock quotes, screening tools, options prices, wire-service news releases, company conference calls, and much more that used to reside exclusively in the institutional domain. Real-time quotes are now commonplace, available to everyone; likewise, other professional perks are delivered to home computers, often free of charge.

3. *Tools.* Tying together high-quality information and market access, new consumer-level tools rival those used in professional investing houses for decades. These tools include software information environments and trading platforms that used to cost a fortune; now they are within the budget of serious home investors.

What does the future look like as the investing revolution proceeds? The utopian scenario envisions a global, 24-hour, always-on, available-to-all securities marketplace. As far as we are from that ideal, it is impressive how far we have progressed toward it. Technology is making investing more efficient, both in price and time. Today's investor can do more in an hour than the previous generation could in a week.

Commissions may not go down any further, or stock brokerage may become commoditized as a free service. Fees are not the main point. The rewiring of Wall Street and the democratization of investing will further empower individuals.

INVESTING AND TRADING

Although online investing is not the mystery it once was to many people, there is still a popular misconception that online investing means stock trading—fast, risky trading. As a generalization, that impression could not be further from the truth. Nimble, daredevil trading certainly has emerged as an information-age hobby, but online brokers just provide an interface. What you do with that interface is up to you.

A basic distinction must be made between investing and trading:

Investing is motivated by a desire to own part of a company. Traditionally, investing is a long-term approach to saving and growing money. Investors consider the *fundamental analysis* of a company and its stock, sometimes disregarding its *technical analysis*. Generally (and in the eyes of the U.S. Internal Revenue Service), a long-term investment is any security held for at least a year.

fundamental analysis involves a review of the company's quarterly balance sheet, which includes data on earnings, assets, and liabilities. Management profiling is part of fundamental analysis.

Trading is motivated by a desire to realize short-term profit through the exchange of securities. Traders consider the technical analysis of a stock, often disregarding its fundamental values. For tax purposes, a short-term trade is any security sold before it has been owned for one year. In reality, traders often hold their positions for a much shorter period—sometimes weeks or days. Day traders typically hold for hours or minutes and usually sell everything off by the end of each day.

technical analysis a stock's technical value is determined solely by price movement and has little or nothing to do with company fundamentals. Pure technical analysis does not even need to know the company's name—its research sphere is populated by price charts and predictive indicators. Technical analysis seeks to predict future price movements based on past and current patterns.

Trading traditionally has been an institutional activity; for decades every major brokerage house has staffed trading desks that lob securities around the globe for company profit. Keeping a flow of securities going helps a broker's customers by providing access to good prices for stocks, bonds, and other investment vehicles. But in the past, the *retail investing* community has not enjoyed the market access to engage in effective short-term trading.

retail investing the buying and selling of securities in the public marketplace by individual investors, as opposed to institutional investing.

Trading has become popular thanks to low commissions and quick executions—the two revolutionary aspects of the Internet as applied to securities. Individuals now have unprecedented access to the markets (once reserved for institutions) and freedom from the burden of high commissions. The shift in focus from mutual funds (which are still popular) to individual stocks (which are a cultural craze) has encouraged the trading phenomenon, too.

But nobody should think that trading is obligatory, despite enticingly low commissions. In fact, some studies of investing practices determine that short-term investing is not as profitable in the long run as the time-honored buy-and-hold strategy. (Consumer stock trading is too new to evaluate definitively, and many home stock traders are quite successful.)

TYPES OF ONLINE INVESTING

There are as many types of online investors as traditional investors—more, in fact, thanks to the additional tools available through the computer. Following is a summary of basic investor types. Look for yourself in this section; knowing your attitudes, intentions, and level of experience is the first step to finding the right online home for your investment assets. (Chapter 11 helps with that search.)

New and Uncertain

This group is populated by folks new to investing, new to the Internet, new to computers, or new to all three. There is plenty of room for the low-risk crowd on the Internet, and in fact the second adoption wave of online investors is far more cautious than the higher-risk early adopters. However, there is also a brazen element to the newcomer demographic—new investors eager to get started and grow money fast in the exciting online realm. Regardless of risk tolerance, all newcomers to investing and online interfaces should proceed slowly, concentrate on education first, and use a broker that provides some hand-holding.

Planning Retirement

The retirement-planning investor is not necessarily new to managing assets or to the online experience and has opened online accounts (or migrated them from offline locations) for convenience and lower fees. For some, investing is all about the retirement nest egg, while for others the long-term, tax-sheltered accounts are part of a bigger picture that includes short-term gains as well. Either way, some brokerages make it easy to maintain retirement products like IRA accounts and stock the investment vehicles typically used in such accounts, such as mutual funds and income-generating instruments.

Fund Connoisseurs

Funds remain the only game in town for some investors, who appreciate the built-in diversity and professional management of commercial portfolios. The Internet has substantial competition from traditional publishers and brokers in the area of mutual funds. Funds have been the main family investment arena for decades, and during that time consumers have been served by publications and helpful discount brokerages. Still, online brokers and publishers make fund research a pleasure and bring information up to date much better than old-time library and magazine resources. In the brokerage realm, some of the traditional fund "supermarkets" operate with full-fledged online interfaces.

Do-It-Yourselfers

This group constitutes the main force driving the growth of online investing. Many investors relish being liberated from human brokers and the institutional grip on information and the transaction process. The most independent investors do not need (or, at least, do not believe they need) stock-picking advice, research assistance, or help with managing and allocating assets.

During the greatest American bull market in history, a new breed of investor strode to the forefront: the amateur expert. The Internet cultivates a sense of empowerment by supplying every type of research and information tool you can imagine. Brokers put the power in their customers' hands by putting the buy and sell switches right on the computer screen. The result is a new class of resourceful investors who perform their own *due diligence*, map their own strategy, and buy and sell their own stock picks. A entire class of online brokers caters to the do-it-yourselfer.

due diligence   practice of researching a stock before buying; known in the lingo of active traders as *due dilly* or simply *diligence*. Performing due diligence involves checking a company's balance sheet, history of business execution, valuation ratios, and (for traders) technical indicators plus any other research that leads to an informed investment decision.

Active Traders

Active traders are involved in following the stock market every day—not necessarily during the day, but certainly on a daily basis. One popular method of active trading is called *momentum trading*, a sort of hybrid style that uses principles of both long-term investing and day trading to profit from medium-term stock positions. Momentum traders try to foresee upward momentum in a stock, based on earnings news, seasonal factors, technical indicators, changes in management, or any combination of events that could move a stock.

> **momentum trading** style of investing that seeks to capitalize on short- and intermediate-term price movements. Momentum traders follow news, earnings cycles, and stock chart readings to anticipate sudden upward or downward price movements. Holding their stock positions for days, weeks, or in some cases months, momentum investors hope to earn about 5 to 10 percent on each investment.

The Internet is conducive to momentum trading because it delivers information fast, letting investors attempt momentum profits without ignoring their jobs or becoming too obsessed with the market. Momentum investors typically hold their stock for days, weeks, or—in the longest scenarios—about six months. Unlike day trading, which bets large amounts of capital on tiny price movements, momentum traders hope for gains of 5 or 10 percent in each position.

Resourceful Adventurers

Online investing has done more than just lower fees. The democratizing effect of the Internet on the securities industry has opened entire new markets to retail investors. Stock and index options, foreign currencies, commodities, short-selling stocks, index funds—these markets and many others are newly available methods of capital creation for individuals. While some fancy investing is hugely risky, the other side of the coin is diversification, and more ways exist for retail investors to diversify assets than ever before.

The adventurous and resourceful online investor is acquainted with vehicles beyond the standard stock-bond-fund portfolio model and typically adds options and short-selling to the mix, at least. It is important for these investors to use a broker with a big assortment of products and to seek out online information sources that help navigate the more exotic markets.

Day Traders

While most of this chapter deemphasizes ultra-quick day trading, there is no denying the almost cultlike popularity of this activity, which has been compared to gambling. While much of the media coverage of day trading is alarming, some individuals have built excellent careers maneuvering nimbly around the stock market. Studies of the alleged futility of day trading for nearly everyone who tries it are controversial.

Successful or not, many day traders avoid the Internet entirely by working in offices that provide direct computer access to the markets. These offices often provide training in addition to computer facilities. However, a new generation of consumer brokers and sophisticated online tools is encouraging new day traders to stay at home.

BENEFITS OF INVESTING ONLINE

For new and experienced investors alike, the question remains: Why do it online? If you have invested assets in a traditional brokerage, what is the advantage of transferring them to the online realm? And why should new investors give up the convenience of walking into a local broker with a check to get started?

The first thing for experienced investors to remember is that your current broker may offer online access to your account, just as many traditional banks provide online services. If you do not want to switch brokers (transferring securities is a little complicated, and besides, you might like your broker), you may not have to.

Many people go online simply because brokerages are not as prolific as banks, and there may not be a local investment office. Opening an online account is a little more complicated than opening a walk-in brokerage account, but once you get it going the online account is easier to maintain.

As mentioned earlier, low fees and more direct access to markets are the two big advantages to investing online. But it is worth noting that being an online investor means more than buying and selling stock over the Internet. In fact, it may not involve transactions at all. The online information flow is a big part of the revolution, and some investors keep their offline investment accounts while making full use of online research sites. That way they become better investors, more informed, and increasingly able to partner equally with their brokers in managing a portfolio.

In the broadest possible terms, there are three realms of online investing, each with specific values and attractions:

1. *Online brokers.* Brokers represent the most important part of the equation, and as a group they catalyzed the entire investing revolution.

2. *Online investment research.* The Internet information flow surrounding investment issues is simply amazing in its breadth and depth. Even if you never buy or sell a stock online, using the Internet to enhance your awareness of the markets can be invaluable.

3. *Online investing communities.* Investment watering holes abound on the Net—virtual clubs where investors gather to brag, speculate, share their research, hopes, successes, and setbacks.

ONLINE INVESTMENT RESEARCH

The depth, range, and quality of investment information on the Web is almost indescribable. One of the most mature areas of online publishing, investment sites make full use of the Internet's timeliness and database facility. Whether you like numbers or stories, audio or text, fundamentals or technicals, play-by-play or summaries, journalism or opinion, the Web can dish up dozens of sites that will bowl you over. Most of it is gloriously free; a lot of the subscription stuff is well worth the money.

I asked the publisher for an extra thousand pages to do this topic justice and was roundly rejected with a reminder that the manuscript was already late. The following section cannot cover investment sites comprehensively, but it does itemize the types of information available to investors, including a few prominent examples in each category.

DAILY MARKET NEWS

The contemporary stock market can be compared to a sporting event, with investors cheering on the sidelines for their favorite stocks and funds. (What this analogy says about the human urge to merge money and sports is a subject for another book.) The euphoria generated by a robust and generally upward-moving stock market and the lack of competition (the more participants the better) create an exciting environment. It is not surprising, then, that the online publications chartered to follow the market seem to provide a sort of play-by-play of the action.

CBS MarketWatch (cbs.marketwatch.com)

One of the most extraordinary and essential online destinations for investors, CBS MarketWatch is an unparalleled news portal and information center. Many investors turn to this site for the market day's first recap. Updated throughout the day, the editorial content here is timely, deep, and covers every possible aspect of the stock market. The editorial focus is on news rather than commentary; the site does employ numerous columnists, but their work plays second fiddle to market play-by-play.

It is easy to get so involved with the packed home page (which automatically updates every couple of minutes) that you forget to investigate the many features linked around the edges. Following are some portions of the CBS MarketWatch experience that should not be neglected. Look for the links in the left-hand page border and at the bottom.

- ✔ *IPOWatch.* Covering *initial public offerings* with a deeper perspective than the usual here-is-what is-coming-next-week approach.

- ✔ *Industry indexes.* Throughout the market day or afterward, this page breaks down the stock market into sectors as defined by institutional indexes. You can see at a glance what industries are up or down, then look at individual companies in those sectors.

- ✔ *After-hours S&P futures.* Get a nighttime glimpse of the next day's market direction by tracking the 24-hour S&P futures trading, the most important leading indicator of the American markets.

- ✔ *Personal finance.* This link resides atop of the home page and leads to a separate news and information portal.

- ✔ *News index.* A consolidated headline list that cuts through the home page's clutter.

initial public offering (IPO)   first issuance of stock by a newly public company. Investors greatly anticipate initial public offerings. During the 1990s, the flamboyant performance of IPOs created a new investing niche and plenty of headlines.

CNNfn (www.cnnfn.com)

As a finance cable-TV channel, CNNfn sits in the awesome shadow of CNBC, which has attained mythic popularity. But on the Internet, the fortunes are reversed, and CNNfn bows to no other site when it comes to market news coverage. Periodic redesigns keep improving this site, which always has been distinguished by tenacious coverage of big issues as well as company-specific stories. International coverage is especially noteworthy.

As is often the case with the news portals, bursting with information as they are, the home page can seem almost intimidating at first glance. Burn through the haze by going first to the Site Index, where you can get a grip on the site's depth.

ZDII (www.zdii.com)

ZDNet Inter@ctive Investor is a perfect home base for anyone primarily interested in the technology *sector* of the stock market. ZDII gets you involved with all the subsectors of the technology revolution that has, to a large extent, driven the American stock markets for years. The home page throws a lot of news in your face, all of it timely and written with an insider's understanding of technology issues.

sector in investing, a selection of stocks representing companies in a single defined industry. The semiconductor sector, for example, contains companies that manufacture computer chips.

Do not leave ZDII without clicking the Industry Indices link—it takes you to the most cogent breakdown of the technology industry you are likely to find anywhere. Each sector niche (semiconductors, broadcasting and cable, information storage, networking, and many others) is profiled with its own home page of news and commentary. Clicking the Quotes link for any sector displays leads to a list of current related stock prices.

CNBC (www.cnbc.com)

The CNBC Web site may not be as fine a virtual portal as CNNfn, produced by its rival cable channel, but there is a truckload of content here. The strategy at this site is to provide a complementary viewing experience to the widely watched CNBC television network. The two outlets promote each other—you can find online versions of favorite CNBC segments and personalities at the site. With many interactive features, CNBC.com invites visitor input.

MoneyCentral Investor (moneycentral.msn.com/investor/home.asp)

MoneyCentral is the renowned financial site produced by Microsoft, and its Investor section is a full-fledged portal in its own right. Featuring exceptionally strong portfolio tools (free with registration), the Research Wizard is also a shining strong point. Probably the most user-friendly stock research service on the Web, the Research Wizard talks you through the important facets of any stock you call up.

In the news and commentary department, this site features good writing and helpful opinions by a small stable of columnists. Aiming for greater accessibility than the advanced editorials of TheStreet.com and Motley Fool, MoneyCentral Investor wins points for clarity and well-chosen topics.

DATA: QUOTES, CHARTS, AND PORTFOLIOS

It is as hard to get a *stock quote* online as it is to see a candle at Lourdes. They are everywhere. No self-respecting financial news site lacks a basic quote server. Stock prices (more often delayed than real-time during *trading hours*) are a commodity, but there are variations in quality. Some quotes are perfunctory; others provide detailed information about the stock's volume, market capitalization, earnings ratios, dividend yield, and much more.

stock quote   price of any stock. Stock quotes are distributed widely online—nearly every investment news and information site displays them.

Furthermore, there is more to stock data than price quotes. Price *charts*, in particular, have become very popular. It seems as if almost every online investor is an amateur technical analyst, poring over historical price graphs to find *support levels*, *resistance levels*, and other indicators.

More Than Just Price

You might think that a stock quote would deliver the price of stock, plain and simple. In fact, most *online quotes* dish up much more, including the following information:

✔ **Volume.** The number of shares traded. This number is updated continually throughout the day.

✔ **Bid.** The price you get when selling a stock.

✔ **Ask.** The price you pay when buying a stock.

✔ **Open.** The price at which the stock opened that morning.

✔ **Previous close.** The price at which the stock ended trading the previous day (not always the same as the morning's open price).

✔ **Day's range.** The lowest and highest price of the stock during the trading session.

✔ **52-week range** The low and high prices during the past 12 months.

✔ **Earnings per share.** The company's total profit divided by total number of shares.

✔ **P/E.** Price/earnings ratio, which measures the stock price against company earnings per share.

trading hours   time during which securities are traded. Trading hours vary depending on the exchange. The American stock exchanges are in the process of expanding beyond traditional daytime hours. Some futures, currency, and commodities markets operate 24 hours a day.

Technical analysts identify stock price ranges beyond which the stock is not likely to move past. Of course, this kind of analysis is always speculative. But since investors and traders all pay attention to the same indicators, these support and resistance levels tend to become self-fulfilling, swaying the buy and sell decisions of active investors. Crashing through its support level is a bad omen, just as rising above a resistance level is a good sign.

chart　graphic view of a stock's price history. Charts are ubiquitous online, often accompanying stock quotes.

support level　a narrow price range below which a stock has not dropped in the past. It is a technical indicator. Stocks sometimes "bounce" off their support levels, if investors believe they have reached a bottom.

resistance level　price above which a stock repeatedly has been unable to rise. It is a technical indicator. Active investors sometimes sell their positions in a stock that reaches its resistance level. Stocks that climb through resistance levels are said to be breaking out, and often attract an investing frenzy.

online quote　quote that displays a stock price. The term is used mostly in the context of Internet investing. Most online stock quotes are delayed quotes, meaning they lag behind the stock market by 15 or 20 minutes during trading hours. Other types of online quotes include insurance rate quotes, bank rate quotes, and loan rate quotes.

Portfolios comprise another form of stock data. We tend to think of portfolios as representing personal holdings, but the ease of creating online portfolios encourages multiple "watch lists" of stocks you may not own but are interested in.

The availability of stock data on the Internet is astounding compared to a decade ago, when almost all information was in text format that was difficult to find and interpret. Now graphics rule the Web, and any investor can understand the gist of data with a glance.

Financial data portal sites combine quotes, charts, and portfolios. Additionally, some sites concentrate on one of those three aspects. The following suggestions are meant as starting points, not final dispositions as to the best of the Web. Before long you will probably find your own favorites.

Yahoo! Finance (finance.yahoo.com)

Yahoo! Finance (see Figure 10.1) is the Wal-Mart of stock quotes. Consistently rated the number-one investing site by sheer traffic numbers, Yahoo! Finance is not pretty, but it is fast and conveys exactly the right amount of information. Speed and lack of unnecessary graphics are hallmarks of the Yahoo! experience in general, no less so in the Finance section.

Investors come here for basic quotes, charts, and portfolios more than for daily market news. Company-specific press releases are conveniently bundled with company stock quotes. You can configure how detailed the quote is—which is very useful when calling up a list of companies all at once and needing only the basics on each. Thumbnail charts are nestled into the quote screen, expandable to larger versions, and somewhat customizable. (Nobody uses Yahoo! for sophisticated charting with technical indicators.) The portfolios are quite good and subject to all kinds of personalization.

Yahoo! Finance delivers millions of stock quotes every day and almost never falters. The site is built like a rock, and although the prices are delayed, investors still turn to Yahoo! more than to any other service.

FreeRealTime (www.freerealtime.com)

It was a great idea when introduced: free *real-time quotes* for everyone. Back then, real-time quotes were rare, and free ones were almost unheard of. Now many online brokers carry free real-time prices for their customers, and other sites display real-time data to visitors willing to pay a small monthly exchange fee (a service fee of a few dollars charged by the stock exchanges).

So is FreeRealTime passé? Nope. The site has matured in all kinds of ways, becoming nothing short of an information and data portal. The real-time quotes are of the snapshot variety, and you can view only one at a time. *Delayed quotes* are also available, and you can get multiple delayed quotes simultaneously.

FreeRealTime really is free—there are no hidden charges or exchange fees. Just register at the site with a user name and password, indicate your approval of some legal language (mostly asserting that you will not sell the quotes), and you are good to go.

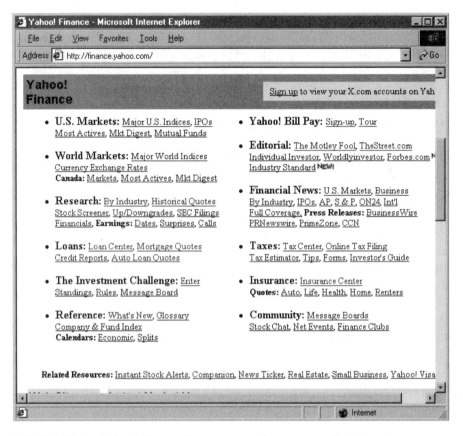

FIGURE 10.1 Yahoo! Finance is not pretty, but most online investors consider it indispensable.

(Reprinted with permission of Yahoo!)

real-time quotes   online stock quotes that are not delayed from the markets. Real-time quotes used to be for professionals only, but the Internet is gradually giving them to individual investors. Anyone can see free real-time quotes at certain Web sites. In addition, very sophisticated real-time market displays are available on a subscription basis.

Next Generation of Data

Web sites do a fine job delivering more securities data than the previous generation of investors could have imagined. Believe it or not, the Web represents just the opening round of quantifying stock information. New services have emerged that use dedicated programs (not the ubiquitous Web browser) to deliver information directly from financial computers.

These new programs have astonishing power, rivaling institutional information flow that used to be reserved for professionals. Although aimed at consumers, the new services are not free (costing $50 to $100 per month in most cases) and are geared to serious, semipro, and professional home investors and traders—those who watch the market nonstop during the day. The information delivered by these high-tech systems includes real-time streaming quote tickers, sophisticated charting, stock price alerts, historical pricing, interactive real-time portfolios, breaking news reports, and much more.

Some of these services offer downloadable demo versions of their software. It is interesting to see all the bells and whistles even if you probably will not buy the service. Following are a few selections:

✔ *CyBerTrader* (www.cybercorp.com)
CyBerTrader™ (see Figure 10.2) was one of the earliest new-generation information services to launch its products. The company is an online broker in addition to providing information products. CyBerTrader includes amazing "five-dimensional" (that is the ad hype) stock screening tools that must be seen to be believed. A downloadable demo uses the previous day's market activity.

✔ *WindowOnWallStreet* (www.windowonwallstreet.com)
A beautiful program for serious traders. There is almost more information squeezed onto its screen than can be humanly absorbed. Features are integrated beautifully. There is no downloadable demo, but the company sends a full-color information packet upon request.

(Continued)

✔ **eSignal** (www.esignal.com)
This innovative program integrates a browser window into its screen, so you can use your online broker without cluttering your screen with windows. ESignal offers a variety of services and pricing plans and covers almost every imaginable securities market.

A few others to check out:

✔ InterQuote (www.interquote.com)
✔ MyTrack (www.mytrack.com)
✔ Quote.com Qcharts (www.qcharts.com)
✔ Quotezart (www.quotezart.com)
✔ SmartMoney's MapStation
(www.smartmoney.com/mapstation)

delayed quotes   online stock or option quotes that show prices 15 or 20 (depending on the exchange) minutes behind the market. Delayed quotes are always available free of charge.

Prophet Finance (www.prophetfinance.com)

This relatively new company has made some waves in the online investing community with its toolbox approach to data. Every few months Prophet Finance announces some new on-screen gadget that raises the bar for free data tools.

Charting is Prophet's big claim to fame so far. The Prophet JavaCharts (see Figure 10.3) is a wonderful Java program that allows users to draw momentum lines right on the chart and overlay all kinds of other technical indicators. The program is presented within the Web browser but can also be placed on the computer desktop, where it sits purring as you go about your online business.

ProphetStation is a subscription product that delivers real-time data, and ChartStream is a dynamic, real-time chart product that draws itself on

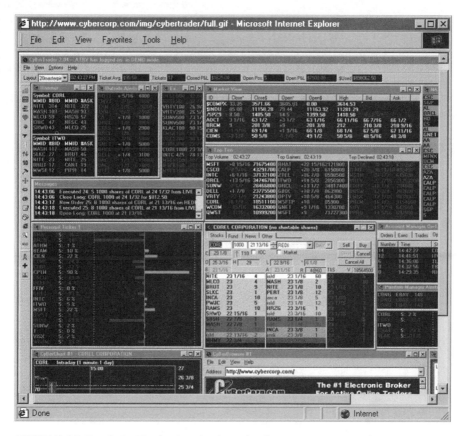

FIGURE 10.2 CyBerTrader is a high-end information service for active traders.

(© CyBerCorp, Inc. 1995–2000. CyBerTrader is a trademark of CyBerCorp, Inc. All rights reserved.)

charting   practice of drawing a stock's historical price movements on a graph. Charting provides an easy way to see a stock's momentum at a glance. Advanced interpretation of charts is both an art and a science, and often involves displaying the price history in several ways simultaneously.

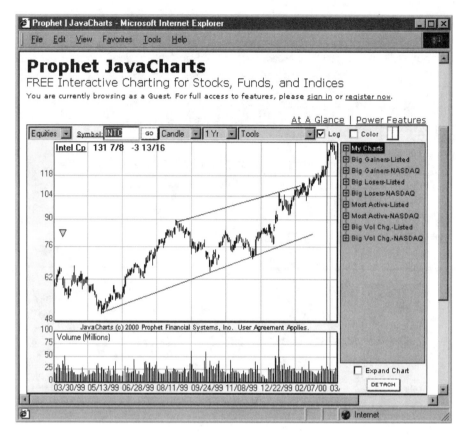

FIGURE 10.3 Prophet JavaCharts is a powerful stock charter that can be torn out of the browser.

(© 2000 Prophet Financial Systems, Inc., www.ProphetFinance.com.)

your screen as the markets trade during the day. The site provides a number of pop-up quote and chart tools. Throughout, Prophet Finance is respectful of users' modem limitations and offers choices of fast or slow downloads.

BigCharts (www.bigcharts.com)

Are bigger charts better charts? That question is best left to metaphysicians, and the BigCharts site is best used by individual investors. This site is a charting portal, delivering plain quotes as an afterthought. Using drop-down menus, BigCharts allows visitors to alter any chart's parameters and displayed indicators.

BigCharts is in danger of falling behind competing chart programs by not updating its tools frequently enough. But user charting is only one aspect of this site. BigCharts is a research institution that presents interesting charts of all sorts that you might never think of drawing for yourself.

Quote.com (www.quote.com)

You know from the name that Quote.com was one of the first Web-based quote servers. Over the years Quote.com has grown and evolved, adding news, various financial services, and subscription products to its lineup. The site is still a good place to get a simple quote. Free registration entitles you to use the clear and understated portfolio section.

The LiveCharts page at Quote.com is legendary. This little Java applet loads into the browser window and streams a live chart during trading hours. (Major indexes are presented in real time; stocks are delayed 15 or 20 minutes.) The beauty of Live Charts lies in its *intraday* configurability—you can set its timing to increments as small as one minute, which active traders love. Even casual investors can get hypnotized by this useful little tool.

intraday   an investing term referring to anything that transpires during trading hours. Intraday charts track stock prices as the day proceeds. Intraday trading refers to quick buys and sells of stocks as their prices shift during the day.

ASK Research (www.askresearch.com)

ASK Research is one of the great underrated investment data sites on the Web. The tools are not fancy, and the data do not stream across your monitor. But the pages are scaled back to their essentials, so they never get bogged down when loading—which is a good thing since they automatically reload every minute or so. (You can alter the frequency.)

You enter a stock symbol on the home page, and the site delivers a beautifully combined quote/chart screen. (See Figure 10.4.) Down at the bottom are several configuration options for the chart. (See Figure 10.5.) You can save your settings, and when you do the site recognizes you on future visits and displays charts just the way you like them.

From each quote/chart page you can link to news headlines and *option chains*. The option prices are conveniently keyed by the stock symbol, and presented with a simple clarity that most dedicated option sites cannot match.

option chains   price quotes for some or all of the options associated with a certain security. Many stocks have dozens of options, each with its own price and expiration date. Option chains sort out all the available options and organize them for easy selection.

ASK Research rivals Yahoo! Finance in speed and reliability—quite a feat.

COMMENTARY AND ADVICE

Objective news is half of the editorial equation at investment sites, and subjective commentary is the other half. Investing is essentially speculative, no matter how conservative the strategy may be. Nobody knows the future, but investing commentators sure enjoy trying to predict it. Some sites specialize in delivering informed opinion, advice, and strategy. It is perhaps ironic that opinion is worth more than reporting, but the fact remains that the best commentary sites cost money to view, whereas the top reporting sites are free.

Following are two subscription sites and two freebies. They all combine high-quality analysis with rock-hard reporting.

TheStreet.com (www.thestreet.com)

Made famous by its irascible founder, James Cramer of CNBC guest-appearance fame, TheStreet.com (see Figure 10.6) is a respected online

FIGURE 10.4 ASK Research provides quick, nicely integrated quotes and charts.
(Reprinted with permission of ASK Research.)

publication presenting the work of top-flight investment writers. Based in New York, the organization keeps its fingers on the pulse of Wall Street, generating up-to-the-minute news reports and shedding light on everything with cogent analysis, opinion, and strategic advice. Cramer himself is hardly a hidden presence here; he contributes his share of editorials that are must-reads for fans of his hotheaded, opinionated, take-no-prisoners style. The other writers do not hold back, either.

In 2000, TheStreet.com announced a change in business plan that

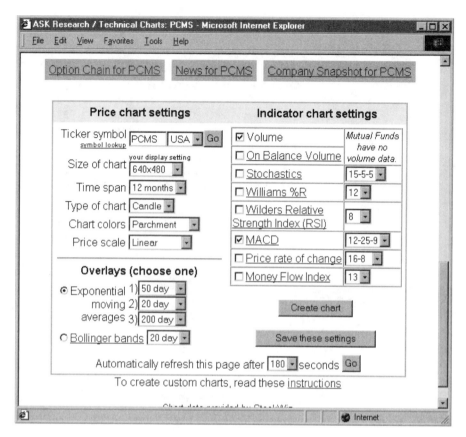

FIGURE 10.5 You can make detailed configuration setting for ASK
Research charts, then save them for your next visit.
(Reprinted with permission of ASK Research.)

would eliminate the subscription requirement and open most of the site
to all visitors. That liberation of content may have occurred by the time
this book is published. Even if not, the site is worth a visit for the free
content that is always presented; a two-week free trial of the subscription
stuff is available.

Motley Fool (www.fool.com)

Started as a small, quirky investment destination within the America Online service, Motley Fool's unique style and smart brand of value investing

FIGURE 10.6 TheStreet.com, one of the most respected investing commentary sites.

attracted hordes of eager followers. (See Figure 10.7.) Eventually the company migrated to the Web, where it operates one of the best investor education and stock strategy sites.

Much of Motley Fool's learning material is stored in the free area of the site, making this a deserving destination even for those who intend to subscribe to a Web site. You can try a free subscription to see if the rest of worth paying for.

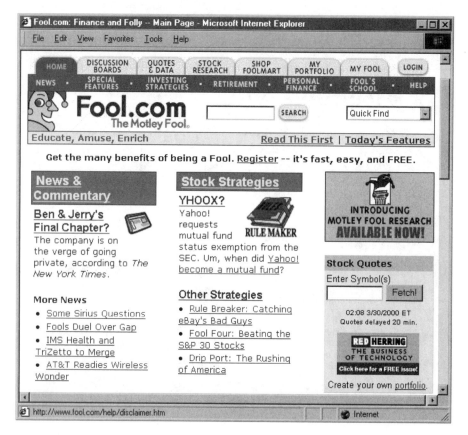

FIGURE 10.7 Motley Fool is a popular publication and community site. (Reprinted with permission of The Motley Fool, Inc., www.fool.com.)

ON24 (www.on24.com)

If you prefer hearing news to reading it, ON24 is for you. Billed as "The Internet Broadcast Network for Online Investors," ON24 lives up to its hype with an astounding range of audio (and some video) programming. The company has collected dozens of analysts who take turns delivering daily commentary on stock questions sent in by visitors.

Breaking news is covered as fast here as at the text portals—a remarkable achievement that owes much to ON24's superb back-end technology that allows almost instantaneous release of audio content. In addition to the analyst shows and news alerts, interviews, round-

Subscribing: Is It Worth It?

The prevailing online ethic is that information is, and should be, free of charge. So how do you assess the notion of paying for access to a Web site? Fortunately, most subscription sites offer a free trial period. But in the long run, is subscribing worth it?

The truth is, online subscriptions can be worth more to you than offline magazine and newspaper deliveries—and they often cost much less. The value of online information is immediacy. The speedy quality of Internet information can be important when reporting on the stock market. Another quality to keep in mind is the searchable nature of online publication—you do not need to hoard paper editions to access past issues and archived articles.

Whether online subscriptions are for you depends on your investing needs and how wired your liefestyle is (how much you want to be tied to the computer). Many folks who are deeply involved with online investing subscribe to at least one site or service and consider themselves lucky to be able to.

tables, and audio opinion columns are featured. ON24 uses the Real-Audio format for its audio streams, so go to this site with a fairly new browser equipped with the RealPlayer plug-in. Each program pops up in a discrete window and can be paused or halted at any time.

ClearStation (www.clearstation.com)

A little subway map drives home the point that this site is a "station," but beyond that cryptic clue the reference is elusive. Nonetheless, ClearStation has emerged from cult status to become one of the most popular mainstream charting sites on the Web. Why is ClearStation appearing in the Commentary and Advice section? Because despite the chart-intensive quality of its pages, this site is essentially a strategy guide that recommends buy and sell points in the stocks it covers. Using an in-house formula of technical analysis, the site generously displays its indicators for free, and even sends entry and exit alerts via e-mail to anyone who wants them.

If any site puts science in the service of opinion, it is ClearStation. Opinion always comes first here, right from the A list of bullish stocks it throws onto the home page. All in all, ClearStation is a fantasy come true for those who prefer technical analysis to company fundamentals, and the site is a Bible of sorts for momentum traders.

COMPANY FUNDAMENTALS

Fundamentals. The very word sounds imposing. This is what investment research used to be all about, and still is for the long-term crowd. Active traders do not have as much use for fundamental analysis, which takes longer than technical analysis and yields more general results suitable to leisurely investing.

Fundamental analysis, which includes earnings ratios, is distributed in detailed stock quotes all over the Web. Digging deeper, into a company's business plan, management profile, and balance sheet, requires some legwork. Three sites, in particular, are indispensable destinations for your bookmark list.

Hoover's (www.hoovers.com)

Hoover's is the brand-leading source of company information. Presented as a series of screens, the Hoover's company profile leaves very little information uncovered. This profound database of company information does not come free—subscribers pay about $15 a month to get the most from the site.

Hoover's has expanded beyond its original charter of providing proprietary company and industry information and is now a comprehensive business portal covering money management, news, and travel. But those company profiles remain the core product of this site, and Hoover's probably will always be associated with high-quality company information.

EDGAR (www.sec.gov/edaux/formlynx.htm)

This homely sounding site is actually the Electronic Data Gathering and Retrieval resource of the Securities and Exchange Commission

(SEC), the U.S. government agency that regulates American investment. EDGAR is the online access point to the SEC's database of company filings. Every publicly traded company is required by law to file certain reports, most famously the quarterly earnings report (called the 10Q).

All SEC-required reports are freely available to anyone who surfs over to look at them. Investors and analysts focus on the quarterlies, viewing the balance sheets as harbingers of the future as well as documentation of the past quarter. There are a few ways to angle into EDGAR; the listed URL takes you to a search form with which you can locate documents by company and report type.

Morningstar (www.morningstar.com)

The legendary mutual fund ratings service has been publishing fund data and evaluation books for many years. The Web site is an extension of Morningstar's core business of helping investors evaluate funds and their managers. Quite a bit of data is available at this site free of charge. For $100 a year, sophisticated fund screening and a portfolio of analytic reports are available. The valuation tools are wrapped in editorial content related to funds—this site is a major portal for fund investors.

ONLINE MAGAZINES AND NEWSPAPERS

Very few printed publications of any popularity have not established some kind of presence on the Web. Whenever a magazine or newspaper extends its publication to the digital realm, it must decide how much to share. Obviously, putting every word of the printed product online removes some motivation to buy the magazine.

Most large publications set up a distinct editorial staff that creates new material for the Web site while borrowing somewhat from the printed product. The degree to which the Web publication duplicates the printed publication varies. Some online publications are mere posters for corresponding magazines, while others are distinct and valuable publications.

Most online magazines and newspapers do not dare charge for entry to the site—too much free online information is available for that gambit to be successful often. A mighty strong brand name is needed to sell information online. Of the publications highlighted below, only one—the *Wall Street Journal*—operates a subscription Web site.

WSJ Interactive (www.wsj.com)

Dow Jones & Company, one of the first (and very few) companies to maintain a successful subscription Web product, produces the Wall Street Journal Interactive Edition. Access to this site costs less than a subscription to the famous newspaper and gives more content. Many investors consider a WSJ.com subscription an essential item in their online investing strategy. The site reproduces the entire newspaper, including the familiar Marketplace and Money & Investing sections (and a distinct Sports section!), plus additional Web-only articles and features. Various e-mail newsletters are available to subscribers. A free trial period helps you determine whether a subscription is right for you.

As with any online publication, stories are enhanced by hyperlinks. In particular, the WSJ.com does a great job with links that pop up current stock quotes for companies mentioned in articles; many sites do this, but very few do it as well. Hyperlinks really come in handy when reading a column like Walter Mossberg's popular technology reviews, from which you can link directly to the site he is talking about.

Money.com (www.money.com)

The interactive arm of *Money* magazine, this deeply resourceful Web site is a distinct, autonomous publication with little reference to the printed magazine. With a reach that goes way beyond investing, Money.com covers real estate, insurance, retirement, and other planning subjects. Scattered features—stock quotes, headlines from CNNfn—are sprinkled around the edges, but the focus here is primarily editorial, just as with a magazine.

SmartMoney (www.smartmoney.com)

Innovation is the watchword at the SmartMoney site. While the printed magazine maintains a leisurely schedule of bimonthly publication, the Web site keeps pace with CBS MarketWatch and other leading news portals.

Fine editorial content would be enough by itself, but SmartMoney.com continually introduces new interactive gadgets for investors. Clever and imaginative stock screening tools distinguish the site, which is also entering the field of information streaming with a subscription real-time quote service called MapStation.

SmartMoney.com covers all the bases, appealing to restless traders and immovable investors alike. As in the printed magazine, fund coverage is outstanding, consistently emphasizing management profiles as opposed to statistical performance alone. For a glittery eyeful, check out the Map of the Market feature, an astounding new way to survey the stock market.

Mutual Funds *Magazine (www.mfmag.com)*

The online version of *Mutual Funds* magazine, this site competes with Morningstar. *Mutual Funds* magazine generously puts some of its current articles into the Web site, there to read for anybody willing to brave the constant subscription ads. Free registration is available to use some of the fund screening tools. The Fund of the Day and Dog of the Day features are always fun, even though funds do not stand up well to close daily examination.

This site is not nearly as data-intensive as Morningstar, focusing instead on editorial content. The two sites complement each other nicely.

ONLINE INVESTING COMMUNITIES

If the development of online services has proven anything, it is that people—even strangers—like to talk with each other. Online investing communities prove that people like to talk about their investments.

The urge to brag is understandable, especially during the bull market in which these communities were born and thrived. But the watering holes described in this section cater to more than just macho braggarts. These investing clubs are resources, support groups, debate centers, and informal social groups. Active traders use online message boards to keep each other company during the long, solitary trading day, and more casual investors use them to catch up with each other's gains and disappointments in the evening.

Investing communities are best approached with open-mindedness combined with cynical caution. Stories you might have heard about investing fraud are true. Deceptive schemes intended to generate widespread interest in a certain stock flourish in the relatively anonymous climate of the Internet. Here are a few rules of thumb for the uninitiated:

✔ *Do not believe everything you read.* A message board *post* is not the *Wall Street Journal.*

✔ *Never buy stock on a tip.* Use tips to spark your own research projects.

✔ *Perform your own due diligence.* That means you should verify any information that influences your investing decisions.

✔ *Take your time.* Get acquainted with any community you join. By doing so you will find the trustworthy voices.

post   message in an online discussion forum. Posts are strung together by multiple users to form a thread, which is a conversation on a particular topic.

With these cautions in mind, take advantage of the fun and useful aspects of the online investment community.

Raging Bull (www.ragingbull.com)

"Leading the Investor Revolution"—that is the motto here. Raging Bull was started in a college dorm room and quickly grew into a bustling, diverse, sometimes fractious community. Members are attracted by the smart messaging software that allows anyone to track the posts of certain people as well as eliminate undesirables from the screen. The system operates similarly to the older Silicon Investor community, whose description follows, but unlike SI, Raging Bull is absolutely free.

Raging Bull (see Figure 10.8) is a hybrid community/news portal, hosting a stable of columnists who report on market events. The editorial viewpoint is relentlessly bullish and revolutionary, reveling in the ongoing empowerment of individual investors. But the main attraction for most people remains the message boards, which are mostly devoted to individual stocks.

Silicon Investor (www.siliconinvestor.com)

Silicon Investor (SI) was one of the earliest online investing communities on the Web, and its population of subscribers is one of its main assets. The level of discussion at SI reaches impressive heights on some boards. You can find almost anything here, from company-specific *threads* to general economic discussions to trading of index options.

FIGURE 10.8 Raging Bull is a combination news site and community of rampant investors.

(Raging Bull is a trademark of Raging Bull, Inc., a wholly owned subsidiary of AltaVista Company. All content is property of Raging Bull, Inc., and may not be used without permission.)

thread a series of posts in a message-board discussion form. Threads define topical discussions on message boards. Each post contributes to a thread; all the threads together comprise the message board.

Silicon Investor is not a professional club; the SI citizens are, for the most part, regular investors who are deeply interested in stocks and determined to perform their own research. Although arguments flame up here and there, a spirit of sharing prevails for the most part. Silicon Investor is free for the browsing, but you need to join the subscription ranks to post a message. While it may seem outrageous to levy a cover charge on the community, the subscription acts as a sort of gate that allows only serious investors through and may help explain the high quality of this community's threads.

Usenet newsgroups (misc.invest.stocks and others)

Usenet newsgroups comprise the native bulletin board system of the Internet, completely distinct from the World Wide Web. Most people read and post to newsgroups using their e-mail program. (Outlook Express and Netscape Messenger both deliver newsgroup service.) The Usenet empire is vast and highly evolved, having predated the Web by many years. About 30,000 topical newsgroups exist on nearly any subject imaginable. Newsgroups are well known as an unregulated realm in which anything goes—manners are quite different from those used by individuals talking face to face.

Considering how enormous the entire Usenet is, the investing groups are surprisingly few and undefined. The most popular is misc.invest.stocks, a breeding ground for raucous and disorganized stock discussions. The newsgroup experience may not be your cup of tea and certainly is not as civilized as Silicon Investor or Raging Bull. But the newsgroups do produce some entertaining discussions.

Usenet   one of the oldest portions of the Internet, Usenet consists of about 30,000 topical discussion forums in message-board format. Usenet contains many investing forums as well as several Web-based online communities for investors.

Yahoo! Messages (messages.yahoo.com/yahoo/Business__Finance/ Investments/index.html)

The investing message boards at Yahoo! are part of a larger message board system, and they comprise one of the most popular gathering places for stock talk. Yahoo! establishes the boards, divided into sectors and individual stocks. It is much harder for an individual to start an original board in Yahoo! than it is in Silicon Investor. Further, the software running the boards is rudimentary, making it hard to follow the thread of discussions.

StockJungle (www.stockjungle.com)

This community is unique. StockJungle provides a platform for amateur investors to look like pros. Anyone can enter the site and submit stock picks, which are then added to the community database of picks. All bets are tracked, and the most successful "analysts" receive lots of glory and even a little money.

StockJungle is not a brokerage; it is a competitive stock-picking community. As a visitor, you may want to participate or just browse. This site suggests many good investment ideas, and any participant who consistently succeeds can be tracked to harvest more good ideas. As always, you should remember always to do your own research and never to invest on a tip.

Chapter 11

Choosing an Online Broker

The most frequently asked question about online personal finance is "How do I choose a broker?" Rampant bewilderment is understandable, considering the sheer number of choices. Over 150 online brokerages exist.

As with online banks, there are two basic types of online brokers:

1. Pure-Internet virtual brokers.
2. Click-and-mortar brokers that grew out of traditional investment houses.

The differences between the two types have dissolved over the years, partly because branch offices are not as important to a brokerage as they are to a bank. Traditional brokerages were always a bit virtual—most of the time you accessed your account by calling a broker on the phone, not by walking into an office. The Internet just eliminates the broker.

TYPES OF ONLINE BROKERAGES

There are no formal divisions of online brokers into categories. But as the field has evolved, certain specialties have emerged. For the sake of organized thinking, look at most virtual brokers as belonging to one of the following types.

✔ Investment portals

✔ One-Stop financial centers

✔ Click-and-mortar brokers

✔ Cut-rate, quick-execution brokers

✔ Next-generation brokers

Investment Portals

A portal, in Web-speak, is a storehouse of content and a gateway to more content. Portals aspire to anchor the visitor's online experience, providing a home base from which productive online expeditions can be launched and within which all the essentials are found.

Investment portals (see Figure 11.1) apply the home-base principle to investing, of course, and those portals operated by brokerages place the buying and selling of securities at the center of the experience. In addition to brokering, these investment supersites stuff their pages with news, research tools, price quotes and charts, and sometimes community features.

Large brokerage centers provide good service for many newcomers and veteran investors alike. Do not expect any strong specialization at an investment portal, since portals emphasize breadth of service rather than depth in any particular feature. Generally investment brokers offer three main attractions:

1. *Products.* Brokerage portals usually deal in several basic kinds of investment instruments: stocks, *penny stocks*, mutual funds, options, bonds. More exotic products, such as currencies and commodities, do not figure in the mix.

2. *Research.* Although research really is not an important part of brokerage service, the portals supply a great deal of breaking company and market news, research tools of various kinds, price quotes (real-time in some cases), and historical charts.

3. *Customer service.* While customer service is always hard to predict in any online brokerage, broker portals at least make an effort to keep you connected to your money in a few different ways. Most of these companies provide multiple ways to access your account, including the telephone and help from human brokers.

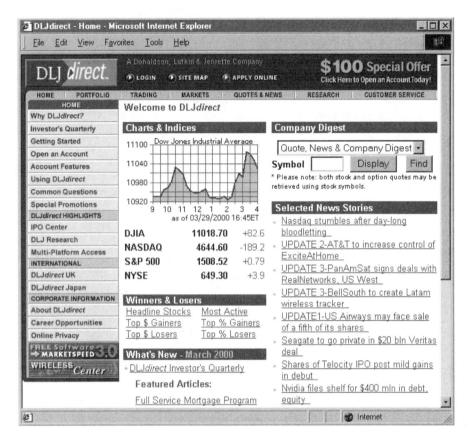

FIGURE 11.1 DLJ Direct is an example of a portal-style online broker that supplies news and research in addition to market access.

(Reprinted with permission of DLJ Direct.)

penny stock   strictly speaking, a penny stock is any stock trading for less than $5 per share. In a more colloquial sense, a penny stock costs pennies, literally—a stock trading for under a dollar.

One-Stop Financial Centers

Another type of broad-based brokerage strives to be a one-stop financial service center, with brokerage tools in the forefront. The main attraction of these institutions is their merging of brokerage and banking features. In this context you have to take the term "banking" lightly. Most brokers that provide checkbooks and debit cards do not operate as full-fledged on-line banks, and in most cases you will not find online bill paying or a wide variety of interest-bearing deposit accounts.

Banking and brokerage services can combine in two ways. One is for online brokers to furnish customers with basic check-writing and cash services; the other is for banks to offer basic stock buying and selling. Neither side of the equation is completely satisfactory, and if you want excellent online banking and brokerage, it is best to use two institutions.

But signing up with a one-stop financial broker definitely has its advantages, first among them the ability to get some money out of your investment account when you need it. Traditionally, *liquidity* is a problem; brokerage accounts are not as liquid as checking accounts—you have to go through a little song and dance to get some cash. Online brokers with check-writing service combine liquidity with investment features, which is a pleasing mix.

liquidity   availability. In a bank account, liquidity is the availability of cash; thus checking accounts are very liquid and certificates of deposit (CDs), which are purchased for a set term, are not. In a stock market, liquidity refers to the availability of stocks and the ease with which investors can buy and sell them.

Click-and-Mortar Brokers

At least one traditional broker—Charles Schwab—understood the power-ful advantages of the World Wide Web early in the game, and established an online version of its service. Perhaps the fact that Schwab had for many years been something of a maverick in the brokerage field (offering dis-count commissions and a populist attitude to investing) inclined it to rec-ognize the benefits of new technology. Some other old-time brokerages were not as quick on the uptake.

Click-and-mortar brokerages, which are the creation of online ser-vices at a traditional brokerage, developed more gradually than pure-Internet brokerages, which leapt into existence with startling speed. In time, though, most of the offline institutions realized that they would lose too many customers if they did not get up to speed with the Internet.

Click-and-mortar brokerages range in quality from the banal to the innovative. Basically, there are two grades of online/offline brokers:

1. *Add-on.* At the most perfunctory level, some brokerages simply tack rudimentary online services to their existing account structures. There may or may not be a discount in commission fees, the hallmark of pure-Internet brokers. The service may comprise a begrudging acknowledgment of the Internet's necessity, with no heart or desire to create a new service profile. In defense of these situations, it is not easy to build an online brokerage, and many customers do not want that many perks anyway. Basic online access to account records is by itself a worthy convenience, just as in online banking. Add-on services are designed to satisfy existing customers more than to attract new customers.

2. *New enterprise.* At the opposite end of the scale are brokerages like Merrill Lynch that have completely redesigned their business to accommodate and leverage Internet technology. Cut-rate Internet brokers have been a difficult reality for traditional firms whose specialty is expert and expensive service. For a long time some of these traditional companies tried to preserve their business models while hoping that online brokers would be a passing fad. With that hope gone, they have transformed into new-service companies. These services are designed both to satisfy existing customers and to attract new ones.

Late to the Party, But Ready to Rock

The big brokerage players, such as Merrill Lynch and Morgan Stanley Dean Witter, may have come to the party late, but they brought their own brand of punch. When it comes to cutting commissions, they are understandably loath to scrape the bottom of the barrel as the impersonal automated brokers do. These companies have introduced innovative commission schedules based on a percentage of total assets as opposed to the per-transaction agenda. In this way, infrequent traders may pay more, but they still have access to the human expertise that these old-time brokerages were founded on. Even Charles Schwab—a discounter from way back—introduced (just before this book was published) a system whereby customers can order expert consultation for a fee.

One advantage of a click-and-mortar brokerage, whether it is Schwab, Merrill Lynch, or another, is the presence of branch offices. But this feature is not as important as with click-and-mortar banks, because investing accounts do not benefit as much from walk-in service.

Cut-Rate, Quick-Execution Brokers

Some virtual brokers aim straight for the bargain-hunting crowd by driving their commission fees down to amazingly low levels. In exchange for nearly free stock executions, customers must cope with very little human service. All online brokers provide some sort of customer service, but personal touches are the first things to go in a high-discount house.

Low commissions usually are paired with fast trade executions. Keep in mind that all online brokers promise near-instant confirmations of stock purchases and sales. Reality tells a different story. Cut-rate brokers know they attract the most active traders who need those low fees to cut their expenses when trading aggressively. Accordingly, those promised swift executions are a necessity, as word gets around fast on the Internet. High-trade customers will find the brokers that provide the best balance of price and speed.

The combination of price and speed is another reason that cut-rate brokers do not offer much customer hand-holding. Their ideal clients—nimble and experienced traders—do not need or want much help or miscellaneous, distracting features. Accordingly, cut-rate brokers often do not provide any kind of banking features, sometimes they offer no mutual funds, and company research often is kept to a minimum. However, fast and accurate price quotes are supplied, often in real time.

Next-Generation Brokers

Low fees, pretty fast executions, and real-time snapshot quotes are not enough for some traders. There is a big void between the package of services provided by the cut-rate brokers and institutional perks the pros use. In an effort to fill that void, a whole new generation of online brokers has set its sights on consumers.

Second-generation brokers are characterized by higher fees and much more sophisticated service. The idea is to approach institutional-level information and execution standards at a fraction of institutional prices. Three major differences set apart these new-style brokers:

1. *Pay for information.* Customers pay for information that is normally free at regular brokerage sites. The cost is justified by the extremely high quality of the information. Real-time quotes are always part of the package, usually in streaming format (like a stock ticker) rather than snapshot quotes. Often the site features direct display of market exchange prices. Extraordinary tools that enable stock screening and market mapping give users an idea of what institutional information flow is like.

2. *Use dedicated programs.* These new brokers do not use the World Wide Web as their operating platform and eschew the Web browser. Instead, the companies provide dedicated programs (some of which can be freely downloaded in demo format) for researching and executing trades.

3. *Instant executions.* Partly because of the avoidance of the relatively slow Web and partly because of direct hook-ups with securities exchanges, users of next-generation brokers enjoy lightning-fast execution of their trades. Often trades are confirmed just a moment after the orders are entered.

Trading commissions at these advanced brokers sometimes do not differ much from regular online commissions. The companies make their money partly by attracting high-volume traders and partly by selling access to the sophisticated information system that runs the program. Next-generation brokers are popular with day traders who wish to work from home.

COMMISSION RATES

The first (and still important) claim to fame for online brokers was lower commission fees than the world had ever seen before. Since the introduction of online investing, a new standard of cost-effectiveness has been established. All online brokers are by definition discount brokers, but over time certain levels of discount have been defined.

By and large, commissions are charged when buying and selling stock, so active traders double the advertised rate when considering the cost of a complete entry-and-exit maneuver. Some brokers manipulate this basic scenario in small ways. A few firms do not charge per-transaction fees at all, preferring either an annual flat fee (rare) or an annual percentage charge based on total assets.

High-Price Online Brokers

At the upper end of the online commission continuum are firms that add a comforting degree of human services to the virtual recipe. Per-trade fees of $30 and up characterize this price level. Click-and-mortar brokers tend to fill this niche, reluctant as they are to match the bargain rates of pure Internet shops. Full-service brokers with banking features also tend to charge rather high commissions.

For those relatively high rates, customers can expect a full array of products and services, including some hand-holding when needed. Whether the firm charges more for human-assisted trades is an open question, but certainly such assistance is available. These brokers have a reputation for reliability, and many customers report satisfaction with higher rates for relatively trouble-free service. By and large, high-price online brokers are used by long-term investors, not the quick-trade crowd.

Mid-Price Brokers

The largest fee category, mid-price brokers charge $15 or $20 per trade, with the possibility of per-share charges for very large orders. If a single mid-price fee can be said to typify the standard commission rate for an online trade, it is $19.95, which the industry has settled on as a kind of hinge point: Anything higher is pricey; anything lower is cheap.

Brokerage portals tend to price their commissions in the middle of the road. A $20 trade implies average features all the way around: good executions (but not great), good research (but nothing outstanding), basic stock quotes (but probably not real-time quotes).

Mainstream Choice

Mid-price brokers are the solution of choice for investors who have some experience with securities and with the Internet but not necessarily expertise in either field. Daring traders need less expensive commissions and more fluid executions. Conservative investors often prefer better service at higher prices. Momentum traders who follow the markets closely and hold stocks for days or weeks can be satisfied paying mid-price commissions.

On the customer service side, mid-price brokers advertise full services but sometimes fail to deliver. Just about all brokers at the mid-price level and below suffer from customer complaints of varying intensity in this department.

Cut-Rate Brokers

Automated service at bargain rates—that is the creed of the cut-rate brokers. These firms charge less than $15 per trade, with the lowest (as of this writing) clocking in at $5. The typical range for bargain commission rates is between $8 and $12 per buy or sell.

Cut-rate brokers make their money through volume and naturally attract restless traders who need to cut expenses with low-fee brokers. Speaking of saving money, cut-rate brokers shave their expenses by minimizing or eliminating nonessential services. Human resources are kept to a minimum, which is just how the high-rolling stock jockeys like it. While pricing information tends to be quite good (as required by active traders), often other research tools are slim—the idea is that traders can go anywhere else on the Web for news reporting, company research, and fancy charts.

New Commission Models

The simple and efficient per-trade model by which online commissions are determined rings true in the computer world. But commissions were not always assessed that way. Percentages are sloppier but still in use both offline and, to a small but growing extent, online.

Some large click-and-mortar brokerages resist per-trade fees. Instead, they offer customers a complete package of broker-assisted trades and financial management services, bundling the whole thing into a fee schedule based on account assets. The brokerage might charge 1 percent of assets per year, for example. In that scenario, an account worth $100,000 is charged $1,000 per year for unlimited trading and access to in-house research and advice. Customers can execute trades themselves, using online interfaces, or by calling a broker the old-fashioned way.

When you break down such percentage systems into per-trade fees, they may not seem favorable compared to the high discounts found elsewhere. Investors who have little interest in Internet trading and are loath to distance themselves from the personalized attention of a full-service brokerage often meet these commission schedules with no complaints.

Active Trading Discounts

Increasingly, mid-price online brokers are concerned about losing customer assets to cut-rate houses that encourage active trading. More than a few successful investors are intent on maintaining their long-term conservative strategies but hanker for a taste of trading. Also, some investors have met with success at relatively tame momentum trading and want to quicken the pace. In both cases, mid-price brokers cannot compete with the low-commission firms without altering the fee schedule.

The solution for many brokers is to set up active trading departments—distinct subsets of their basic service plans. Customers who qualify by trading at certain levels (of volume, not success) get special commission rates. Often two or three qualifying levels exist, each with a separate commission schedule. The more you trade, the cheaper the commission for each trade.

These active trading discounts offer not only better prices but often better trading tools as well. Active traders have access to special programs and information platforms that provide a somewhat sophisticated on-screen trading environment.

EVALUATING ONLINE BROKERS

Shopping for an online brokerage is baffling to newcomers and not much easier for more experienced folks. Many investors spread their assets over two or more online accounts—you do not need to be rich to see the sense in that. Brokers have specialties, just as grocery stores do, and a longtime user of one online broker might decide to open a trading account, or a retirement account, with another broker. But the vast selection of competing companies can paralyze a person's decision-making powers.

Television ads abound. Online promotions flow across your screen like a rushing river of conflicting claims. The truth is, some brokerage features are more important than others. Different things are important to different investors. And the advertising claims cannot always be taken at face value—there are hidden aspects to the hype.

The following sections describe what you should keep in mind when deciding on a brokerage and exposes some pitfalls of online investing prior to signing up. Use these sections to sharpen your awareness of what online brokers offer, then look at the rundown of popular brokers later in this chapter.

An Important Truth

The sad fact is that you cannot truly audition the reliability and friendliness of a brokerage before opening an account. If you frequent the investing forums, you may hear buzz about one broker or another, including horror stories and vociferous complaints. Take all this buzz with a grain of salt. Remember that, usually, the most complaints come from the largest customer bases and do not represent the thousands of happy users.

Ranking systems (described later in this chapter) attempt to quantify customer experience at online brokers. Aside from those rankings, when it comes to selecting a broker, go with the features you want that are listed in black and white.

Range of Products

Know how you want to invest and make sure your brokerage supports your strategy. All online stock brokers deal in stock, naturally. You also might want to consider the mutual fund lineup, if any—there is wide variance in mutual fund support from one broker to another. Even more specifically, investigate the range of no-load mutual funds.

Even within the realm of stocks, some brokers offer more coverage than others. If you are interested in penny stocks (those costing less than $5, and sometimes literally pennies, per share), make sure you use a firm that trades on the Nasdaq Bulletin Board—an offshoot of the main Nasdaq exchange populated with low-price stocks. Canadian stocks are harder to find, and participation in European, Asian, and South American exchanges (aside from mutual funds) is almost impossible to find.

If you have experience with many types of investment instrument, consider opening more than one account. The best option broker for you may not be the best stock broker or the best mutual fund supermarket.

Execution Quality

How reliably are your stock transactions accomplished? How quickly are your trades executed and confirmed on your screen? The crucial issue of execution quality is, unfortunately, difficult to determine before

Beyond Stocks

Beyond stocks, a world of possibilities exists, some of which may interest you. If you hedge your stock investments using options, make sure your prospective broker carries stock (and index) options. You may be surprised at which ones do not! Online brokers do not universally provide bonds. Currency speculation, futures, and commodity trading are left to specialized brokers for the most part—these arenas may enter the online stock brokerage scene in the future, but do not bother trying to find them now.

you get and use an account. For conservative investors, the good news is that these questions are not really that important; long-term strategists who hold stock for months or years do not need instant confirmation of trades.

Traders who execute momentum positions or intraday maneuvers do need a broker that can execute orders quickly and efficiently. Otherwise, buy and sell points can be missed, leading to much gnashing of teeth. The only evaluation tools at your disposal are the brokerage review services (detailed later in this chapter) and customer buzz on the investing message boards. (See Chapter 10 for a look at online investing forums.)

Take a cue, also, from the way the brokerages position themselves in the marketplace. Those that advertise quick executions and are attempting to attract traders rather than investors generally fulfill their promises much of the time. This is not to be glib or naive—there are technological means of providing quick executions, and brokers who specialize in that feature invest in those technologies.

Site Reliability

Next to robust trade executions, a sturdy Web site is vitally important. If one complaint has been leveled universally against online brokerages, it is that they sometimes flake out when the going gets tough. Specifically, during very busy market days, when account activity is peaking across the board, brokerage sites can become temporarily unavailable to many people. The sites crash, leaving customers without access to their accounts and trading screens.

What to Do When Your Broker Crashes

Crashes are almost inevitable if you are an active trader. Despite the improvements to Web site stability in the field, every online broker crashes now and then, leaving customers with no access to their accounts, unable to place buy or sell orders. A site crash can be financially damaging. If you own a stock that is going down, and you cannot sell it, your broker may be liable for part of your loss. Establishing liability for the inability to buy a stock at a certain time is more difficult.

If you ever feel your broker has lost you money, contact customer service and request compensation. Such requests are successful more often than you would guess. Online brokers know they are under a negative public relations spotlight when their service goes down and usually are eager to make amends after a serious crash. For that reason, you may have more success attaining a rebate after a well-publicized service outage than if you experienced temporary glitches on a normal day.

Once again, as with execution reliability, there is not much you can do to determine a broker's interface stability. If you snoop around the forums, you may notice that customer complaints center on a few companies. And the review services touch on this point.

When brokerages seriously crash—leaving their customers without access for an hour or more—the event receives media coverage. Often it is the most popular brokerages that suffer during high-traffic days, and these may be exactly the firms that suit your needs best in other ways. Putting up with occasional outages may become part of your game plan. If you are not an active trader, you may not even notice site disruptions.

A secondary issue related to site reliability is how the interface performs when it is operating normally. With brokerages as with any other type of Web destination, some sites are more streamlined than others. Whether you are eager to trade or merely checking your balances, nothing is more frustrating than tapping your fingers while graphics-laden pages slowly load on your screen. Fortunately, you can test this factor simply by exploring the brokerage site before opening an account.

Site Interface

Reliability questions aside, how a site presents important screens is vital to the online investing experience. Think of the brokerage site as an environment for your eyes; if the view is confusing or jarring, you may end up unsatisfied. Scrutinize two parts of the site:

1. Order pages. Order pages are where you buy and sell stocks. (See Figure 11.2.) Newcomers should look for explanatory links that define order types and unfamiliar terms. The page should load quickly and be free of distracting graphics. Function is far more important than beauty on the order page.

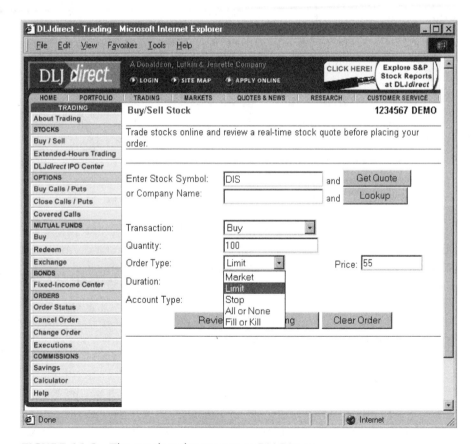

FIGURE 11.2 The stock order screen at DLJ Direct.
(Reprinted with permission of DLJ Direct.)

2. *Portfolio pages.* This is where your positions are listed and tracked. The portfolio page is a sore point for many online investors. It should be clear and, ideally, link each holding to the order page.

Generally, find out in advance whether the site operates well for you. Is navigation clearly marked? Do you have trouble finding your way around, or are the departments well marked on each page?

Commission Rates

Broker fees were explained in detail earlier in this chapter. When absorbing brokerage hype from TV ads and Web banners, consider a few points:

✔ *Varying commissions.* Commissions for market orders often differ from fees for limit orders. Market orders (in which you cannot specify your high and low buying and selling prices) usually are cheaper than limit orders (in which you determine the uppermost you are selling to pay when buying, and the lower figure you will accept when selling). Naturally, the advertisements usually mention the market-order commission, even though most traders always use limit orders.

✔ *Escalating commissions.* If you plan to deal in penny stocks, watch out for escalating commissions. Some brokerages charge a flat per-trade fee up to some number of shares—perhaps 1,000 or 5,000—then a low per-share fee for additional shares. The result is that a 50,000-share purchase of a 30-cent stock can cost a bundle. Do not expect to see ads mention this little item.

✔ *Other fees.* Low stock commissions do not imply low prices for other transactions. A super-discount online stock broker may not carry many no-load mutual funds and may charge exorbitant rates for options. This is another reason that some people work with multiple brokers.

✔ *Commissions for active traders.* Active intraday traders might want to look for commission structures that charge just a single commission for multiple trades of the same stock on the same side (buy or sell) during the same day. Multiple trades sometimes are intentional moves by traders and sometimes are the result of the brokerage failing to fill a large order all at once. Either way, paying commissions for each partial execution can get expensive.

✔ *Human assistance.* Many brokerages let you call a human broker to buy or sell a security, instead of using the on-screen interface. Commissions are usually higher for human-assisted trading.

Margin Fees

Brokerages lend money to qualifying customers, up to a federally regulated limit of 50 percent of a stock purchase. Accounts with such automatic credit are called *margin accounts*, and borrowing half the cost of a stock purchase is called margining. Whether margining is right for you depends on many factors, but if you want that credit line, investigate how much the broker charges for the loan. The interest rate for securities borrowing is called the *margin rate*.

margin account investing account with an automatic line of credit. By American securities law, investors may borrow up to half the cost of a security from the purchasing brokerage. Doing so is called buying on margin, and the brokerage charges interest on the loan, known as the margin rates.

margin rate rate of interest charged by a brokerage when lending money to customers. The margin rate is usually some small amount above the broker loan rate.

Margin rates are expressed as a certain percentage above the *broker loan rate*, which is the interest rate charged by banks when they lend money to brokers. The closer you can get to the broker loan rate, the better; you may be able to find a firm charging the flat broker lending rate, with no markup.

Margin rates are important only to high-capital investors and traders who lean heavily on their broker for equity financing.

broker loan rate interest rate charged by banks when lending money to investment brokers. Brokerages add a bit to this rate when providing the margin rate to their customers.

To Margin or Not to Margin?

Margin accounts are an easy way to leverage your existing cash. Maybe too easy. Some consumer advocates feel that margin requirements should be toughened so that ordinary investors—who may not be sufficiently aware of the risks of trading—cannot obtain lines of credit so easily from online brokers.

When using margin to purchase stock, the worst thing that can happen is the stock goes down, and your broker asks you to put more cash in your account to cover your loan (since the value of the stock is no longer sufficient collateral). If you do not fund the account quickly, the brokerage is entitled to sell your stock and repay itself from the proceeds. In that case, you suffer an investment loss.

Most people should use margin loans with discretion and caution, if at all. Remember that having a line of credit does not necessarily mean that you should use it.

Real-Time Data Services

Time was, real-time price quotes were a glamorous aspect of *institutional investing*, rarely seen on a home computer. The rest of us tolerated stock quotes delayed 15 or 20 minutes behind the real market action. It was like living in a time warp, and still is at many sites. Today inexpensive or free real-time quotes are prevalent and probably soon will be available for free everywhere, just as other types of once-costly information are. In the meantime, this perk is a shopping criterion when selecting a broker.

institutional investing   the buying and selling of securities by brokerages and investment banks.

A few things to keep in mind:

✔ Your online broker is not the only source for real-time stock quotes. If you need up-to-the-minute pricing, and a broker does not offer it, do not eliminate that broker from your consideration. A number of nonbrokerage Web sites provide the service, either free or for a monthly subscription. (One dedicated free site is Free Real Time, at www.freereal-time.com.)

✔ An online broker may provide real-time quotes to its customers but not to its visitors. Read feature descriptions carefully, because the service may not be immediately apparent.

✔ All stock quotes, whether delayed or real time, come in two forms: *snapshot* and *streaming*. Snapshot quotes require reloading to update the prices, while streaming quotes appear as an on-screen ticker, automatically updating. Most free real-time quote are in snap-shot format. People who need current pricing sometimes need the streaming format, so check with the brokerage to see which version is available, if either. If a brokerage you like doesn't offer them, you can purchase streaming real-time quotes and other sophisticated information elsewhere.

✔ Consider whether the whole issue of real-time quotes is important to your investing style. Traders need instant pricing. Slower investors can use limit orders to specify the exact price they are willing to pay and wait for the market to match that price. Furthermore, some brokerages that do not feature continuous real-time quotes do show you a real-time price before you send an order.

snapshot quotes   style of online stock quote that must be refreshed in order to see the latest price.

streaming quotes   style of online stock quote that resembles a stock ticker. Unlike snapshot quotes, streaming quotes do not need to be refreshed manually.

One other real-time service is important: portfolio updating. Some firms update your on-screen portfolio once a day, at night (U.S. time). Others, by contrast, update your positions whenever you trade. It is also nice to see real-time updating of the prices of your holdings throughout the day.

Many nonbrokerage Web sites provide portfolio services, but it is important that your brokerage give you good portfolio tools that show your trading activity.

Customer Service

The big question about customer service at online brokers: Is there any? That is a joke, but not much of an exaggeration. This area is a flagrant bone of contention between brokers and their customers. Lack of responsive human service is most pronounced at high-discount shops that automate most services. But all online brokers experiencing rapid customer growth have had trouble keeping up.

It is a good idea to test customer service in advance by asking a few questions by phone and e-mail. It does not matter what you ask; the important thing is how fast and helpfully they answer. Requesting information about opening a new account is a tried-and-true tactic, especially if you order application forms in the mail. Another method is to e-mail or phone the company to ask about some of the features discussed in this section.

Customer service and human-broker service are related but separate departments. No matter what you think of customer service in advance of opening an account, you do not know how easy it might be to get a human broker on the phone when you want that service. There is no way to test that service in advance.

Multiple Interfaces

The Web is a fine interface if you happen to be sitting in front of a computer. And that is enough for investors who do not trade a lot. But even moderately active traders who travel need an alternative means of accessing their brokerage account. Many brokerages allow human-assisted trades, at higher commissions, over the phone.

The resolute do-it-yourselfer should look for alternative interfaces. Touch-tone phone service is a prevalent solution—cumbersome but learnable and effective. A few brokers (and their number will surely increase) offer paging service and cell-phone screen interfaces in partnership with certain cellular providers.

Minimum Initial Deposit

Most, but not all, online brokers require a certain amount of money to open an investment account. This requirement can be an obstacle to new investors who wish to get started with a small amount of savings. Fortunately, in the competition for customers, the initial requirement has scaled down to nothing in some cases and as little as $500 at other firms. Some other brokers hold steady at the $1,000 or $2,000 level, or higher.

Clearly, having a small nest egg limits your choice of brokers. Over time, as your assets accumulate, your choices expand and moving to another broker is always possible. After the initial deposit, every brokerage accepts subsequent deposits of any amount.

Banking Features

Does the online broker you are considering provide rudimentary banking service? Often all investors want is a little liquidity—checks that draw on the investment account do the trick. Remember that checks can draw only on cash in the account, not the cash value of held securities. Some brokers go a little further in emulating banks by furnishing debit cards. And some institutions, whether they started as banks or brokerages, offer a full range of services on both sides of the fence. But generally, good online brokers have at least limited banking features.

Research Tools

Online broker advertisements make a big deal of promoting their in-house, on-site research tools. (See Figure 11.3.) Images of thoughtful investors, faces bathed in monitor light as they study stock charts, are meant to secure our confidence that the broker provides everything we need to invest knowledgeably. That may be true, but it is unimportant.

Obviously, researching investments online is very important. But where you do it does not matter much. Every destination on the Web is one click away from every other destination. Browsers can open multiple windows displaying multiple sites. Always remember: The Web is the portal, not the broker.

Brokers do have a good selling point when they provide subscription content to their customers free of charge. In such cases you are getting good value. But when it comes to basic company research, historical charts, and wire news services, do not be swayed. That stuff is ubiquitous.

Demo

The best brokers are not afraid to show their stuff to visitors. When visiting sites of potential brokers, look for a demo of its order, confirmation,

FIGURE 11.3 National Discount Brokers provides a wide range of investment research tools.

(Copyright © 1999 National Discount Brokers.)

and account screens. You do not need a multimedia dazzler, just examples of what your investing experience will look like. Brokers that do not provide that basic demo have a lot to make up for. Do not let them off the hook easily.

After-Hours Trading

The trading day is not what it used to be. After decades of gradual expansion, the roof is about to be blown off the business day—before long stock trading may transpire in a 24-hour marketplace. In the meantime, several technology companies license computerized trading systems to brokers with the intent of letting consumers trade in the evening and early morning (Eastern U.S. time).

If you live on the West Coast of the United States or in another country, after-hours trading might be an important consideration. In fact, some East Coasters with regular jobs appreciate the ability to trade in a market that is still open after work.

Some brokers subscribe to an after-hours system and some do not. The adoption of after-hours investing has proceeded more slowly (as of this writing) than many expected, so it is hard to predict when all the brokers will get up to speed. If you do wade into the after-hours markets, proceed cautiously. Prices tend to be volatile, and not necessarily tied to daytime valuations. Furthermore, since trading volume is still slim in the evening, orders sometimes go unfilled.

Initial Public Offerings

Every individual investor would like to get an initial public offering (IPO) into the account—before it hits the open market. The rocketing valuations of high-tech IPOs make retail investors drool with envy, but the institutional stranglehold on share distribution makes it hard for individuals to get IPO shares.

Nonetheless, some online brokers obtain pre-IPO shares of imminently public companies for distribution to their customers. The brokers accomplish this feat through affiliations with the underwriting investment houses that bankroll IPOs. However, average investors, even those with accounts at these participating brokers, do not usually get any of the slim IPO action. In most cases the high-asset accounts get the prized shares first.

ONLINE BROKERAGE RANKINGS

With over 150 online brokers clamoring for attention, customers, and assets, investors need some objective source of information that sorts out the bubbling brew of Internet investing services. Fortunately, a number of review sites come to the rescue with methods for ranking online brokers. Before long there may be so many of these ranking sites that we will need other services to rate *them*. For now, here are descriptions of six important sites that everyone shopping for an online broker should know about.

Gomez.com (www.gomez.com)

Gomez has evolved over the years into a broad consumer reporting service that helps online citizens make better destination choices. The service started as an online broker ranking service, and the site's core is its personal finance section. Gomez evaluations of brokers, updated seasonally, are widely quoted in advertisements and by users. This service remains the brand leader in brokerage rankings and manages to stay a nose in front of competitors in quality.

The heart of the Gomez system involves breaking down ratings according to different criteria, in recognition of the differing needs of investors. The Overall Score list is the most prestigious, and brokers that place near the top of that elite ranking earn valuable grist for the advertising mill. Other criteria, including Ease of Use, Customer Confidence, On-Site Resources, and Overall Cost, generate distinct rankings.

The entire range of data Gomez collects is further parsed into lists intending to point certain types of investors to the right broker—this may be the most valuable part of the site. Hyper-Active Traders, Serious Investors, Life Goal Planners, and One-Stop Shoppers get independent recommendation lists.

The brokers on each list are linked to their own review pages, which spell out specific strong and weak points. A community section allows visitors to add their personal experiences with the broker, but in most cases that feature is pretty empty. (Better to keep your eye on the investment forums for the latest broker buzz.)

Gomez does not canvass the entire universe of brokers, and indeed, no ranking service is comprehensive. At last count, Gomez investigated 53 brokers. The findings are not without controversy, and it is always a good idea to check out a few ranking sites if you want a rounded (if possibly confusing) impression.

XOLIA.com (www.xolia.com)

XOLIA.com (see Figure 11.4) is a new and impressive entry to the broker-rating field. The company has developed database technology that allows users to compare one broker's features against another effectively. The service is designed to be licensed to other Web sites, but its owners generously make it freely available to all visitors.

XOLIA's strong point is its depth of detail. Dozens of criteria are applied to each surveyed broker. The interactive software allows you to view results by individual broker or to compare as many as three brokerages side by side.

Try using XOLIA in tandem with Gomez. Use Gomez to get a broad portrait of a broker's strengths, then shift to XOLIA to fill in the details.

FIGURE 11.4 XOLIA.com provides detailed comparisons of up to four online brokers from its database of several dozen.
(Reprinted with permission of XOLIA.com.)

Keynote Web Broker Trading Index (www.keynote.com/measures/brokers)

Keynote provides a unique and valuable service that seeks to quantify a single aspect of the online investing experience: brokerage site response. Slow pages at the brokerage site can really drag you down, especially if you trade fairly actively.

Keynote attempts specifically to measure response times of order pages. The service stops short of buying and selling stock to determine order efficiency—an important but distinct issue. Instead, Keynote times the speed with which the order page and its confirmation page appear on the screen. Any experienced investor knows that plenty of aggravating delay can lurk in that space between getting a quote and sending an order.

The Keynote service is updated weekly and lists about 20 of the most popular brokerages. Each current table lists the present week and the previous week. You can look at earlier tables stretching back many months to get an ongoing picture of any broker's long-term reliability. Technically astute visitors appreciate the information (in a separate table) about each broker's Internet access backbone and Web server software.

SmartMoney Broker Meter (www.smartmoney.com/si/brokermeter)

SmartMoney takes an approach similar to Keynote's but does not delve as deeply into each broker site. Instead, the Broker Meter measures general brokerage access by timing the link speed to the home page from various American cities. The results are packaged in an interactive Java display that shifts and rearranges itself before your eyes when you change a variable.

The results may correspond to your personal experience surfing to various brokerage sites. At any rate, the snazzy display is worth looking at.

Kiplinger (wwa.kiplinger.com/magazine/archives/ 1999/November/ebroker.htm#data)

Kiplinger makes a good effort to sort information about online brokers by broad criteria and by brokerage destination. Drop-down menus make it easy to choose an individual broker or a sorting category. The criteria include Commissions, Margin Rates, Statement Clarity, Broker Knowledge, and Overall Rank. Obviously, some subjectivity is involved in the rankings, and no information about the methodology is offered.

Each broker page at Kiplinger divulges the company's commission rate, minimum initial deposit, margin rate, and the availability of real-time quotes, check-writing, and touch-tone trading.

Kiplinger's results are interesting and thought-provoking, but no newcomer should rely on this ranking service alone to choose a broker.

Choosing a Discount Broker (www.sonic.net/donaldj/query.html)

If there is one underground, cult-status broker-rating site, this page is it. For years, this site has provided a totally noncommercial information page that dishes up some uncomfortable truths about online brokers. Many online investors regard this page as a bible of sorts and submit their own experiences. The site quantifies this feedback and integrates it into more objective findings.

There are no graphic niceties at this site—it is pure text, organized in one long page through which you must slog somewhat painfully. But the effort is worth it. Far more comprehensive than other rankings, this page dredges up brokerages you may have never heard of and organizes them into categories that are important to an investor's daily life. This page is the only location where you can find lists of the top brokers in several unusual categories, including:

✔ Brokers with the same commission rates for broker-assisted trades.

✔ Best commissions for penny stocks.

✔ Best broker for Canadian stocks.

✔ Best commissions for option trading (with separate lists for 1-, 5-, and 10-option contracts).

✔ Best margin rates.

✔ Best brokers for no-load mutual funds.

✔ Best fee structures for IRA accounts.

✔ Best service plans for real-time quotes.

✔ Best after-hours trading systems.

✔ WebTV-compatible brokers.

Suffice it to say, Choosing a Discount Broker is an incredible resource, modestly presented. This site provides a terrific service. One of its beauties is the contrary nature of the findings—it is not afraid to slam a broker or remove it from a "best of . . . " list on the basis of numerous

Which Broker Is Most Popular?

You see it all the time: "the number-one Internet broker." Ads and media reports both throw this distinction around. How true are such claims? It is difficult to measure broker size, simply because different criteria are equally legitimate. Do the claims refer to number of accounts, or cumulative total of account assets? The two values do not necessarily coincide. With the growth of active retail stock trading, another measure comes into play: trade volume, which reflects how much money the brokerage is making on commissions.

customer complaints. Since the site is more in touch with the sentiments of the active investing community than with the corporate rating services, its lists are worth paying attention to.

INCOMPLETE DIRECTORY OF ONLINE BROKERS

With so many brokers online, a complete rundown of all their pros and cons is out of the question. Diligent shoppers should prowl through the ranking sites mentioned earlier, although no site rates *all* the virtual houses.

The following section sketches the services of a handful of the most popular and well-known brokers.

E*Trade (www.etrade.com)

The undisputed brand leader of purely virtual brokers, E*Trade is a mid-price, middle-of-the-road institution with an exceptionally broad selection of products and services. Styling itself as a full-featured investment portal, E*Trade gives its customers a generous range of research services that normally would cost subscription money outside of the site. It is good choice for do-it-yourself investors with Internet experience. Note: Customer service has never enjoyed a good reputation.

✔ *IRA accounts:* Yes

✔ *Real-time quotes:* Yes, snapshot

✔ *Banking:* Free checks

✔ *Active trading plan:* Yes

✔ *Mutual funds:* 5,000+ funds, 230+ families

✔ *After-hours trading:* Yes

Charles Schwab (www.charlesschwab.com)

This click-and-mortar is the largest online broker by some measures. Traditionally a discount firm in pre-Web days, Schwab is now on the high-price end of the commission scale compared to other online brokers. The company enjoys a fine reputation for execution reliability, site stability, and customer service. A new program lets account holders avail themselves of personal consultations. It is a good choice for a new online investor who likes the human touch.

- ✔ *IRA accounts:* Yes
- ✔ *Real-time quotes:* Yes, snapshot, limited number
- ✔ *Banking:* Free checks
- ✔ *Active trading plan:* Yes
- ✔ *Mutual funds:* 1,650+ funds, 200+ families
- ✔ *After-hours trading:* Yes

DLJ Direct (www.dljdirect.com)

Clarity, ease of use, and great site performance distinguish DLJ Direct. Several account tiers attempt to attract different levels of investor, from affluent and slow-moving to ambitious and quick-trading. This is a do-it-yourself broker for people who do not need hand-holding.

- ✔ *IRA accounts:* Yes
- ✔ *Real-time quotes:* Yes, limited number
- ✔ *Banking:* Free checks
- ✔ *Active trading plan:* Yes
- ✔ *Mutual funds:* 7,000+ funds
- ✔ *After-hours trading:* Yes

Ameritrade (www.ameritrade.com)

Ameritrade is continuing to grow its reputation with innovative perks, such as tracking the account-opening process at the site, a trick borrowed from the online lenders. Penny stocks can be traded only over the phone—bad news for penny-stock Webheads. A good customer service reputation and low commissions make this an increasingly popular brokerage. It is a good choice for the bargain-hunting do-it-yourself investor.

- ✔ *IRA accounts:* Yes
- ✔ *Real-time quotes:* Subscription only
- ✔ *Banking:* Free checks
- ✔ *Active trading plan:* No
- ✔ *Mutual funds:* 7,000+ funds
- ✔ *After-hours trading:* Yes

Fidelity Investments (www.fidelity.com)

This is the online department of a famous click-and-mortar brokerage, featuring moderately expensive commissions, exceptional customer service, a sluggish site, and the renowned Fidelity mutual funds. Account screens could use improvement. It is a good choice for the fund connoisseur who wants human expertise on demand.

- ✔ *IRA accounts:* Yes
- ✔ *Real-time quotes:* Yes
- ✔ *Banking:* Free checks
- ✔ *Active trading plan:* Yes
- ✔ *Mutual funds:* 3,300+ funds, 330+ families
- ✔ *After-hours trading:* Yes

Datek (www.datek.com)

Datek, the original day-trading online broker, has been displaced by next-generation, high-tech brokers. Still, the company is distinguished for good execution speed and rock-bottom commissions for the frequent trader. Datek owns its own after-hours trading system, a big draw for the addicted. The firm continues to promise option trading, but it still had not arrived by this book's deadline. Neither can you trade penny stocks here. It is a good choice for the very active stock trader ready to dedicate some money to pure trading without distractions.

- ✔ *IRA accounts:* Yes
- ✔ *Real-time quotes:* Yes, streaming and snapshot
- ✔ *Banking:* No
- ✔ *Active trading plan:* No
- ✔ *Mutual funds:* 3,200+ funds, 60+ families
- ✔ *After-hours trading:* Yes

National Discount Brokers (www.ndb.com)

A complex, attractive site (see Figure 11.5), National Discount Brokers (NDB) has a well-regarded customer service department and caters to active traders with its one-commission policy on certain multiple trades. The company provides a way to track new account applications before the

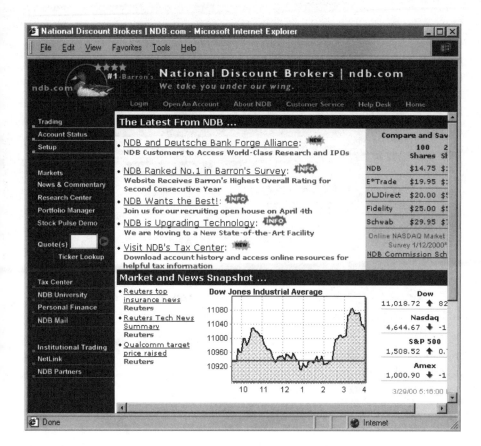

FIGURE 11.5 National Discount Brokers maintains a complex and attractive site.

(Copyright © 1999 National Discount Brokers.)

account opens. It is a good choice for investors who want a well-designed site, moderate commissions, and ongoing software introductions to serious traders.

- ✔ *IRA accounts:* Yes
- ✔ *Real-time quotes:* Yes, unlimited
- ✔ *Banking:* No
- ✔ *Active trading plan:* Yes
- ✔ *Mutual funds:* 9,500+ funds, 600+ families
- ✔ *After-hours trading:* Yes

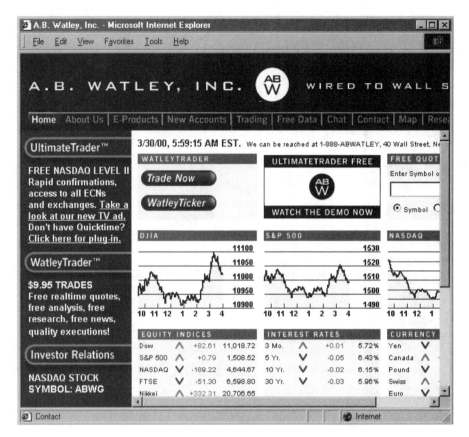

FIGURE 11.6 A.B. Watley is a good broker for aggressive traders.
(Reprinted with permission of A.B. Watley.)

A.B. Watley (www.abwatley.com)

A haven for cutting-edge traders, Watley (see Figure 11.6) is constantly advancing and refining its service. On-site customer service chatting is unusual for an investment broker, and customer service in general enjoys a good reputation. Superlative information and research services are for customers only. This is a good choice for the serious trader who is not ready to join a day-trading firm.

   ✔ *IRA accounts:* No

   ✔ *Real-time quotes:* Yes, unlimited

   ✔ *Banking:* Yes

✔ *Active trading plan:* Yes

✔ *Mutual funds:* No

✔ *After-hours trading:* Yes, offline only

Morgan Stanley Dean Witter (www.online.msdw.com)

Formerly Discover Brokerage, Morgan Stanley Dean Witter is a high-end broker with high-end commission fees. Unearthly customer service for an online broker makes the high fees worth it to loyalists. Wireless trading access is provided. It is a good choice for current customers who do not want to change and for new investors who value vintage service at any price.

✔ *IRA accounts:* Yes

✔ *Real-time quotes:* Yes, unlimited

✔ *Banking:* Yes

✔ *Active trading plan:* No

✔ *Mutual funds:* 5,000+ funds, 180+ families

✔ *After-hours trading:* Yes

Suretrade (www.suretrade.com)

Attempting an integrated financial experience, Suretrade provides wireless trading, insurance quotes, mortgage quotes, Internet telephone connections for contacting customer service without logging off, and other perks. Suretrade tries to buck the industry trend by concentrating on customer service. On the downside, as of this writing Suretrade did not update trading portfolios in real time. It is a good choice for the cost-conscious investor who wants a broker that tries to please.

✔ *IRA accounts:* Yes

✔ *Real-time quotes:* Yes, limited

✔ *Banking:* No

✔ *Active trading plan:* No

✔ *Mutual funds:* 7,500+ funds, 80+ families

✔ *After-hours trading:* Yes

Glossary

archives previous content stored for future reference. Online bill-payment services archive their customers' bills and payment records. Online banks archive monthly account statements. Information sites archive past articles. In all these cases, customers may have varying access to the archived material.

assets property, investments, and cash that have worth. An asset can be anything, from a certificate of deposit to a family heirloom. For most people, assets are measured by totaling personal property, investments, and deposits, then subtracting debts.

ATM networks automated teller machine systems. Traditional banks either own or are affiliated with networks of ATM machines, offering customers a way to get cash without paying an annoying service charge. Most virtual banks do not enjoy such network ownerships or affiliations; thus they cannot offer their customers no-fee ATM access. Some, however, rebate the cost of using the ATM networks of other banks.

ATM rebates rebates used by virtual banks to make up for the fact that the cyber banks usually do not own ATM networks. Because of that lack, virtual bank customers are subject to withdrawal fees at every machine they use. Many virtual banks pay back the equivalent of one withdrawal fee a week, thereby footing the bill for a reasonable amount of ATM use.

authorization form form giving permission to access an account. Customers complete authorization forms when setting up online bill-management accounts, allowing the service company to access their checking account to pay bills.

bank rates interest rates paid by banks on certain types of accounts. Traditionally, banks pay interest on savings accounts and other long-term deposits. Online banking has started a new tradition of paying attractive interest on checking account deposits.

biller any organization that bills its customers. Typical billers include utility companies, credit card issuers, and mortgage lenders. The term is used in online bill-paying systems.

bill management usually refers to online services that receive, schedule payments for, and send payments to pay a person's monthly and sporadic bills. The

275

most sophisticated online bill-management services take near-total control of recurring bills, storing them and notifying customers when bills have arrived and when payments are due. Such services usually cost less than $10 a month.

bill paying *see* **online bill paying.**

bill presentment refers to the method in which you receive your bills. Online banks that offer bill payment do not present your bills to you—you continue receiving them through the mail. But third-party bill-management systems actually receive your bills and *present* them to you in digital form, as scanned images.

bookkeeping programs *see* **financial software.**

brick-and-mortar a slightly derogatory term that refers to physical institutions such as banks. Brick-and-mortar companies have not extended their services to the online realm. Those that have are known as click-and-mortar businesses, offering both online and offline access to accounts.

broker a intermediary between a consumer and a financial service. Stock brokers (human or virtual) connect investors to the stock market; insurance brokers match consumers to insurance providers; loan brokers create relationships between borrowers and lenders. Although the Internet is famous for removing intermediaries, many types of online brokerages are thriving.

brokerage a company that serves as an intermediary between a consumer and a financial service. A brokerage can help consumers purchase and sell stocks, options, insurance, real estate, and loans.

brokerage account investment accounts through which securities are bought, held, and sold. They are called brokerage accounts because traditionally such accounts have been administered by trained securities brokers, agents who accessed the trading markets on the behalf of individual investors. Such human agents may or may not intervene in modern online brokerage accounts. Where such assistance exists, it is invisible, and customers use on-screen interfaces to buy and sell securities.

broker loan rate interest rate charged by banks when lending money to investment brokers. Brokerages add a bit to this rate when providing the margin rate to their customers.

CD account an account that holds certificates of deposit (CDs), which are low-yield, conservative investments. The certificates give the issuing institution (usually a bank or virtual bank) access to your money for a predetermined period, during which time the bank hopes to create a better return than it is paying you. CD yields are on the low side compared to many other investments, but they are extremely safe and a popular way to park money that is not needed immediately.

chart graphic view of a stock's price history. Charts are ubiquitous online, often accompanying stock quotes.

charting practice of drawing a stock's historical price movements on a graph. Charting provides an easy way to see a stock's momentum at a glance. Advanced interpretation of charts is both an art and a science, and often involves displaying the price history in several ways simultaneously.

click-and-mortar traditional financial institutions that have extended their products and services to the virtual space. Such institutions have not abandoned their physical presence (the mortar) but have added online interfaces (the clicks). Institutions that have not (yet?) ventured online are called brick-and-mortar companies, and the term is not entirely complimentary.

closing consummation of a business or financial agreement. Most typically, closing refers to the final step in the home-buying and mortgaging process, at which all contractual documents are signed, the deed is handed over, and the mortgage check is delivered. Closing is almost ceremonial in its complexity, and is attended by buyer, seller, attorneys, and lenders.

closing costs charges and fees associated with finalizing a real estate and mortgaging transaction. Most closing costs are charged by the mortgage lender and are used to pay for assessment services and to compensate the lending institution for its risk.

commission fee charged by every brokerage (online or offline) for the service of assisting in securities transactions. The most common commission at online brokers is the stock commission, charged when buying and again when selling stock. Broker commissions usually are charged on a per-transaction basis; less often they are charged as a per-share calculation or a percentage of assets.

customer service customer service on the Internet can be provided in digital formats such as e-mail and on-site chatting, or by traditional means such as the telephone. The financial sites usually provide two types of customer service: help with site navigation and help with financial products offered by the site. Online banks and stock brokers are famous for poor customer service compared to walk-in banks and brokerages.

cyber cash the cyber cash concept is designed to simplify the present credit card system and make payments more secure. Electronic currency schemes are a sort of Internet equivalent of smart cards, whereby an online account is funded with deposited cash, then used to pay for online merchandise. (See **electronic cash**.)

day trading the practice of buying and selling securities (usually stocks) rapidly in an attempt to capitalize on small price movements. Typically, day traders do not hold any stocks overnight. Day trading is a high-pressure and controversial method of investing. Day traders often work in offices set up to access the stock markets efficiently, but new online brokers and information services are encouraging some to operate from home.

debit deduction from the balance of a deposit account, such as a bank checking account. Debits can be withdrawals, check payments, finance charges, or any other action that reduces the cash balance of the account.

debit card plastic cards, similar in appearance to credit cards, that deduct money from a checking account for purchases. Debit cards often are branded by prominent credit issuers, such as Visa or MasterCard, but in fact do not extend a line of credit to their owners. Users employ the cards in ATMs to get cash and in shops and restaurants to make cash purchases.

debt consolidation debt counseling and renegotiating are both bundled into this term. To add further confusion, there are two types of real debt consolidation: loans and renegotiations. Loans provide consumers a way to refinance several ongoing bills at once and are used in cases where credit may be troubled but is not seriously delinquent. Renegotiation is used in dire scenarios to avoid personal bankruptcy.

delayed quotes online stock or option quotes that show prices 15 or 20 (depending on the exchange) minutes behind the market. Delayed quotes are always available free of charge.

demo a demonstration. The term is applied to both software programs and on-screen illustrations of financial services. Demo versions of stock-tracking programs help users evaluate the products before buying. Demos of virtual bank account screens assist in evaluating virtual banking service.

deposit account one of several types of account in which cash is placed with some degree of liquidity (availability). Typical deposit accounts include checking accounts, traditional savings accounts, certificate of deposit (CD) accounts, and money market accounts.

deposit yield percentage of gain on deposited money. Deposit yield differs from dividend yield associated with some stocks.

direct deposit paperless method of depositing regular paychecks into a bank account. Direct deposit has been used for years in certain high-volume administrative situations, such as Social Security payments. The method has gained additional popularity with the advent of virtual banking, where direct deposit is sometimes the easiest way to get money into the online account.

direct lender a bank or other institution that lends money directly to consumers. On the Web, direct lenders are distinguished from loan brokers, who match loan applications with products offered by many lenders. Direct lenders, as a group, lag behind brokers in establishing Internet sites.

due date date on which a bill payment must be received in order to avoid penalty or interest charges.

due diligence practice of researching a stock before buying; known in the lingo of active traders as *due dilly* or simply *diligence*. Performing due diligence involves checking a company's balance sheet, history of business execution, valuation ratios, and (for traders) technical indicators plus any other research that leads to an informed investment decision.

electronic bills bills that avoid the printing and sending of paper statements, just as electronic payments circumvent the need for paper checks. Electronic bills are delivered directly and instantly to virtual bill-payment systems, where they are presented to you online for examination and payment. If you want a paper record of the statement, you can print the bill directly from your Web browser. Electronic bills usually are paid using electronic payments.

electronic cash alternative forms of payment used on the Internet. Electronic cash (e-cash) is a new field and has yet to capture the public imagination, but some cutting-edge virtual banks are experimenting with electronic cash accounts and e-mailed money.

electronic payments near-instantaneous transfers of funds when paying a bill. Electronic payments are initiated by an online bank, bill-paying service, or individual, to only those companies that are equipped to accept such payments. A harbinger of the future, electronic payments are becoming more prevalent.

encryption scrambling of data for security. Encryption does not protect information from being intercepted on a network, but it can stop that information from being read or used. Encryption exists for all kinds of online content, including e-mail. Web sites and browsers use encryption to protect all kinds of personal information that people type when applying for and using online finance accounts.

equity options *see* **options.**

execution completed order to buy or sell securities. Using an online broker, you can buy or sell stocks; when your orders are confirmed as filled, the execution is complete. One of the ways online brokers are rated is by execution speed.

FDIC Federal Deposit Insurance Corporation. The FDIC insures deposit accounts (checking and savings) against bank failure.

financial software financial software, or accounting software, is a program that resides on a person's computer and helps manage his or her accounts. When using this book it is important to understand the difference between stand-alone programs that are bought and installed in a computer and Internet programs that people use interactively when online. Web sites and their features are also software, but people do not own them or house them in their computers.

fixed rate permanent interest rate charged to credit card purchases after the teaser rate period has expired. Also known as the go-to rate.

forms documents that collect and submit information. Financial institutions use online forms to gather information about you and submit that information as part of the application process. Short forms are used for all sorts of tasks, including entering your user name and password when logging on to an account. Long forms are used to apply for credit cards, online banking accounts, and instant insurance quotes.

fundamental analysis involves a review of the company's quarterly balance sheet, which includes data on earnings, assets, and liabilities. Management profiling is part of fundamental analysis.

go-to rate *see* **fixed rate.**

grace period period of 20 or 25 days within which no interest is charged to credit card purchases. If the full card balance is paid within the grace period each month, interest charges never accrue.

hackers individuals who interrupt, steal, or alter the flow of information in a network. Most hacking is illegal and involves remotely breaking into other people's computers. In theory, hackers can pirate financial information, but actual losses due to hacking are extremely rare.

HMO health maintenance organization. A group insurance plan affiliated with a network of hospitals and doctors. Customers stay with the healthcare network and trade monthly premiums for low-cost healthcare.

home equity loan loan backed by ownership of real estate. Home equity loans can be used for just about any purpose, from home improvements to vacations.

initial public offering (IPO) first issuance of stock by a newly public company. Investors greatly anticipate initial public offerings. During the 1990s, the flamboyant performance of IPOs created a new investing niche and plenty of headlines.

instant approval instant acceptance of new accounts available through some online application procedures, especially credit card applications. The approval may be displayed on the screen in which you completed the application or sent by e-mail.

instant quote a quick price display in response to a submitted form. Used by online insurance brokers and mortgage brokers, instant quotes give visitors a fast and detailed view of the type of insurance or loan products that might fit their situation. Instant quotes come early in the shopping and application process when buying insurance or a mortgage online.

institutional investing the buying and selling of securities by brokerages and investment banks. Compare to **retail investing.**

insurance carrier a company that provides insurance coverage directly to consumers, as distinct from an insurance broker, which acts as an agent between consumers and many carriers.

interest rate defined percentage at which money appreciates (grows) over one year. The extra money is called interest, and can accrue (in the case of a savings account, e.g.) or be owed (as in the case of a mortgage). Accordingly, a high interest rate is favorable for savings accounts, and a low interest rate is sought for loans of all kinds.

interest rate lock *see* **rate lock.**

intraday An investing term referring to anything that transpires during trading hours. Intraday charts track stock prices as the day proceeds. Intraday trading refers to quick buys and sells of stocks as their prices shift during the day.

IPO *see* **initial public offering.**

links (more formally: hyperlinks) on-screen navigation items that take you to new destinations on the Web. Links can be words or images and are distinguished by the changing shape of the mouse cursor on most computers. Text links are often (but by no means always) underlined.

liquidity availability. In a bank account, liquidity is the availability of cash; thus checking accounts are very liquid and certificates of deposit (CDs), which are purchased for a set term, are not. In a stock market, liquidity refers to the availability of stocks and the ease with which investors can buy and sell them.

margin *see* **margin account.**

margin account investing account with an automatic line of credit. By American securities law, investors may borrow up to half the cost of a security from the purchasing brokerage. Doing so is called buying on margin, and the brokerage charges interest on the loan, known as the margin rates.

margin rate rate of interest charged by a brokerage when lending money to customers. The margin rate is usually some small amount above the broker loan rate. See also **margin account.**

message boards interactive community features that allow users to engage in protracted written discussions. Financial message boards transpire on the Web and in the Usenet portion of the Internet and are especially popular among investors. Community sites allow investors to share research and discuss their stock picks.

momentum trading style of investing that seeks to capitalize on short- and intermediate-term price movements. Momentum traders follow news, earnings cycles, and stock chart readings to anticipate sudden upward or downward price movements. Holding their stock positions for days, weeks, or in some cases months, momentum investors hope to earn about 5 to 10 percent on each investment.

money market account deposit account that pays a modest investment return approximating the yield of a Treasury bond. In fact, money market accounts are partly invested in Treasuries and other kinds of conservative debt. People often use these safe accounts as temporary depositories for spare cash, located in both banks and investment brokerages. Some online brokers automatically sweep spare cash into a money market account, where it remains available for investments.

mortgage broker agency that matches home buyers with lenders. Mortgage brokers have flocked online. Online mortgage broker sites let visitors apply for preapproval online, then send the necessary paper forms to complete the application.

mutual fund professionally managed securities portfolio open to contributions by individual investors. Mutual funds are pooled investments, the most popular of which control billions of dollars in assets. Open-ended funds do not have a determined number of shares but create shares as investors buy into the portfolio. Closed-end funds do have a determined number of shares and trade very much like stocks.

online accounts refers to online access to accounts. Financial accounts always exist in the computers of real institutions. Online accounts are those accessed through an online interface, and offline accounts are accessed through branch offices, ATM machines, and other offline means. Many modern financial accounts can be accessed by both online and offline methods.

online application Internet forms submitted to virtual banks, insurance brokers, and other financial institutions. These forms require pretty much the same information as paper applications. Online applications result in the initiation of an online account, a price quote, or the preapproval of a loan.

online banking involves access to checking and savings accounts through a personal computer. Typically, online banking services include access to account statements, money transfer functions, and online check writing. Traditional banks often provide customers with online account access; virtual banks exist online only, without walk-in branch offices.

online bill paying one of the most popular and intriguing aspects of Internet banking, online bill-paying services let the bank (or independent company) write and send the check for standard monthly bills. Some bills can be paid electronically, using fast bank transfers. Whichever method is used, the advantage is freedom from manually writing and sending checks. Online bill-paying interfaces are partly automated and easy to use.

online broker broker that provides on-screen interfaces for buying and selling stocks, mutual funds, and other securities. Low fees, account convenience, and more direct access to the securities markets give online brokers (or brokerages) an advantage over their brick-and-mortar cousins.

online calculators interactive tools that help determine one's financial goals and their attainability. Presented within the Web browser, these calculators often are small Java programs that take up to a minute to appear. Popular and useful online calculators help users plan retirement, figure out affordable mortgage scenarios, compare auto loan and leasing possibilities, and calculate the advantages of Roth IRA accounts.

online insurance a fairly complex and quickly evolving field in which consumers can search out, compare, and apply for certain types of insurance policies. Life insurance is best represented on the Internet, but health and property insurance is available, as well. Some insurance carriers sell policies directly over the Web, but most of the action is through Internet-based insurance brokers.

online investing to most people, "online investing" means online brokerage. But in fact online investing means taking advantage of any aspect of the investment information and service revolution. That could mean researching investments online while continuing to use an old-style broker. Online investing is characterized by a wealth of free information, inexpensive brokerage, and unprecedented access to the securities markets. All kinds of investing styles, from day trading to retirement planning, can be pursued online.

online payment any payment of a bill that originates or is ordered online. Online payments are not identical to electronic payments. Not every online payment is an electronic payment, but every electronic payment is an online payment. The other main type of online payment is a check created and mailed by an online bank or payment service.

online quote quote that displays a stock price. The term is used mostly in the context of Internet investing. Most online stock quotes are delayed quotes, meaning they lag behind the stock market by 15 or 20 minutes during trading hours. Other types of online quotes include insurance rate quotes, bank rate quotes, and loan rate quotes.

online transfer a method of moving money from one Internet-accessed account to another. Ideally, online transfers are as easy as using a mouse and occur within minutes. When implemented well, online transfers between two accounts at a single institution occur almost instantly.

on-site chatting mobile and nimble technology that can be applied to a single site. It often is associated with chat rooms. On-site chatting lets you "talk" with a customer service representative through typing, without logging off the Internet or using your phone.

option chains price quotes for some or all of the options associated with a certain security. Many stocks have dozens of options, each with its own price and expiration date. Option chains sort out all the available options and organize them for easy selection.

password used to access online accounts. Passwords and user names form a two-step key that opens the door to an online account. Passwords never appear on-screen; when you type your password a series of asterisks appears instead, shielding your private password from curious eyes.

payee *see* **biller.**

penny stock strictly speaking, a penny stock is any stock trading for less than $5 per share. In a more colloquial sense, a penny stock costs pennies, literally—a stock trading for under a dollar.

personal broker a human broker, sometimes employed at an online brokerage. With the advent of online investing and automated virtual brokerages, personal brokers comprise a special service category. Many online brokerages provide personal brokers when customers do not want to use the online interface for some reason. Commission fees are usually higher when ordering through a personal broker.

personalization an important feature of some financial service sites, by which you can save and retrieve your unique information. The most common type of personalization occurs when you open an account and can view your account screens. Beyond simple account access, personalization is applied at research sites and insurance brokers, sometimes by allowing visitors to save incomplete applications for later completion.

points cash increments of 1 percent of a loan amount, usually a mortgage. Points are variable items in the negotiation of mortgage terms, with each point usually worth 0.25 percent of interest rate on the loan. So paying 2 percent of the loan amount up front (2 points) can reduce the loan's interest rate by a 0.5 percent.

portal home-base Internet destinations that link to all kinds of information, both within the site and elsewhere on the Web. The big generic portals, such as Yahoo! and Excite, provide many types of information on almost every subject imaginable. Smaller portals also exist, focusing on specific topics and industries. This book refers to financial service portals in the fields of online banking, investing, insurance, and loans.

POS point of service. A health plan that gives customers a choice of using a network of healthcare providers (at low cost) or a doctor outside the network (at higher cost).

post message in an online discussion forum. Posts are strung together by multiple users to form a thread, which is a conversation on a particular topic.

PPO Preferred Provider Organization. A network of healthcare providers that provide services for a flat rate to covered members of an insurance plan.

preapproval more definite than prequalification, but still not a firm deal, preapproval is part of the loan-approval process in which the prospective borrower's financial condition has been verified and the basic terms of a future loan have been agreed on.

prequalification a preliminary step in the loan process, prequalification tells a prospective borrower that, according to the personal information submitted so far, a certain type of loan is likely to be approved. Prequalification is based on just the barest information, and is not usually verified with a credit check.

presentment *see* **bill presentment.**

privacy refers to a Web site's policy regarding how it handles your personal information. Privacy and security are the two issues that determine how safe it is to engage in online personal finance. Most responsible Web-based financial services publish privacy and security statements that detail what measures are taken to keep your personal information private.

provider an institution that renders concrete service—such as a bank, a direct lender, and a virtual investment brokerage. Many of the sites described in this book act as intermediaries between you, the visitor/shopper, and providers affiliated with the intermediary site. Other sites profiled are produced by providers themselves to market their services directly to consumers.

rate lock guarantee of a certain interest rate, for a certain duration, when taking a loan. The lender guarantees low rates for short periods and higher rates for longer periods. Rate locks are important when negotiating a mortgage—ideally the lock period is long enough to close the real estate purchase but short enough to assure a low rate.

rate monitor online display of current interest rates. Rate monitors are found at insurance sites, loan sites, and bank sites as well as at information portals that track rates of all kinds.

real time refers to financial information that is absolutely current. In the world of online finances, often price, portfolio, and account information is delayed for one reason or another. Obviously, delayed information is inferior to real-time information, but the distinction matters more in some situations than in others. Delayed quotes are a nuisance for online traders, for example, whereas mutual fund prices delayed until the end of the day generally do not cause any grief. Real-time information is sometimes available as a subscription product, but in many areas of online finance it is becoming cheap or free.

real-time quotes online stock quotes that are not delayed from the markets. Real-time quotes used to be for professionals only, but the Internet is gradually giving them to individual investors. Anyone can see free real-time quotes at certain Web sites. In addition, very sophisticated real-time market displays are available on a subscription basis.

refinancing replacing one loan with a new, more favorable loan. Refinancing takes advantage of interest rates that are lower than they were when the first loan was taken. In most cases, the new lender pays off the first loan and lets the customer repay the money at a better rate.

resistance level price above which a stock repeatedly has been unable to rise. It is a technical indicator. Active investors sometimes sell their positions in a stock that reaches its resistance level. Stocks that climb through resistance levels are said to be breaking out, and often attract an investing frenzy.

retail investing the buying and selling of securities in the public marketplace by individual investors, as opposed to institutional investing.

savings account traditionally, an alternative to a checking account, where you can stash money you will not need for a while. Savings accounts generally pay higher interest rates than checking accounts but offer lower yields than CDs and money market accounts. Savings accounts may or may not require a minimum balance.

sector in investing, a selection of stocks representing companies in a single defined industry. The semiconductor sector, for example, contains companies that manufacture computer chips.

security refers to the integrity of network connections and the impenetrability of information traveling over the network. Security is an important issue in online personal finance, because many Internet services require input of personal information. Security measures like encryption make that information difficult to intercept and decode.

shareware software that may be downloaded from the Internet and used, free of charge, for a predetermined trial period. After the trial the program must be purchased and registered or deleted from the computer. Financial shareware includes accounting programs and credit card management programs.

SIPC Securities Investor Protection Corporation. The SIPC insures brokerage accounts—not against bad investing but against brokerage failure.

snapshot quotes style of online stock quote that must be refreshed in order to see the latest price. Contrast to **streaming quotes.**

stock quote price of any stock. Stock quotes are distributed widely online—nearly every investment news and information site displays them.

streaming quotes style of online stock quote that resembles a stock ticker. Unlike snapshot quotes, streaming quotes do not need to be refreshed manually.

support level a narrow price range below which a stock has not dropped in the past. It is a technical indicator. Stocks sometimes "bounce" off their support levels, if investors believe they have reached a bottom.

teaser rate initial interest rate charged to purchases made with a credit card. The teaser rate is sometimes as low as 0 percent and usually lasts from three to six months, after which a fixed rate begins.

technical analysis a stock's technical value is determined solely by price movement and has little or nothing to do with company fundamentals. Pure technical analysis does not even need to know the company's name—its research sphere is populated by price charts and predictive indicators. Technical analysis seeks to predict future price movements based on past and current patterns.

third-party companies companies that act as intermediaries providing specialized services. One prominent example is online bill paying. Virtual banks provide that service, but dedicated third-party services are taking some of that business.

thread a series of posts in a message-board discussion form. Threads define topical discussions on message boards. Each post contributes to a thread; all the threads together comprise the message board.

trading hours time during which securities are traded. Trading hours vary depending on the exchange. The American stock exchanges are in the process of expanding beyond traditional daytime hours. Some futures, currency, and commodities markets operate 24 hours a day.

transaction sale or purchase. To investors, a transaction is a filled order to buy or sell a security.

trial period test period in which a financial service or subscription is provided at no charge. Online bill-payment services and virtual banks market trial periods aggressively. Also, investment subscription sites frequently offer no-charge trials of two weeks or a month.

tunnel linear progression of Web pages that takes you far from a site's starting point. Tunnels are navigational inconveniences seen in many online application forms.

unsecured debt debt not backed by any collateral, such as a security deposit, an automobile, or a house. Generally, unsecured debt refers to consumer credit card debt.

Usenet one of the oldest portions of the Internet, Usenet consists of about 30,000 topical discussion forums in message-board format. Usenet contains many investing forums as well as several Web-based online communities for investors.

user name part of a two-step security process for accessing online accounts. Most online banks and brokerages protect the privacy of your account with a user name and password. In most cases, both can be of your choosing, although some brokerages assign user names and passwords at first, then let customers change them.

virtual banks some terms do not have industry-wide, exact meanings. For the purposes of this book, a virtual bank is a branchless institution that operates online and only online. Click-and-mortar banks that have branch offices and on-screen services are considered online banks but not virtual banks.

virtual credit card a card provided by an Internet-only company, not a traditional bank, that is made of plastic and used in the usual fashion. Online products like this let you manage and pay your account online.

World Wide Web the hyperlinked portion of the Internet. Other distinct portions of the Internet include e-mail and Usenet newsgroups. The Web is distinguished by its navigation system, which is based on clickable links (hyperlinks), each of which displays a new screen, or destination.

Index